EAT THE RICH

EAT THE RICH
& Other Interesting Ideas

Peter Werbe

Black & Red Books
Detroit

EAT THE RICH
& Other Interesting Ideas
Peter Werbe

No Copyright 2023

Black & Red Books
PO Box 02374
Detroit MI 48202
www.BlackandRed.org

Cover and interior design: Ralph Franklin

Cover photo: Millard Berry – Demonstration against Pres. George H. W. Bush, Dearborn, Michigan 1990 www.millardberry.com

Back cover author photo: Rebecca Cook

Author contact:
pwerbe@gmail.com
www.peterwerbe.org
www.facebook.com/peterwerbe67

ISBN: 978-1-948501-26-2

Also by Peter Werbe:
Summer on Fire: A Detroit Novel (2021)

For Fredy Perlman
(1934-1985)

Contents

INTRODUCTION 1

OPENERS
Escaping from Europe 7
James Baldwin 14
History of the Fifth Estate 19
What Does Fifth Estate Mean? 28

POLITICS
Selecting a Master 31
Republicans: Get Out of Town 37
Revenge of the Nerds 39
Burn All Flags 48
Getting Back to Zero 49
Clinton: Greater Danger to Peace 54
The 2020 Election 57

CULTURE
Will Marijuana Save World Capitalism 65
Surreal Life 72
The Vegetarian Myth 75
Looking at Animals 81
Getting Off the Road 88
R-E-V-O-L-T 92
What a Day It Wasn't 98

RELIGION
Christ's Body Found: Easter Cancelled 105
Has George Bush Doomed Christianity? 109
Godless 112

TECHNOLOGY
We Get a Computer and Hate It! 119
Turn It Off! 127

DIRECT ACTION
Occupy Confronts the Power of Money 137
Recycling and Liberal Reform 145
In Defense of Self-Defense 156
Anarchists & Guns 160
Anarchist Violence or State Violence 166
Fifth Estate A-Gassed 171

MUSIC
No Dance; No Revo 177
Dancing for Our Lives 179
Will Success Spoil Chumbawamba 182

WAR
All Wars are Lies 191
Hiroshima: First Shot of World War III 201
Wartime Wildcats 205
The Empire Exists Iraq 210

WILHELM REICH
Sexual Repression & Authoritarianism 219
Sex Economy 226

CAPITALISM
Confronting Poverty and the Poor 233
World-Wide Crisis 237
I'm Sticking with the Union 243
Coffee Keeps Us Rolling 253
Marxism: Obscuring More Than It Reveals 258
Isn't All Money Fake? 263

ON THE ROAD
An Anarchist in Cuba 267
Cuba: From State to Private Capitalism 279
An Anarchist at the World Social Forum 289

FINAL WORDS
Interview with Peter Werbe 300
Eat the Rich 303

DETROIT POLICE DEPARTMENT
INTER-OFFICE MEMORANDUM
INTELLIGENCE SECTION
SECURITY UNIT

CONFIDENTIAL

Date: May 25, 1972

To: Commanding Officer, Intelligence Section

Subject: SECURITY UNIT SOURCE # 142   (*Indicates previous contact with subject by Security Unit.)

On May 24, 1972, Detective Sergeant Allen Crouter received the following information from S.U. SOURCE # 142:

On May 18, 1972, Source attended a meeting held at the FIFTH ESTATE offices located at 4403 Second. Source identified the following FIFTH ESTATE members as being present:

███████* ███████*
███████* ███████* (aka ███████)
███████*

General financial matters were discussed regarding "sagging" FIFTH ESTATE sales.

Also discussed were demonstrations planned for May 27, 1972, (MICHIGAN ███████), and May 29, 1972, (███████).

The FIFTH ESTATE, along with ███████*, 6100 West Vernor, were concerned because of the possibility of violence during the march and rally by members of DETROIT ███████ (███████ coordinators of the MICHIGAN ███████.

Leaders of ███████ have assured both these groups that the march and rally will both be non-violent.

Source is going to attend the Second '72 ███████ ███████ scheduled for May 26th through 28th, 1972 at the University of Miami, Miami, Florida. The purpose of this meeting is to formulate plans for the disruption of the Democratic and Republican Conventions to be held in Miami Beach, Florida: (Democratic: July 9, 1972 through July 13, 1972; Republican: August 21, 1972 through August 25, 1972.)

Source will furnish a complete report as to the results of this meeting upon his return to Detroit. (See attached article.)

The Detroit and Michigan State Police and the FBI maintained a program of illegal surveillance and disruption of radical groups and publications, such as the *Fifth Estate*, during the 1960s and '70s. Several groups, including the newspaper, sued for release of documents related to police activities and recovered documents such as the one above. Names of informers were redacted before their release.

Introduction

The essays contained in this volume reflect the issues I addressed in my 2021 book, *Summer on Fire: A Detroit Novel*.[1] —particularly racism, violence, war, anarchism, the consequences of sexual repression, fascism, and other subjects that shape the modern world. That text was a fictionalized memoir depicting the summer of 1967 and the activities of the staff of the *Fifth Estate* newspaper, the publication in which most of the writing in this volume originally appeared.

Reprinting previously published essays commenting on events and controversies in the past run the risk of having them seem irrelevant today. Commentary written with an immediacy, as a reaction to the moment, often doesn't carry well into the future. However, with this collection, you as the reader and me as the writer, we have decided to take the risk that there is current value to what I've published over the last several decades.

The political perspective reflected in the articles is in the tradition of revolutionary anarchism. Both revolution and anarchism are terms that now have little fixed meaning, and may evoke a misunderstanding or even trepidation in some people to whom an explanation is warranted.

When revolution is discussed in these pages, I attempt to recreate the spirit, ideas, and accomplishments of the short-lived anarchist Spanish Revolution. This mostly ignored event occurred within the context of a civil war fought in Spain between 1936-1939 when the rule of Capital and the political state were overturned for those few years.[2] During my lifetime, the same qualities of revolt came to fruition during the 1960s freedom struggles, particularly among Blacks, women, and Native and LGBTQ people, as well as the anti-war and environmental movements, all of which continue today.

Anarchism is often used in the fearmongering corporate media as a synonym for chaos and rioting when nothing constrains an individual or a mob. Black-clad anarchists feature heavily as scapegoats for opportunist politicians. Although now, with great distrust of government across the globe, declaring oneself an anarchist is quite widespread and, in some circles, almost fashionable. However, beyond superficial trappings, anarchist ideas and desires continue to appear in community-based projects, with anarchists always on the front lines fighting against the worst excesses of capitalism and the state—racism, police violence, patriarchy, globalization, assaults against the environment, and fascism.

However, anarchists don't advocate reforming an oppressive system, but the entire elimination of both the political economy of capitalism and its armed guard, the state. In its place would be a system of decentralized direct democracy that ends all forms of hierarchy including those based on class, race, gender, or sexuality.

These ideas that I and others advocate aren't as obscure as one might assume. A half-century after John Lennon's popular song, "Imagine," was recorded, it's astounding that a song with such radical lyrics—"no countries," "nothing to kill or die for," " no religion," "no possessions"—has carved out a permanent place in popular culture. His words define anarchism with a message that resonates with millions of people around the world. Its plaintive melody and quiet piano allow the unambiguous words to be clearly distinguished, expressing what so many people try to imagine.

Almost all of the thoughts developed in these essays are part of a collaborative process shared with friends and comrades who were and are staff members of the *Fifth Estate*. They contain the ideas of contemporary political theorists, radical historians, ones gleaned from classic anarchist figures such as Emma Goldman and Peter Kropotkin, the radical psychoanalytic theories of Wilhelm Reich, and the writings of activists within the Native people, Black, and women's movements. The works of these thinkers were, and still are, part of conversations in which the *Fifth Estate* group and friends discuss how they can be made real.

With a few exceptions, my essays aren't cheery ones. Rather, they are meant to confront the ruling ideas that are the foundation of a system based on cruelty, exploitation, and destruction of the planet. Hopefully, you will find they bring some new perspectives to things often taken for granted — ones that need to be replaced by those we can imagine; ideas being the precursor of action.

"I hope someday you'll join us" is in the last stanza of Lennon's song. I have hope that the next collection of my essays will reflect a world-wide movement that has put what we imagine into being.

The following essays appeared in the *Fifth Estate* unless otherwise noted. The date of the issue in which they appeared is below their title. Those from the *Fifth Estate* are accessible in digital format at FifthEstate.org/archive.

Notes:
1. Information about my novel, where to purchase it, plus online footnotes and a soundtrack are at peterwerbe.com.
2. I wrote an introduction to a reprint of *Objectivity and Liberal Scholarship*, by Noam Chomsky, perhaps the best-known anarchist public intellectual. It might be difficult to imagine a duller title, but the book is an exciting description of the revolution Spanish anarchists brought into being until it was suppressed by a combination of fascists, Stalinists, and liberals in the late 1930s. It's published by Black and Red – Detroit (blackandred.org) and is available from them as well as PM Press (pmpress.org).

Chapter 1
Openers

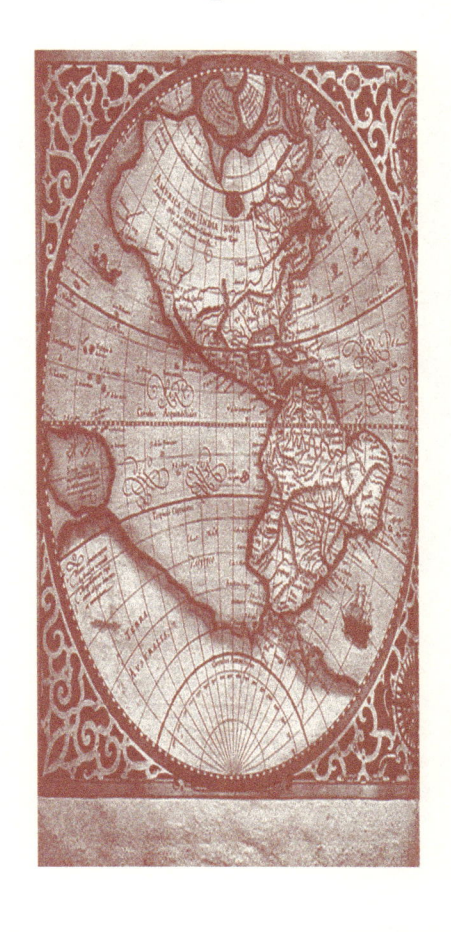

Escaping From Europe
Why Our (White) Ancestors Came Here in the First place
Spring 2008

"The Arawaks...brought us parrots and balls of cotton and spears and many other things, which they exchanged for the glass beads and hawks' bells. They willingly traded everything they owned ...They were well built, with good bodies and handsome features.... They do not bear arms and do not know them...They have no iron. Their spears are made of cane...They would make fine servants."
Christopher Columbus, ship's log, October 12, 1492

This, written by that courageous Italian navigator and explorer sailing under the flag of Spain, describes his welcome by a gentle and guileless people upon his first day in the Americas. It ominously presaged all that followed.

Thus begins the oft-told tale of the ignoble and ignominious entry into the New World (new to the bewildered sailors of the three ships who thought they had arrived in Japan) heralding the commencement of the European invasion and occupation of the Western hemisphere.

Most know the story of the greed, oppression and mass murder that resulted in the largest and most sweeping ethnic cleansing in history, resulting in the deaths of perhaps 30 million Native Americans.

The discovery of Columbus by the Arawaks was fortuitous as the three ships might have made landfall almost anywhere else on the continent that lay between the explorers' intended destination in eastern Asia. The random meeting had deadly consequences for the tribal people who had cheerfully welcomed their strange visitors. They suffered a total genocide. The flourishing culture of the Arawak/Taino people was entirely eliminated after the establishment of the first Spanish colony on Hispaniola following Columbus' second voyage.

The nearly naked Arawaks were fascinated by the clothing covering the entire body of their strange visitors, but particularly by the metal armor the soldiers wore. At ease in their land and their bodies, they didn't realize the murderous potential of these armored men whose steel didn't just cover and protect their corporeal beings. The invaders also possessed heavily armored personalities–extensions of an eons old culture of domination and submission, of hierarchy, patriarchy, state society, acquisitiveness as substitute for intimacy, a symbolism replacing living life directly. An inferior culture met a superior culture, but the rigidity and arrogance of Columbus and his men blinded them to the reality of their historic encounter.

Rather than shedding their clothing and armor, stopping their obsessive search for gold, ceasing Columbus's desire to possess every piece of land or water he saw by naming it in honor of their horrid religion, they saw these gentle people as objects to be eliminated or enslaved, their land to be confiscated, and their wealth to be looted. Thus, they destroyed the opportunity they must have at least vaguely glimpsed that offered them a chance for psychic revolt and renewal from the pathogen of European culture they carried with them. Columbus and his men could have shed their emotional and metal armor and embraced the people as the New World rather than the land.

The reasons for the brave voyage across a dangerous and uncharted sea are well known to all, and stated even in the most unapologetic versions of the Columbus navigations: the quest for riches and to spread the Christian Gospel to people who already had a mytho-poetic spirituality that was life-affirming as opposed to the cult of execution, sacrifice, sin, renunciation of the flesh, and repression demanded by the European death cult religion.

But it was the expedition for new sources of wealth for the

motherland which framed the Columbus voyages and the subsequent ones of the other intrepid explorers of that era. This, of course, is not an unusual motive for a representative of a nation-state.

Since capitalism's establishment 4,000 years ago as a mode of production and exchange, with the simultaneous rise of the State as the guarantor of the class-and-rule racket, its rapaciousness has been ceaseless. Capitalism, by its intrinsic nature, necessitates continuous expansion; stasis is ruinous to it. By the late 15th century, driven by a profound society-wide crisis, Europe began to push beyond its historical geography.

Classic capitalist theory and its Marxist critique usually don't mark the rise of this form of political economy until thousands of years later. But when societies operate under a sign of valorization, where labor is sold, when commodities are exchanged and wars are fought to control more of all this, it is capitalism, and it began with the first nation states.

There was the inherent tendency, in fact a necessity, to expand capital's domination wherever possible for the different nation states of Europe, most of which were in constant conflict with one another for trade, resources, and goods. By Columbus's time, Portugal, Spain, England, Holland, and France had begun a frantic world-wide search for wealth outside the boundaries of their continent.

Readers with even a scant historical knowledge of the political, environmental, and cultural circumstances in Europe during the period of the so-called Great Discoveries–the heroic sea voyages of Columbus, Magellan, Cabot and others–already know this story. However, it's important to describe what was occurring at the time to understand why expanding beyond their borders was a necessity for European nation states if they were to continue their culture as it was constituted.

Most of the regimes of medieval Europe were broke by the end of the 15th century; wealth creation was stagnant, constant wars drained treasuries, and feudalism was collapsing. It's a charming little tale that Queen Isabella of Spain pawned her jewels to finance Columbus' journey in hopes his discovery of gold would refill the country's coffers, but it is more indicative of the precarious economic situation the rulers faced.

The continent was environmentally ruined, in good part through the destruction of its forests which were toppled to supply the basic materials of daily life. Wood was used for heating, cooking, construction, and fuel for metal smelting and rudimentary industrial energy. Deforesting of many regions occurred early on in the metal ages. Cyprus cut down its forests so completely to supply metallurgic centers with fuel that the island remains treeless today, 2,000 years later. In his book, *Internal Combustion*, author Edwin Black reports that on the shores of the Mediterranean, there "are some seventy to ninety million tons of slag from ancient smelting."

So deforested was Western Europe that by the reign of William the Conqueror beginning in 1066, the new king of England ordained the repressive Forest Law which forbade commoners from using wood for any purpose. Violation was punished with severe torture. The mythical Robin Hood, who is said to have lived and taken sanctuary in King John's Sherwood Forest, was a powerful legend of resentment by the common people to this restriction. The prohibition is usually put forth as an example of kingly arrogance and selfishness, but the tale was motivated by the extreme scarcity of wood. Wood and timber scarcity only worsened in Europe by the 15th century.

Rivers were heavily polluted from human and industrial waste, and food was often adulterated by unscrupulous merchants. With the use of wood suppressed by the elites, and the newly discovered energy source of coal becoming the fuel used by common people (in England, peat), the unrestricted burning by increasing urban populations produced a palpable smog that was one of the contributing factors to plummeting quality of life and health standards and diminished life expectancy.

As large numbers of peasants, freed from feudal bondage, streamed into cities, what had been small towns swelled to unmanageable, filthy, polluted, crime- and disease-ridden metropolises. The great cities of Medieval Europe became the spawning ground for the wide-spread plagues of the era. Bubonic Plague—the Black Death—produced three major epidemics in the

6th, 14th, and 17th centuries causing the death of an estimated 137 million victims.

Religious fervor was rampant, frequently to the point of mass hysteria, beginning with the Crusades in the 11th century. Ostensibly with the goal of freeing Jerusalem from Muslim control, but in actuality it was more about looting Middle Eastern and Asia Minor territories, and forcing open new trade zones. The succeeding centuries were followed by incessant, decades-long internecine warfare among the European powers that impoverished nations and created a permanent class of maimed battle casualties and deaths that significantly decreased the number of able-bodied men.

Pogroms against Jews were frequent, often encouraged by the authorities, both secular and religious, including Martin Luther. Jews, who were the money lenders of Christian Europe, were often expelled from their host nation, such as Germany and Spain when royal debts to them got too high. Christian worship obsessively pervaded almost every aspect of daily life although the Catholic Church, the largest landholder in Europe, was rife with corruption and hypocrisy.

Authoritarian monarchies constituted political rule across the continent which was always arbitrary and often incompetent. The culture, both official and convivial, exhibited intense cruelty marked by institutions such as the Inquisition whose innovation of water boarding (or, the Water Cure as it was known for centuries) was utilized to extract confessions of deviltry.

Beginning in the mid-14th century and continuing for three centuries, nations were consumed by a panic over witches, mostly women, in their midst. Witch-hunts, especially in Central Europe, resulted in the trial, torture, and execution of tens of thousands of victims during the period described as the "Burning Times."

Capital punishment was inflicted for even minor transgressions, particularly as an element of State terror to instill in the disrespectful rabble the sanctity of the property rights of the emerging bourgeoisie. Hideous tortures were exacted upon prisoners, brutal sports which included animal fighting were popular, such as bear baiting and dog fighting, and constant clashes between people at any public gathering marked the era.

Madness and mass hysteria were common particularly as feudalism imploded and no alternative communal social structure was allowed to arise that could encompass the peasants set adrift by its breakdown. Outbreaks of mass, collective dancing such as the tarantella swept parts of Europe where populations of entire villages whirled manically for hours until collapsing in fits of exhaustion. This phenomenon has interesting and positive qualities to it such as outlined in Barbara Ehrenreich's *Dancing in the Streets: A History of Collective Joy.*

As Michel Foucault notes in *Discipline and Punish*, insanity and cruelty were commonplace, and as leprosy disappeared, the mad were herded into the former leprosariums. Ehrenreich reports that an epidemic of "melancholy"—what we now call "depression"— arose during that period.

Crime, banditry, brigandage, assaults, murder, and robbery were all endemic on the common level, and corruption, bribery and payoffs defined every government on the continent. Even undertakings on the part of royal houses, such as provisioning the ships of the first great explorers, weren't secure from the most corrupt practices. Naval historian Stephen Morrison, in his classic *The European Discovery of America: The Southern Voyages, 1492-1616*, relates how the merchants of Seville shortchanged Magellan's ships as they set out on what they supposed would be a year and a half's journey to Asia. Upon arriving at what the Captain-General dubbed Tierra Del Fuego, it was discovered they had only been given less than half the rations they thought had been stored aboard, and much of that was spoiled.

And so, we return to that moment in 1492 when two peoples stared across a great cultural divide—one at peace with themselves and their environment, and the others, representatives of a toxic culture that was in the throes of disintegration that lacked the ability to live harmoniously with each other or the planet. Columbus and his men had the option of throwing off their armor and their restrictive clothing, feasting on the abundance of the island and adopting the ways of a free and happy people, but we know what they chose—"They would make fine servants"—and the world has suffered for it since.

Had the *terra incognita* of the New World not become available as a source for expansion and looting, Europe would have been forced to deal with the rot at the core of their society at home. Instead, they were able to gain a new lease on life by resuscitating only one aspect of what confronted them–their economic dilemma. All else remained the same until other social forces were unleashed in the next few centuries.

We are at the point where the extended life of that toxic culture 500 years later has invaded and dominated all continents and defines planetary consciousness. The conditions that characterized the Middle Ages appear in the modern era with a similar destructive ferocity and threatening potential, and in most aspects, even worse.

What now? Maybe we should be heartened by the recent news reports that Russia may beat the U.S. to Mars? A colony in space now that we've ruined this planet? At least there are no native inhabitants to enslave or kill.

Or better yet, how about fixing what we already have?

Suggested reading:

Black Ghost of Empire: The Long Death of Slavery and the Failure of Emancipation, Kris Manjapra, Scribner, 2022

A People's History of the United States, Howard Zinn, Harper Perennial, 2015

The Strait, Part I and II, Fredy Perlman, Black and Red-Detroit, 1986 and 2023

James Baldwin
3 Friends & Race in America
Summer 2017

Film Review: "I Am Not Your Negro" (2016). Director: Raoul Peck; Writer: James Baldwin; Narration: Samuel L. Jackson

The title of this documentary about novelist, playwright, poet, and essayist James Baldwin is not spoken as such in the film. Where the line is uttered in this excellent film by Haitian-born director, Raoul Peck, Baldwin tells a British audience, "I am not your..." and uses the "N" word to complete his sentence.

It's not written here because it is the worst word in the English language, one that should never be printed or spoken. Besides its use to demean and dehumanize African Americans in general, it was often the last word heard by a black man about to be lynched, or today, beaten or shot by a racist cop.

Director Peck obtained permission from the Baldwin family to use the author's 1979 30-page letter to his literary agent describing an uncompleted project about race relations. The text of Baldwin's letter, originally titled, "Remember This House," is voiced by Samuel L. Jackson, the highest paid actor in Hollywood.

The reference to the movie star's wealth is to suggest that his participation in this project must, at least in part, be motivated by the realization that no matter how much money he has, as a black man, he can still hear that "famous word," as I once heard it described.

The film employs historical footage of Baldwin talks and scenes from Selma to Ferguson to draw a chilling portrait of how race still defines America even so long after Baldwin's death 30 years ago.

This isn't a biopic. It opens with startling scenes from recent protests against police killings, but quickly defines the film's touchstones—the murders of Martin Luther King, Jr., civil rights activist, Medgar Evers, and Malcolm X, all of whom Baldwin counted as friends.

Baldwin, speaking through Jackson's sonorous and dramatic reading, says he is embarking on a "journey to tell the truth." This simple declaration in America is both subversive and revolutionary. To do so is to attack the fundamental myths of the nation that began as a slave republic, as we are reminded by essential historian Gerald Horne, and which enslaved and bred for slavery millions of human beings, as we are reminded by historians, Ned and Constance Sublette.

The slavers had such a hand in writing the celebrated U.S. foundation document guaranteeing freedom (to some), but which also institutionalized slavery and set up an electoral mechanism for choosing a president that allowed the modern iteration of the Founding Slavers to recently assume the presidency.

The Slavocracy was so integral to the economy of the entire U.S., but particularly the South, that it waged a catastrophic civil war to maintain their "peculiar institution," the echoes of which are still heard today every time a black person walks down the street.

You may say, "I know the same history as you do. I'm anti-racist." You're right. Maybe this readership is the wrong audience for the film although the drama of Baldwin's words and Peck's presentation is so intense, witnessing what we think we know is a stark reminder all of us can use.

The film would best be seen by the majority of Euro-Americans who have voted for Republican candidates for president since 1968 almost solely on the basis of race. However, they probably would have to be strapped to a chair, eyes forced open with clips, "A Clockwork Orange"-style, and forced to see the scenes in this film of their forebears, their historic counterparts, at lynchings, resisting integration in the 1950s, waving White Power signs and swastikas when Dr. King marched in Chicago in 1968, cheering militarized police attacking peaceful demonstrators, and advertisements featuring a slew of appalling Aunt Jemima-style ads.

The images should make those of us who are white sad, angry, and ashamed, since regardless of our anti-racism, we are the beneficiaries of white supremacy. This is not said to instill guilt. Quite the opposite. It is a call to realize the obligation of the debt we owe by continuing our anti-racist work.

With the election of Donald Trump, we are living in a modern version of a 1970s Rhodesia. A white colonial nation based on horrors that dreams of an imagined greatness that never was. Slavery seemed like a bright idea to bring riches to a few, and an economy that involved millions profiting to some degree, but ignored the human toll.

The one chance for truth, reconciliation, and justice, was smashed following the end of the Reconstruction Era in 1877 by the same social forces that bolster white supremacy today.

The film comes at a time when Baldwin's writing, received exceedingly well during his lifetime, but having gone into something of an eclipse, is experiencing a recent renaissance. His 1963, The Fire Next Time, spent 41 weeks on The New York Times best seller list and not only spoke for the organized civil rights movement, but also presaged the rebellions that, indeed, brought fire to a nation unwilling to bring about "liberty and justice for all."

Baldwin's work approached race and other forbidden topics beginning with his first novel, Go Tell It on the Mountain; a collection of essays, Notes of a Native Son appeared two years later. His second novel, Giovanni's Room, caused some outrage because of its explicit homoerotic content. Others that followed, Another Country and Tell Me How Long the Train's Been Gone, dealt with themes of being black and gay overlaid with the violence and unrest of the 1950s and '60s.

The footage of Baldwin speaking before primarily white audiences contains an electric sense of the period—everything was then open for examination; anything could be changed. Everything needed to be examined and changed. But, the Rhodesians weren't about to easily give up the world in which they ruled. They killed three men Baldwin loved and countless others just to keep separate drinking fountains and see other people as the word which will remain unwritten here.

There is much in "I am not..." about media representation of black people, from films like "King Kong" or the stereotype frightened or grinning Negroes in Charlie Chan films, TV series like "Amos and Andy," and ads depicting happy servants. Visuals like this and the 10,000 collectibles in Prof. David Pilgrim's Jim Crow Museum of Racist Memorabilia, located at Michigan's Ferris State University, are part of a contemptible cultural creation which attempted to convince both blacks and whites that the races were in correct relationship to one another.

The majority of whites still support the same policies of repression and believe the same myths. The overwhelming majority of blacks never did; almost none do today. This makes for an explosive social mixture.

It is worth the price of admission alone just to see Baldwin standing amidst a white audience at a 1965 Cambridge University debate declaring his humanity. In The Fire Next Time, Baldwin asks the question, "Do I really want to be integrated into a burning house?"

The American Rhodesians are breathing their last. Many of their children want justice as an ethical imperative as much as black children want it as a practical imperative.

The only question that remains is, will the Rhodesians burn the house down on their way out?

Suggested reading:
The Counter-Revolution of 1776: Slave Resistance and the Origins of the United States of America, Gerald Horne, MJF Books, 2018
The American Slave Coast: A History of the Slave-Breeding Industry, Ned and Constance Sublette, Chicago Review Press, 2017

18 | *Peter Werbe*

Spring 2019 Fifth Estate issue. The publication began in 1965.

History of the Fifth Estate
Part 1: The Early Years
Spring 1996

"The Fifth Estate supports the cause of revolution everywhere."
FBI Report

In my estimation, the above nine-word summary by the nation's secret police serves adequately as an abbreviated history of this paper on the occasion of its 30th anniversary.

However, it will definitely not satisfy my friends and comrades on the FE staff who urged me on our 20th and 25th anniversaries to write a comprehensive account of the newspaper's long existence as a radical publication.

It is not due to an inflated sense of self-importance that people feel the story should be recounted, but rather because the history of this paper mirrored a period of large-scale rebellion in its early years and continues today to give expression to a body of ideas which find little exposure elsewhere.

The FE was started by Harvey Ovshinsky, a 17-year-old Detroiter who previously self-published in high school what was then called a fanzine. After visiting California in 1965 and spending a summer working on the *Los Angeles Free Press*, the first of what was to be dubbed the Underground Press, he returned to Detroit filled with enthusiasm for a similar effort here. Our founder also brought back the title for his paper, named after a coffeehouse he frequented on Sunset Strip. The owner later threatened to sue the *Fifth Estate* for appropriating its name from his shop.

Ovshinsky assembled a staff of his siblings and a few friends at his parents' suburban home, and borrowed money from his father to pay the printer. The inaugural issue of the Fifth Estate, dated Nov. 19, 1965, proudly announced on its masthead that it was "Detroit's New Progressive Biweekly Newspaper." It was produced on a portable typewriter, taking advantage of the so-called off-set printing-revolution, which meant anyone who could type and had scissors and glue, could publish a newspaper. Previously, typographic technology meant only those with specialized equipment or a goodly amount of money could see their views in print.

The first issue featured a critical review of a Bob Dylan non-acoustic concert[1], a "borrowed" Jules Feiffer cartoon, a hip events calendar, and an announcement of a March on Washington to end the war in Vietnam. The finished product was passed out to friends and concertgoers. When I received a copy of the first edition at a University of Detroit Mr. Bo blues concert, I was amazed that a paper with radical content could be produced by young people like me.

Such a publishing venture doesn't seem so out of the ordinary today, but 30 years ago, with the exception of a few newspapers like New York City's *Village Voice*, little similar to this was being printed anywhere. The mainstream press didn't review Dylan, or publish calendars (certainly not for poetry readings and the like), and articles critical of the growing U.S. involvement in Vietnam was unheard of' except in a few socialist papers.

The fledgling FE stumbled along for a few issues, (changing its self-description by the second issue to "The Voice of Liberal Detroit") covering the emerging alternative arts, culture, and political scene.[2] But in early 1966, after Ovshinsky moved the paper's office from his parents' basement to a mid-town Detroit storefront near Wayne State University, it became almost a one-man operation. The move, however, saved the paper from an early extinction when it was quickly discovered by young activists from the newly-formed Detroit Committee to End the War in Vietnam, the Detroit Artists Workshop, and others in what was a bohemian, arts, radical politics, student, youth ghetto. Overnight the paper's office became a bustling center of writers, photographers, and artists, all anxious to contribute their efforts.

As the anti-war, civil rights, hippie, New Left and alternative culture movements grew in Detroit, so did the paper. Our pages became a forum for the new and rebellious ideas that characterized the era. By late 1966, the FE relocated to a high-visibility, hippie hang-out area known as Plum Street where we opened a bookstore above our offices. The early paper's content was a mix of articles about psychedelic drugs, the anti-war movement, rock and roll, the alternative culture, and anything that was anti-authority.

Though the 1960s have received a bad name in some quarters for hyperbole in writing and excess in action, they are exactly what attracted me to it. When I look back through crumbling early issues of the FE, with their colorful psychedelic artwork, articles denouncing "The Man" and "the pigs" and "Amerikkka," and photos of exuberant young people holding up clenched fists or dancing with abandon at a Love-In, much of the writing and ideas still look good to me even after the passage of a generation.

The nation-wide underground press movement was enormous in scope, with at least 500 regularly appearing tabloids by 1970, and perhaps hundreds more which disappeared after only an issue or two. The FE office's mimeograph machine was used by numerous high school, civil rights and anti-war groups, dissident union caucuses, and even GIs, to print newsletters. To the horror of their officers, active-duty GIs circulated hundreds of anti-war papers and newsletters at U.S. bases, on ships, and even in Vietnam.

Liberation News Service in New York City sent out twice-weekly news packets with reports of protests and features from around the world including much from the North Vietnamese side of the war. The Underground Press Syndicate was established to coordinate connections between the papers and promote their distribution. It was estimated the combined weekly circulation of the alternative papers was two million.

On FE publication day, thousands of papers were distributed to local stores by a collective specializing in the distribution of radical periodicals. Hundreds were mailed to GIs in Vietnam who apparently were not offended by either our call for the victory of their enemy in the field, or for them to mutiny as a way to end the war. Soldiers often wrote to tell of how our papers were passed along from unit to unit throughout the war zone or in the U.S.

Also, a small army of street sellers would assemble at our offices to grab a bundle of papers for resale at demos, concerts, and shopping malls. The cover price was 15 cents and the sellers kept a nickel. We had to fight constant battles with cops, military brass, security guards, principals, and foremen for the right to distribute our paper without harassment. Later, 80 FE coin boxes were installed across the city.

The early paper reflected the lives of people who thought either the Age of Aquarius or World Revolution (or both) was at hand, and who believed that we were a vital part of it. Maybe this sounds like youthful foolishness today, but in the 1960s the empire appeared to be unraveling at home and abroad. We saw ourselves at once as the allies of Third World guerrilla movements which were assaulting U.S. foreign bastions, and as the leading expression of revolution at home, "within the belly of the beast," as we glamorized it in those days.

To us, making love and revolution to the sounds of the MC5, the Stooges, and other seminal Detroit rock bands was fun as well as a serious calling. Add the entire psychedelic experience and we were a long way from the lifestyles of either our parents or from the last generation of revolutionaries who had their origins in the 1930s labor movement.

The edge of fun began to diminish, however, with the advent of events such as the massive 1967 Detroit uprising (the FE offices were tear gassed by the National Guard) and other urban black insurgencies, the police rampage at the 1968 Chicago Democratic Convention, the escalation of the U.S. war against the civilian population of Vietnam and revelations of massacres like that at My Lai, the domestic counter-insurgency murders of Black Panther Party members, the assassinations of Martin Luther King (to halt his potential for labor organizing and antiwar opposition) and Bobby Kennedy (who would have beat Nixon handily in the 1968 elections and probably ended the Vietnam war), the Tet Offensive, the murder of the Kent and Jackson State students, and the 1970 declaration of martial law in Canada to combat Quebecois separatists. These and other similar events came down on us child revolutionaries with an intensity we hadn't anticipated.

We suddenly realized that the Empire we had characterized as a house of cards was fighting back tenaciously and with deadly force. Our publishing efforts reflected this change. There was less "fun" and more "struggle" in our pages. We became a weekly with a circulation of 15 to 20,000; strident calls for revolution became standard fare on our covers with frequent images of armed Black Panthers or Viet Cong guerrillas. By 1969, our founder, feeling increasingly isolated by the radical fervor of the staff, quit the paper following his disagreement with a vote to print a front cover taken from a Cuban poster featuring an array of guns and the quintessential one-word slogan of revolutionary impatience, "NOW!," in six-inch letters.

During that period, FE staff members traveled to North Vietnam, Cambodia, and Cuba to meet with the enemy in a show of solidarity with those at the forefront of combating U.S. Imperialism. Although we may have exhibited a large degree of naiveté about the nature of the Stalinist regimes we glorified, the fact that young people in their teens and twenties took on the tasks of internal opposition to a monstrous war machine still seems admirable to me.

Every important social and political current of the '60s found expression in the pages of the Fifth Estate. The anti-war, civil rights, gay, feminist, youth and labor struggles, were cumulatively referred to as The Movement. In retrospect, it seems incredible that the rug could have been pulled out so quickly from under a social phenomenon of such breadth and depth. Although the reasons for the dissolution of the movements of that era and the collapse of the underground papers are complex, I would date the watershed event as the 1972 elections to mark the official end of the "60s."

The emergence of the 1970s Me Generation and the Reagan years began with the massive defeat of presidential peace candidate George McGovern, and the landslide re-election of the war criminal, Nixon. Our realization that the American voting public was unwilling to elect a Democrat with a barely tepid anti-war platform, and instead chose to return to office the person responsible for the mass slaughter in Vietnam was a blow from which the anti-war movement and the New Left never recovered.

The dreaded Nixon, who had won office by less than a percentage point four years previous, had actually improved his popularity despite all the returning body bags and illegal bombings of North Vietnam and Cambodia. Also, the ending of the hated draft and the Vietnamization of the war began to erode public support for The Movement which had become increasingly more radical in its beliefs and actions.

Those at the core of the resistance and publishing projects began to burn out. By 1972, the FE had resumed its twice-monthly schedule after appearing weekly for almost a year—a schedule, which combined with our intense political work, had nearly destroyed our brains and bodies. For five or six years, many of us had literally done nothing else night and day other than movement work, never taking a vacation, rarely even a trip to the movies. (People were dying in Vietnam; how could one justify entertainment?)

Relentless contestation—unending rounds of meetings, demonstrations, rallies, occupations, deadlines, conferences, arrests, courts and the like—took its toll.[3] Although these activities contained the positive moments of an oppositional movement (being at a march with a million people or with thousands of young men burning their draft cards is indeed a rich and memorable experience), they were also emotionally grueling.

People throughout the movement began bailing out. Jobs, families, gurus, rural communes, even Leninist sects, plus a host of other activities were sought to provide some respite from years of relentless revolutionary agitation. Alternative papers across the country began folding at a rapid rate as internal disputes, lack of purpose, financial problems and official repression took its toll. By 1975, Liberation News Service and the Underground Press Syndicate had disappeared and all but a few radical publications ceased publishing within a very short period.

In 1974, I joined the exodus, leaving the paper after eight years, for a combination of the above reasons (with the exception of a guru and Leninism). Rather than endure what one staffer suggested would be a "dignified death," the remaining FE members began thrashing about for a new identity and took on a fortunately short-lived perspective of labor militancy influenced by the International Socialist group before managing a burst of energy in what was to be a precursor to the many fashionable alternative arts and political weeklies that exist today. For about a year the FE was a lively and innovative bi-weekly publication, both editorially and in its design.

Soon, numerous internal contradictions began to crash in on the paper, and by 1975 it was almost terminal, deeply in debt to printers and suppliers, almost devoid of staff following several serious personality clashes, and dependent upon commercial advertising including X-rated movies and cigarette ads for revenue and salaries. The remnants of the staff printed a notice in the paper that they would soon close up shop unless they received an influx of new participants.

A number of us, including several other former staffers and friends, who were influenced by the writings of Fredy Perlman, Jacques Camatte, Jean Baudrillard, council and left communists, and the Situationists, answered the call. Eleven of us had constituted ourselves as the Eat the Rich Gang and undertook a number of projects in 1974 through '75, including publishing *Wildcat!*, and *The Irrational in Politics* at the Detroit Print Coop, producing a number of Fifth Estate inserts, setting up study groups, as well as some sabotage activity and radical pranks.

When our group arrived at the Fifth Estate office, the three remaining staffers were less than enthusiastic about us rejoining the paper. But, by an 11 to 3 vote, we (the new staff) decided to become a monthly, to no longer accept ads (they were the voice of capital, we said), and to stop paying salaries. The three holdovers were horrified and left after a few issues.

Unlike those remainders of the '60s who devolved into dreary workerism or cynicism, we were enthusiastic about the ideas we had discovered and were happy to discard Marx, Lenin, political parties, unions and all of the rest of what the left held dear.[4] In my estimation, the readiness on our part to adopt new and challenging analyses of what constituted revolutionary activity is what accounts for our maintaining one of the few newspapers to survive the 1960s.

Although the University of Michigan's Labadie Collection of libertarian and radical materials lists us as the oldest continually publishing anarchist paper in American history, when we set out on our present course in Summer 1975, we had no idea any anarchists had survived the 1930s, nor did we identify ourselves as such. We were quite surprised to discover a small, but thriving anarchist movement whose activity was primarily confined to publishing journals.

We were soon contacted by a group of older comrades who were the remaining participants of the 1920s and '30s anarchist movements with whom we established cordial and rewarding relationships. These stalwarts of another era have almost all passed from the scene, but their memory as committed, militant, unswerving proponents of "The Ideal" remains with us as a model of resistance and vision.

Articles in the new monthly Fifth Estate were based on the ultra-left perspectives gleaned from our readings of Camatte, Jean Baudrillard, the Situationists, Wilhelm Reich and others. Other perspectives developed from exciting discussions hosted by Fredy and Lorraine Perlman at their home where we furiously debated and discussed ideas contained in the books and pamphlets published at a rapid pace by Black & Red.[5]

By 1980, we decided the dictum, "All isms are wasisms," was correct and began extending the anti-authoritarian critique beyond the obvious oppression of capitalism and the state to uncover deeper roots of the repression of the human spirit and the biosphere. This led us to the positions often characterized as anti-technology and anti-civilization which this paper is best known for advocating.

Writing the last two sentences makes me realize this may be a good place to end Part I of this history. Our story from 1975 to the present is much more difficult to relate quickly and simply since it involves the development of complex ideas as well as events. Also, in a sense, we're still in the midst of it.

Notes:

1. Dylan's use of amplified instruments was very controversial at the time since he was considered a folk artist, not a rocker, who backed himself with only acoustic guitar and harmonica. When he began his second set at Detroit's Masonic Temple in 1965 accompanied by The Hawks, a full rock band, a portion of the audience began chanting, 'We want Dylan," and a handful walked out. Laconic as always, Dylan responded from the stage, 'Who'd ya come to see?"

2. At some point in the 1970s, our definite article, "the," literally fell off the layout when we adopted our current masthead. This deletion caused the Post Office to list us as *Fifth Estate* which is how many readers refer to us as well.

3. Many underground papers, including this one, had become dependent on ad revenue from record companies who correctly saw our publications as the best venue for tapping into the emerging youth culture. However, as mainstream media got "hipper," and rock papers, such as *Rolling Stone,* more corporate, the radical press was left high and dry with ads falling off to almost nothing.

4. In 1974, The Eat the Rich Gang helped organize a successful demonstration against an assemblage of Detroit's wealthy and distributed a cookbook we produced for the event entitled, *To Serve The Rich.* It contained recipes calling for human ingredients and included dining on Split Priest Soup, Rocky Mt. Oysters Rockefeller, a Hearst Patty, and others named after long gone politicians and corporate heads.

A disdainful Marxist we knew advised us we'd have better spent our time on a pamphlet about socialism. "Socialism is about work," he sternly reprimanded us. "I thought it was about utopia," I said. "No," he assured me. We took him at his word and looked elsewhere for a political philosophy.

5. Lorraine Perlman's memoirs of Fredy, *Having Little, Being Much* is an excellent resource for an understanding of this period. Also, FE back issues (now available in a digital format at www.FifthEstate.org) contain the ideas which are the wellspring of our current publishing efforts and the original form is certainly superior to their being summarized.

Suggested reading:

Scratching the Surface: Adventures in Storytelling, Harvey Ovshinsky, Wayne State University Press, 2021

Having Little, Being Much, Lorraine Perlman, Black & Red-Detroit, 1989

What Does Fifth Estate Mean?
Spring 1996

People always ask about the origin of the paper's odd name. It is odd, and for our purposes over the last twenty years, an unfortunate one. The title refers to the three powerful French estates at the time of the 1789 revolution—the aristocracy, clergy, and common people. A wag in the 1920s quipped that the popular press exercised such power over public opinion, it was literally a fourth estate—so, apparently the fifth is one up on the fourth. It has become a generic term for all non-corporate, non-mainstream media.

When CBC-TV began an investigative documentary program using that name in 1975, we wrote the Canadian station telling them since we already had used the name for ten years, why didn't they find another. The channel never responded.

We've been saddled with that name for three decades which seems all the worse in later years since the quantification of life is nothing we are fond of and we oppose estates of any sort. Although we've often considered changing the title, it seems more trouble than it's worth, particularly since we still encounter people who remember us fondly from the '60s and are glad we are "still keeping the faith." Also, the name signifies a continuity we don't want to lose.

Chapter 2
Politics

Selecting a Master or Ousting a Tyrant
Spring 2004

I haven't voted for a president since the 1968 quadrennial fraud where one war criminal, Hubert Humphrey, lost to Richard Nixon who would become one. I plunked my ballot down for Black Panther leader, Eldridge Cleaver, on the Peace and Freedom Party ticket. I suspect that was the last time I will enter a voting booth.

Humphrey had disgraced himself, stating infamously, "Vietnam is our finest hour," even though the extent of the imperial slaughter had already been widely exposed Also, this once famous liberal was nominated beneath the truncheons of the Chicago cops at the uproarious and repressive 1968 Democratic Party convention.

The Democratic Vice-President wasn't a candidate who could be made more palatable by invoking the phrase, "the lesser of the two evils," when compared to the dreadful Nixon. In fact, Humphrey was perceived by many of us as being the greater evil, given the Johnson administration's merciless prosecution of its war against Vietnam, and its failure to stop attacks on black leaders and communities.

Did we guess wrong? Nothing could have been worse than Nixon's mad escalation of the war which finally left 3.5 million Vietnamese dead as well as 58,000 of the invaders. Humphrey lost by a mere one half of a percentage point and those abstainers, including me, could have conceivably made a difference in the election's outcome. This, of course, assumes Humphrey would have done anything differently.

In the previous election, some radicals backed Lyndon Johnson over the arch-conservative Barry Goldwater, fearing that he represented the extreme anti-communist wing of the Republican Party and, if elected, would involve the US in a large-scale ground war in Southeast Asia. It was the liberal Democrat, as it turned out, who did just that. Electoral history is replete with other such examples of how the lesser of two evil voting produced the very evil most feared.

Electoral activity as it relates to somewhat authentic reform doesn't have much of a track record either. One has only to recall the election triumphs of the left in 1936 Spain and 1970 Chile to be a bit apprehensive about what such victories achieve. When the will of the people was expressed through the official means provided by the state apparatus, it spurred a fascist revolt followed by decades of repressive dictatorship in Spain and 17 years in Chile. It gives even greater weight to the old anarchist saying, "If voting could change anything, it would be illegal."

The question of voting by those opposed to the state and capital arises again as we confront the damage to people and the planet caused by the vile Bush regime in just over three years. However, many of those who should know better have bought into the anti-Bush rhetoric to the extent of accepting the prevailing left/liberal mythology that the 1990s under the Clinton/Gore administrations was some sort of Golden Age with a booming economy and peace.

But this means ignoring NAFTA, de-industrialization and job loss, "welfare reform" (a polite phrase for kicking the poor off the rolls), more cops, one environmental sell-out after the next, and, if we want to keep score of dead Iraqis (and we should), our great liberal icons are responsible for hundreds of thousands of civilian deaths through the enforcement of economic sanctions and thousands of bombing raids on that country. Bush's toll makes him a piker compared to the mountain of corpses Clinton produced.

There's no disagreement that Bush and his corporate and right-wing sponsors have turned the system entirely into a racket for the rich (rather than the crumbs it previously provided). The only positive aspect of this is that it neatly illuminates the true function of government—an apparatus to loot the populace and protect society's rulers.

But Bush policies are so egregiously shortsighted that even the financial sector of the U.S. elite class worry that the greed and messianic drive of the dominant right-wing ideology threaten the long-term interests of capital itself. When the International Monetary Fund (IMF) warns that Bushonomics endanger the entire world economic system, it is a clear signal that big capital is worried about policies that maximize short term profit over long term financial stability.

That government is based on organized force and looting is nothing new. The state arose thousands of years ago as an institution to protect wealth and hierarchy and little has changed subsequently. The fact that a few governments in the last 300 years have given a thought to the needs of the ruled is a late development and one which is currently being reversed, particularly in this country. So-called democratic governments are but a footnote in the repressive history of the political state.

BushCo shovels the swag into the maw of the greedy corporations in an unprecedented manner because the opposition is so symbolic. Imperial Rome knew that it needed to provide bread and circuses for the masses so they would ignore the conditions of their subjugation. Now, Bush offers only television circuses in the form of terror alerts and wars against the empire's great enemies no matter what pipsqueaks they really are, plus the usual fare of media titillation.

There are no grand movements of opposition even as the country's infrastructure deteriorates, schools close, prices rise and more and more jobs move to areas in which the wage structures are what the capitalists hope will soon be the world norm.

This will not be altered by the election of what has traditionally been the other half of the ruling political con game. George W. Bush, and John Kerry, the presumptive Democratic presidential candidate at this writing, are fellow members of the secretive, upper class, good old boy, Yale-based Skull and Bones society, and it is unclear whether the latter's election would signal an abrupt change in the disastrous Republican policies, or just a change of faces.

Gwendolyn Mink, author of Welfare's End, and currently writing a book on the Democratic Party, said, "The Kerry campaign seems to be focused on demonstrating the candidate's martial virtue to win over the warrior electorate. Combined with his unapologetic defense of his vote giving Bush carte blanche to invade Iraq, the masculinist Kerry campaign raises disturbing questions about just how much he would change current foreign and military policy."

It would be an excellent sign if the American people at least showed enough collective fortitude and plain common sense to handily reject someone who is destroying their standard of living, lied about the reasons for war, and is giving the store away to the rich. But screw voting as a means of stopping Bush. The real question is, "Why aren't there hundreds of thousands out in the streets banging pots and pans demanding social and economic justice such as we've seen in South American countries?" The answer is stuff for another article, but ultimately it is the most important question we face.

Those who oppose the state on principle, but are willing to abandon the concept based on a perceived need to defeat Bush, should probably just go ahead. Particularly if they can get past the sequential humiliation of wage work, followed by voting on the day designated for choosing your ruler.

However, I wonder what those people in the anarchist milieu think they will accomplish by casting an isolated ballot that matters little in the aggregate total. There certainly aren't enough of us to constitute an anti-authoritarian bloc of voters, and I doubt if we'll see an Anarchists for Kerry committee being established to urge disaffected radicals to register and vote.

So, at best, voting is an empty gesture born of an understandable frustration of being unable to accomplish our goals through traditional anarchist direct action and community building, but at worst, it is a sacrifice of principle for nothing in return.

Author Postscript: This essay was written prior to the 2004 Bush/Kerry presidential election. It reflects the traditional anarchist position of abstention from participating in the electoral process by voting or supporting political parties.

Since 2008, as the Republican Party became increasingly racist, misogynist, and fascist, I have voted in elections with a sense of doing harm reduction to protect the most vulnerable communities under attack from the right wing. This doesn't mean my critique of the political system and its mechanisms has lessened. Only that until we have effective means of protecting our communities from what the right wing intends, this is what we're stuck with.

The *Fifth Estate* distributed this single-sheet extra at the 1980 Republican National Convention held in Detroit's Cobo Arena. It shocked and enraged the Republican delegates, but delighted city residents.

Republicans: Get Out Of Town
Fall 1980 Convention Extra

REPUBLICANS!

We mean it! Pack your bags and leave Detroit! Take your vile political party, your cadaverous candidate, your stinking love for the state, your vicious racism, your blatant sexism, your hatred for the poor, your insane war plans, your nauseating patriotism, your putrid Christianity, your antiquated sexual morality, your contempt for the rest of the world, your millionaire officials, your middle-class sensibilities and your pathetic lack of vision and get out of our city!

Daily life is bad enough around here without your two-ring circus turning this city into a mini-police state decorated with balloons and pennants. Don't be fooled by the pervasive media hype that would like to convince both you and us that your appearance is "good for Detroit." Most of us know it is your fellow Republicans like Henry Ford II, Lee Iacocca, Max Fisher and the rest who have produced the current depression in Detroit (and, in Detroit, it is a depression and not a recession like back in your suburban enclaves). No one cares about your shrinking political gang and its attempt to wrest control of the state apparatus from the clowns currently occupying the White House. The last time your slimy party elected a President, only 13 percent of the U.S. population even bothered to vote for him and he turned out to be a crook!

Your very appearance—your fat, white faces, beady-eyed,

dreaming of an America that never was and never will be is an insult to all of us who have made possible your average delegate income of $47,000 a year! The city you think so ugly and violent is constructed just that way so as to allow you to enjoy your American Way of Life while we and the rest of the world exist on what's left. Even walking down the street you are a provocation in a city which has been gutted of much of its human characteristics and replaced instead by that which you adore—architectural monstrosities, factories, machines, freeways, and offices.

Your desire to defend this grotesque world plucked clean of its human meaning, its sensuality and its joy with MX missiles, neutron bombs, new manned bombers and even more nuclear weapons, makes you our implacable enemy! We want you out of here and fast! Go to Miami Beach where most of you wanted the Convention to be held in the first place. It is a fitting place for the living dead.

Your stay in Detroit only serves to incite our rage at this society and at you—the cheerful robots who sing its praises. We are filled with desire for a free and full life which will mean you and everything you represent being swept from the Earth. You insult our dreams with every moment you remain! Leave!

Revenge of the Nerds
The Republican Victory
Winter 1995

"*Consider the average intelligence of the common man, then realize 50 percent are even stupider.*"
   Mark Twain

"*I am nothing, a cloak of skin with a mouth saying, Don't kill everything so soon.*"
   Mick Vranich and Wordban'd

Wouldn't the headline, "61% of Electorate Avoid Polls; Conservative White Men Elect Right-Wing of Political Racket to Power," after the Nov. 8 Republican sweep of Congressional seats have been more accurate than those in the media which trumpeted, "Americans Vote for Change?" Admittedly, mine is not exactly snappy, nor would it fit well as a banner headline, but it's closer to the truth.

At some level of consciousness, even the 39 percent of the voters who overcame the lethargy, cynicism, despair, disgust, and resignation to vote, must know their ballot will do little to change daily life.

Also, the Republican victories did not represent the change in American political character anywhere near what the media pundits and right-wing talk show hosts would have it. The difference between the results of this election and the 1992 Congressional races was created by only a two percent shift to the Republicans spurred on by the gun lobby and right-wing talk radio, plus decreased participation by the traditional Democratic base.

As it was, the Republican national vote was a scant 50.5 percent of the total, but they obviously had the numbers in the right places. Most importantly, although both parties were Political Action Committee-dollar driven, in the end it was the Republicans who generated greatly vaster sums which translated into victories. This is what created the so-called landslide for the right. The actual number of voters who wanted right-wing Republicans to run the government probably comes in at only around 20 percent of the adult population. In many ways, the election was a parliamentary-style, well-deserved vote of no-confidence in the Clinton government rather than assent to the Republican's murky Contract with America.

But regardless, the rightists now have the levers of political power after 40 years of center-right control by the Democrats and although the Republicans are no less part of the reigning political racket, this is the first time in over a generation they will be positioned to derail the political trajectory of liberal statist social programs begun in the 1930s. For most of the population nothing too much will change in material terms from what would have occurred if there had been a Democratic victory. The slow economic squeeze being suffered by most of the middle- and working-class will go on unabated regardless of which party is in office.

The rich will undoubtedly get richer as Republicans vote to repeal the capital gains tax and figure other ways to get more cash to the high side of the trough. However, the most significant result of the Republican "revolution" will be that the poor will get poorer and their lives much more miserable. The fingernail grip many have on life will likely be stomped on.

The Republican victory is not just the revenge of the nerds—those resentful, goody-good, pious churchgoers who never got in on what they saw as the sex- and dope-soaked, anti-authority generation of the 'sixties. It's also the revenge of the Delta Sigma Pi's—the rich, handsome, party animal, frat boys who were also out for a good time, but who hated hippies, drank, rather than smoked dope, and whose social conscience ended at putting a buck in the collection plate at their Presbyterian church service.

Together, the Delta Sig/nerd coalition has announced plans to wage a two-front battle against the poor and the "counter-culture McGovernites," as the new Speaker of the House of Representatives frothed before the election. The rabid Pat Buchannan already set the terms of engagement earlier at the 1992 Republican convention in Dallas when he shouted a battle-cry from the speaker's podium: "There is a religious war going on... We must take back our cities, and take back our culture." He's talking about the poor and us! In Washington, giddy, newly elected Republicans are sharpening their knives to disembowel the Democratic side of the racket. In Michigan and other states, ex-paintball players run around in camo, toting exotic assault weapons forming unofficial state militias and talk of arresting the (old) Congress for treason. The stench of fascism is in the air, even if it's not on the immediate political agenda.

But the reason for all this thunder on the right is mystifying. If it is proto-counterrevolutionary with the ominous state militias echoing the Freikorps, para-military bands which roamed post-World War I Germany attacking the left, what revolution are these current guys the counter to? Have these authoritarian statists suddenly come out of the closet with an almost anarchist apprehension of government? Is it only they who are able to discern that the Clintons are really leftists under their centrist, opportunistic, corporatist facade who mask their plans for One World Government by selling out to the corporations on everything from trade agreements to the redwoods to health insurance?

Fascism always contains a strong quantity of twisted psychopathology—exaggerated hatreds, resentments, and fears— as one of its essential building blocks, but its appearance on the historical stage in the 20th century has traditionally been linked with very specific opposition to an upsurge of the left or the trade unions or the demand for minority rights, not their collapse as we are currently witnessing. Fascist sentiment will probably remain as such, rather than be mobilized as a movement which seeks the power of the state since capitalist classes in other countries have had bad experiences with this political philosophy and only turn to it in cases of extreme emergency. They have no need to up the ante of political rule if current methods of government serve to secure their interests.

Although only a small percentage of what motivated Republican votes could be accurately fascist sentiment, it is out there in surprising numbers. Where it surfaces, it presents itself as a bizarre psycho/politics with hysteria, rage, and threats reserved for phantom enemies, having no authentic ones about. This prototype can perhaps best be seen in the membership of rapidly forming unofficial state militias. However, beneath the militaristic bluster and bravado, and bristling armaments, fascist personality types are psychic chickenshits who cower before authority, ache to be submerged in hierarchies, and are spineless when it comes to confronting the real source of their economic misery and social angst. Hence, they aim at the wrong target—those in the classes below them.

At the right's most ragged edge, you can hear national talk shows, computer bulletin boards, and newsletters consumed with whacko chatter about an imminent demonic New World Order, where U.S. sovereignty will be lost to the United Nations and our cities patrolled by Blue Helmets—UN police. Callers into talk shows insist they have incontrovertible documents to show the foreheads of newborns will be imprinted with bar codes beginning with 666, that 100,000 Hong Kong cops will be brought here after the colony reverts to China in 1997, that mysterious all-black helicopters are patrolling our skies, that a government plan to totally disarm the people is at work, that road signs are already in place for a network of concentration camps for patriots, etc., etc.

Certainly, these nuts are not totally off the wall with their fears of centralized government; it's a position anarchist anti-statists share. But theirs is an authoritarian and paranoid rejection of politics, one which dares not examine the fundamental character of this society, its culture, and its economy. Rather than looking at the authentic crimes of capitalism and the state, they wind up with liturgical recitations of the Constitution and pathetic conspiracy theories which leave daily life intact—the job, TV, the mall—and a call for politics which only affirms everything which brought them and the rest of the world the problems we all face.

At the respectable edge of this reactionary wedge are the Republicans, (and even Clinton and many Democrats) who plan to dismantle the social safety net—those entitlement programs which have to do with feeding, housing and caring for the tens of millions of poor this system pushes to its margins. The Republicans, impervious to an impending Christmas season, sounded in late 1994 like a cliché from a 19th Century Dickens novel as they called for a $60 billion welfare cutoff to families, sending children to orphanages, and re-opening poor farms. With their insistence that poverty emanates from the ill-habits of penury rather than the greed of the rich, and their triumphal, smug arrogance and loathing of the poor, they loom as a Frankenstein-like resurrection of Rev. Cotton Mather, Thomas Malthus, and The Great Gatsby stitched together into one great social monster seeking the vengeance of the Lord on the least fortunate.

This is not to say that Congress and government are not a corrupt cash cow for special interests. Just that the Republicans are no less a part of the apparatus and the only real special interests being served are no different than they ever were; the wealthy, the corporations and the politicians themselves. Nor should this be taken as a defense of the hideously dehumanizing, bureaucratic welfare system which liberals once correctly assailed as demeaning to the poor. But now, with the debate moved ever farther to the right, liberals are shocked about talk of its reduction or outright abolition and, rather than remain critics of welfare, have become its staunchest defenders. "What will become of the poor," they correctly inquire?

Conservatives couldn't give a shit what happens to them. The poor rarely vote. When they do, it's predominately Democratic. So, beating up the destitute and powerless makes good political sense for the Republicans who, in this way, can assuage the massive economic and social anxieties felt by the middle-class. The Republicans know those in the middle-class who bother to vote for them love punitive politics (the death penalty, the military, abortion prohibition, welfare cut-offs, etc.). This could mean goodbye anti-poverty stuff or at least a massive scaling down.

The liberal criticisms of the welfare system are certainly correct, but so are some of the conservative ones: huge chunks of money go into corrupt programs which amount to little more than payoffs to big city Democratic political machines with the main recipients being office holders and poverty program bureaucrats, rather than the poor. However, for those who depend on state stipends for the wherewithal of life including the basics of food and shelter (such as the Women, Infants and Children [WIC] feeding program), the pittance received, accompanied by the humiliation of the system is hardly the rip-off the middle-class grumbles about, but that misperception is what translates into votes for attack dog politicians.

Right-wing critics of welfare charge that everything from New Deal to Great Society programs have failed to elevate the poor, but rather have created an "enduring culture of poverty" where generations have come to expect the state dole. In conservative parlance, "the government takes from the productive and gives to the unproductive."

This modern restatement of 19th century Spencerian survival-of-the fittest Social Darwinism is the perfect ideology for this era. Although we are assured by the corporate media that the economy is expanding domestically and within regional and international trade zones and tariff agreements, it is viewed with apprehension by many that good paying jobs are disappearing and the future is uncertain. In this context, it is easy to understand why advocating the withdrawal of generosity from bygone eras seems so popular.

This misses the seemingly obvious. Poverty in capitalist society is created by a class system which distributes wealth disproportionately to different sectors. The contention that poverty is caused by poor education, lack of job skills, poor motivation or the like, gives credence to the pernicious idea that poverty is self-generated. Both conservatives and liberals think, if only they'd get a GED or some job training, they could fit right into the nearest suburb. That's ridiculous. If somehow everyone in the country obtained a Ph.D., it would simply mean the McDonald's counterperson would have a degree in French renaissance literature and the garbage collector a graduate degree in anthropology. Is it really beyond so many people's comprehension that the attributes of the poor are symptoms of poverty, not its cause?

Also, the Horatio Alger rags-to-riches mythology continues—"Anyone can make anything of themselves, blah, blah." I informed one lunkhead I had the misfortune of talking with recently that statistics demonstrate quite clearly the existence of an ironclad, permanent caste/class system. Those born into a social/economic category stay there with few exceptions—the poor are born and stay poor; the same for the rich. But no, he began, "Anyone can..."

This social blind spot acts as a convenient anchor for denial about the maldistribution of income. If the poor are responsible for their own plight, what responsibility does the hard working, white male bear in the situation? None, is increasingly the answer. The punitive nature of the response becomes even more obvious when one points out the enormous quantity of public money going to subsidize corporations and the rich. You hear in return, "Oh, I'm against that, too," he or she will say, but then votes to deny aid to children and the elderly.

Classic fascists used to resent and fear the rich—the big bourgeoisie—as well as the lower orders. This current crop of conservo-fascists loves the rich and famous and scurries about devising rationalizations for the disparities in income. Since the number of poor is increasing and beggars and homeless are permanent features of our cities, it becomes necessary to explain why so many people are doing so badly in what we are continually reminded, "is the richest nation in the world.".

One explanation currently being debated in the media is that it's not only social habits which disable the poor from upward mobility, but in the case of people grouped under the heading of black or African-Americans, a genetic failing as well. This canard always surfaces whenever great disparities of wealth appear. At the turn of the century, wealthy New Yorkers were convinced by science that Jews and other Eastern Europeans (the poor of the Lower East Side) were genetically deficient.

For over a hundred years, the same analysis, under a variety of pseudo-sciences, has been applied to the descendants of the slaves brought to the New World. The latest manifestation, *The Bell Curve* by Charles Murray and Richard Hernstein, postulates intelligence is largely controlled by genetic inheritance and that blacks have lower cognitive abilities (that is, they are dumber) than whites as measured by IQ tests.

I have no intention of refuting the scientific and social foolishness of this contention as others have done it more than adequately and thoroughly recently in numerous liberal and radical publications. In one such endeavor, Adolph Reed Jr., in a Nov. 28, 1994 highly recommended *Nation* article said, "It is both beneath my dignity and politically unacceptable to engage in a debate that treats as an open question that I might be a monkey," and then proceeds to prove Murray and Hernstein are (with apologies to our simian friends).

Even liberal commentators recognize the underlying social and political purpose of this debate. If the recipients of social largess are genetically incapable of improving their lot through the assistance of social programs, why throw money at the hopeless?

However, even if we were to grant validity to the spurious claims of these racists, what then should be made of their conclusions? If, in fact, you had a genetically disadvantaged population sector, shouldn't they be given special consideration just as we give to those with physical disabilities? The lie of it all can perhaps best be seen when one compares the difference in the IQ scores between whites and blacks the authors report, and realize it doesn't explain the much vaster differential between white and black income and wealth. Race in America is the first way income is disproportionally distributed and depends on the maintenance of theories like Murray and Hernstein's to perpetuate the myths of racism. Hence, the explanation and importance of racism's indelible permanence.

Even though the Republican "revolution" is based on a minority of the population and perhaps could have been thwarted by the participation of only a few more good-hearted voters, it still makes sense that most anti-authoritarians joined with the vast majority in boycotting the polls.

Although democracy is only one variant of capitalist rule, it isn't the worst. So, the question often arises regarding electoral abstention by anarchists. Someone will always argue, wouldn't it have been better to have swallowed our principles and sent all the

Republicans down to defeat as happened to the odious, authentic fascist, Oliver North, in Virginia? Since voting is so passive, why not submit to the sequential humiliation of working followed by a trip to the voting booth to forestall the coming to power of right-wing creeps who will be around for the next two years bashing the poor, the gay or anyone not on the white, up-tight and Christian right?

Firstly, the traditional anarchist, anti-statist arguments against voting are valid in this election no less than in others. This critique of voting is accurate as to how little efficacy the act contains. Also, since voting only matters in the aggregate, if we were really to be effective in the electoral arena, not only should we vote as individuals, but also organize others to do similarly. It's easy to see where this path leads: Anarchists for Sen. Charles Robb—North's corrupt and slimy Democratic opponent. I think not.

Secondly, the Democrats got what they deserved, much like all of the ruling parties did in Italy in 1993. And, like Italy, voters reached to the right for a solution rather than daring to take on the totality of the ruling racket. Clinton, an opportunist corporatist who has received high approval ratings from the *Wall Street Journal* for his pro-business stances on NAFTA and GATT, and the Democrats are not an opposition to the right, but its partner. This can be seen by the President and his party's post-election weaseling remarks on prayer and middle-class tax cuts (with apologies to weasels).

As the corporate media in this country witnesses the formal political power shift, it obligingly cranks out the Republican message: the People have turned to the right; they want less government, less taxes, etc. None of this necessarily represents the deep and authentic concerns of an unhappy and anxious people, but will be treated as such by those who create the dominant images and those who willingly consume them.

For our part, anti-authoritarian projects and our resistance aren't part of the ruling equation. By their nature and our desire, they are autonomous of the governing apparatuses. The challenge for us to continue building communities of resistance and confront the megamachine at the points of its worst abuses is no different than before the election charade.

Burn All Flags
Bad Attitude – Summer 1995

On March 21, four people demonstrated at the Federal Bldg. in downtown Detroit for the right to be anti-patriotic. While so doing, they burned a small American flag, much to the outrage of passersby and security guards.

We give full support to all acts of flag desecration and encourage others to commit similar provocations.

All flags are rags. They are symbols of the nation state that traps the human spirit within artificially established boundaries guarded by men with guns. Flags cause people to lose their common sense. They make men willing to kill other men who wave a different flag. They cause people to hate those who live in a different nation state rather than hate those who rule us.

Flags make people forget that the interest of rulers everywhere is to protect their own wealth and privilege and to expand the territory and people they control. Flags make people love an abstraction called "my country" and forget that in real life we are ruled by a rich, selfish, swinish elite who think of us as dog meat for their industries and businesses, and cannon fodder for their wars.

Only the U.S. has such a compulsive flag-waving mania, and no country since Nazi Germany actually insists on a pledge to a flag. Free people have no need of flags; only the slaves of nation states do. Even the red flag of revolution is waved by police state bureaucrats and those who aspire to be. The black flag of anarchy could easily suffer the same fate.

Forget the symbols of revolution. Burn all flags! Be anarchy!

Getting Back to Zero: The Day Before The 2016 Election
Summer 2017

There have been long standing political and theoretical debates about whether a particular political movement or leader is fascist. It often can come down to hairsplitting. Is Trump a fascist? Was the Spanish dictator, Francisco Franco? Or, Argentina's Juan Peron? Or, is the term fascist applied indiscriminately to any oppressive government and politician?

Mussolini certainly was and declared himself as such. The Italian dictator made the fasces, a bundle of sticks featuring an axe indicating the power over life and death, the original symbol of fascism, hence, the origins of the term. The figure, taken from Imperial Rome, also appears on the U.S. $1 bill.

Pure fascism was rooted in a philosophy of creating social harmony by ending the endemic class conflict of the 19th and early 20th century under the rule of a strong state and leader. Its aim was to resolve social antagonisms by enforcing the vertical integration of classes whereby, in theory, the state both protected capitalism from revolutionary workers, but also supposedly mitigated exploitation of workers by capital. In reality, the first tenet was much more forcibly adhered to, with the latter given scant adherence. War, nationalism, and racism figured heavily into the equation.

However, with all of the attempts at defining fascism and who fits into that category, when authoritarian rule becomes dominant in a society, do the formal definitions really matter? No one labels Stalinist Russia as fascist, but when an "enemy of the people" was sent to a Gulag or shot in the basement of a Cheka prison, compared to a similar scenario involving the Nazi SS, would it really matter to the victim, or to the larger society what the political label was?

What we are seeing now in the American political landscape doesn't rise to the level of historic fascism, but its social base certainly comes close to what has been described as the "crazed hordes of the petty bourgeoisie." The vertical integration of classes under a strong warlike state, with a large portion of a population whipped up in racist frenzy, which worships militarism, and encourages personal self-actualization through identification with the leader and the state, sounds like a definition of Trump supporters.

Perhaps the good news is that the majority of American voters felt they were rejecting this in the last election where Hillary Clinton received the most popular votes. However, as it has been since 1968, the majority of whites voted for the Republican presidential candidate mostly on the basis of addressing the question: Do black lives matter? They answered, no.

The same would have been true with any Republican candidate, but because of Trump's extraordinary history of racism, xenophobia, and sexism, there is heightened moral indignation at his election and an outpouring of expressions of condemnation. This was seen in the almost immediate organizing of huge demonstrations not seen since the 1960s. While the outrage at a personally and politically horrid figure being elevated to the position of the world's most powerful man should not be diminished, it's hard to imagine that such a sizable opposition would have occurred had the winning Republican candidate been one of the other terrible politicians from their party.

If the 2016 election hadn't been stolen from Clinton by the suppression of minority voters, Russian hacking, FBI malfeasance, and the Electoral College, there probably would have been only a handful of the usual suspects (that would be us) protesting the election of a Wall Street warmonger (that would be her).

When so many people are mobilized in opposition to the government, anything is possible, but most of it so far has been a struggle to get back to zero; that is, what life and politics was like on Nov. 7, 2016, the day before the election.

Rather than policy, this election particularly was a referendum on what was to constitute the dominant social narrative. In those terms, the Democrats constitute the continuing expansion of the bourgeois revolution which began as narrowly inclusive, contradicting its motto of "liberty and justice for all," or the even better expressed French version: liberty, equality, fraternity." The struggles against slavery, including the Civil War, women's suffrage, the labor, civil rights, feminist and LBGTQ+ movements fit into the fulfillment of these slogans, but always within capitalism, and never completely bringing the visionary triad into complete fulfillment.

The Democrats represent (the importance of the verb needs to be stressed) tolerance and inclusion, while the Republicans are a 21st century version of 1970s Rhodesians hanging onto a fantasy of white supremacy and a world that barely existed even for them.

The new Republican administration has begun a right-wing wish-list repealing of reforms of capitalism that go back as far as the Roosevelt New Deal and 1970s protection of the environment and a women's right to choose. At this writing, they have only begun to unravel social safety nets and restrictions on capital accumulation by the wealthiest.

However, these are not fascist moves, nor is defunding Planned Parenthood or the National Endowment for the Arts or ending financing of programs for the Great Lakes or Bay Area water restoration. Even Muslim bans and increased border madness isn't. They are just plain awful and it is understandable why the resistance is as great as it is.

But, where is the resistance going? Occupy, the last great moment of opposition, essentially collapsed because it had nowhere to go after claiming public spaces. The right-wing Tea Party found a comfortable home in the Republican Party to the point where their policy goals became dominant and they elected a president.

The developing resistance to the far-right conservative presidency is still in its infancy, but most of it is aimed squarely at replicating Tea Party success by capturing the Democratic Party. Much of the resistance advocates what they define as a progressive agenda, that is, defending the social gains of the last 85 years and adding to them with policies such as a national health care plan.

Even employing a term like resistance with its resonance to the World War II partisan fight against the Nazis suggests something may be different than the usual call for reforms. However, when you go to michiganforrevolution.com, one finds a call to join the Democratic Party.

The Republican executive orders and legislation have already hurt a great many people, and more injurious rollbacks of liberal policies that have made capitalism less onerous than it was before the 1930s are planned.

A key component of fascism as well as the American state is its culture of militarism that is the bulwark of war Keynesianism, a huge transfer of wealth from taxes to fuel the U.S. economy through war production. This economic policy brings with it the American empire being perpetually at war, a situation exacerbated by Obama and Clinton's military confrontational policies at Russia's borders, something even the darling of progressives, Bernie Sanders, didn't challenge.

So, what is to be done? Revolution was simple for our radical forebears. Workers produce all wealth; all wealth should go to the workers. Workers of the world unite; you have nothing to lose but your chains. The working class and the employing class have nothing in common. When those slogans were devised, the proposed solution to capitalism was to get rid of the owners and rulers and have a democratic and equitable society managed by workers councils.

Now, with industrial/petro/chemical capitalism reaching its tipping point of making the planet unlivable, its continuation under a different mode of administration seems fatuous. Plus, are the majority of workers now less organized than ever since capitalism's origin, the agency for revolution? Can the same productive apparatus remain after a revolution, but only substituting a Flatulence Filtering Underwear (actual product) Workers Council for the capitalist boss, and in other industries producing thousands of other useless items manufactured to keep capitalism humming?

The question to address is where is the locus of revolutionary organizing? Anywhere? Everywhere? Maybe that's the best we can do right now for self-guidance. What not to do is obvious. Back into the arms of the Democratic Party as a bulwark against Trump leaves us where we started, at zero.

Regarding right wing policies and actions? Call them fascists or not, we will fight them.

Clinton: Greater Danger to Peace
Spring 2018

It's hard not to be distracted by the right-wing Shit Show presently playing in the White House with its daily exposures of corruption, racism, xenophobia, and discrimination.

The most glittering of all the baubles dangled for our horror and enjoyment is Russian interference in the 2016 election and the collusion of the Trump campaign with President Vladimir Putin's operatives. The accuracy of this charge is strengthened almost daily and denied only by the Trump camp, Fox News, and a surprising number of leftists and news sites like *CounterPunch*.

However, the question is almost never asked, why did Putin consider it such a high priority that Donald Trump, a sleazy and stupid real estate investor, become president over a sophisticated, policy-wise, seasoned politician like Hillary Clinton?

It's difficult to imagine that a U.S. president who seems worse than George Bush and Ronald Reagan combined, could have a better position on the critical issue of peace than Barack Obama and Hillary Clinton, but Trump trumps both of them when it comes to Russia.

Before recently capitulating to the U.S. intelligence services' view of Russia as a hegemonic rival, Trump proposed what the old Khrushchev-era Soviet Union called "peaceful coexistence" between the two countries. The liberal champions, Clinton (who voted for the Iraq war, and Obama, an undeserving recipient of a Nobel Peace Prize), ramped up Cold War II during their administration, endangering the world with the prospect of war in Europe more threatening than anything Trump has done with N. Korea.

Whether Trump advocated peaceful relations with Russia because Putin has the rumored video tape of prostitutes peeing on him, or since Trump didn't expect or want to win the presidential race, and was setting himself up for future real estate deals in Russia, he didn't want an adversarial relationship in Eastern Europe. He couldn't care less about Crimea, eastern Ukraine, or the nature of Putin's rule. As the Godfather rasped, "It's only business."

Putin's intervention in the U.S. election was based on the defense of his country from Western threats, ones which are of a significant nature. Once again, the West is at Russia's doorstep, intent on surrounding it with hostile nations and offensive weaponry.

Putin is a ruthless dictator without a single admirable trait, but his moves annexing Crimea and intervening in eastern Ukraine do not threaten the U.S., 4,000 miles to the west.

Before leaving office in January 2017, Obama sent 3,600 U.S. tanks and 4,000 battle-ready troops to Europe and held military maneuvers near Russia's borders. What would Obama have thought if the Russians had done something similar in Canada or Mexico?

Perhaps more ominous is the building of another American missile defense system in eastern Poland, following the placing of a U.S. Aegis Ashore system in Romania, an act that Russia called "a direct threat." And, that is a correct assessment. Missile shields are a component of first-strike nuclear strategy.

When Mikhail Gorbachev, the last head of the Soviet Communist Party, essentially dismantled the USSR, he did so with hope for a peace that ended the decades long Cold War and nuclear stand-off which the West launched following WW II.

NATO and the Warsaw Pact were to be disbanded and the eyeball-to-eyeball stare-down between the two blocs would end. Instead, the U.S. has expanded NATO up to Russia's borders.

That Trump's desire for détente with Putin was brought to heel was demonstrated in the December issuance of a National Security Strategy paper which identifies Russia in terms of the U.S. intelligence services' reflexive hostility to Russia. Maintaining traditional Western belligerence fuels the Military/Industrial Complex, and creates job security for the enormous intelligence and military apparatus.

Military spending in the U.S. is one of this country's economic pillars; it ruined the Soviet Union. The U.S. needs an enemy to justify its $643 billion yearly military budget, and irregular fighters with AK47s don't fill the bill. So, the symbiotic relationship between Russia and the U.S. war economy began its resuscitation into Cold War II by Obama/Clinton (supported by Bernie Sanders) and increased in Trump's latest war budget (it's not defense).

The corporate and mostly liberal media attacks Trump for his overtures to Putin acting out their fealty to the warfare state. CNN refers to Russia as "our implacable enemy," liberal talk show host, Stephanie Miller identifies the country as a "hostile power," and former director of national intelligence, James Clapper, calls Trump a "Russian asset."

The corporate media outlets are the megaphone that justifies the extension of American military power across the globe that threatens not only Russia, but the world with an unimaginable war.

Concentration on the politics and technology of Russian electoral interference while ignoring the reasons for it, misses the chance for understanding and exposing traditional cross-party warmongering.

A radical anti-war movement should call for the withdrawal of American military from all countries around the world as a minimum demand. Ultimately, we want the disbanding of all armies.

The 2020 Election
What to do while waiting for the Revolution
Spring 2020

The 2020 Michigan presidential primary on March 10 marked the end of the progressive fantasy that the American political landscape could be altered by supporting U.S. Senator Bernie Sanders as the Democratic Party nominee.

Instead, it was bye-bye, Bernie, as Joe Biden swept every county in the state as voters overwhelmingly went for a candidate they thought had the best chance of defeating the execrable Trump in November.

The Democratic Party establishment was determined not to allow Sanders to transform it from its traditional center-right, pro-corporate, militarist policies into even a tepid social democratic one. Biden is the perfect candidate for the party. He is of the same mold as Obama, Clinton, Carter, Johnson, Kennedy, or Truman, all who harken back to Franklin Roosevelt's New Deal in the 1930s. They all recognized capitalism as the heart of economic policy and defense of the empire as the keystone of foreign policy. That is not going to change through the electoral system and certainly not through the Democratic Party.

These are considerations when thinking about the relationship of anarchists to the 2020 election. We are a small, very loosely affiliated movement of people who think the political state and contests for its power are the problem. So, how do we engage in this period when the presidential contest will be the major political focus at least as presented through the media?

Saying we are loosely affiliated is even an exaggeration. As small collectives, we work in local projects and struggles, organize info shops, bookstores, theater festivals, performance spaces, book fairs, and produce publications and online news sites. Anarchists are involved in any number of admirable resistance and revolution-building efforts, and often have influence in excess of our numbers.

Think of how often mass movements such as Occupy or pipeline defenses utilize the techniques developed over the generations of collective leadership, affinity groups, and direct democratic decision making. However, our efforts have little or no impact on the current crisis within the state governing apparatus where a civil war has broken out between sectors of the ruling class. This is not to say both sides are equal, although there is much more fundamental agreement than often seems obvious.

Although committed to empire and capital, the Democrats come closer to European social democratic political formations that advocate reforms to reduce the worst features of the economy and the social structure it produces. Whatever we may say about the function of reforms being the co-optation of revolutionary demands, life within capitalism is less miserable with the reforms that have been fought for and granted over the last century and a half.

Although many changes have been enacted, the struggle to bring reforms into being often exacted a great toll from those who campaigned for them, such as the labor movement and in the Civil Rights era.

As long as the fundamental rules are followed by reformers, that is, not challenging capitalism or the state, the system has enough flexibility to grant at least a portion of what was being demanded. Ultimately, it was to the benefit of the rulers to allow reforms. From 1848 to 1939, intense class warfare grew to such proportions that it made revolution a possibility had reforms not been granted.

Today, that is ancient history. The Trump administration is committed to rolling back many of the elemental reforms won over generations. His election has also energized a resurgent fascist movement. Anarchists are quick to state that Trump should be contested or removed through direct action, but it's clear that large demonstrations and occupation of public space aren't enough to stop political rulers once they are committed to a policy, such as war.

So, what are our alternatives while waiting for new forms of radical struggle and formulas for resistance to emerge? Undoubtedly, there are many being created within small venues that are prefigurative, post-capitalist relationships, and innovative forms that can be effective in the real world eventually. But, there's an election in November that at this moment appears to be the only mechanism by which the U.S. can rid itself of the damage Trump has done, and which will increase if he is re-elected.

As anarchists, we can vote, but that brings shudders of indignation to those demanding adherence to a generations old principle of non-involvement in electoral or party politics. The point has been made previously in these pages that there are so few anarchists in America, whether we all vote or none of us vote, little or no difference in outcome will occur. The best argument against voting is that it erodes the traditional anarchist critique of the state if one participates in its processes.

However, it's a secret ballot and with permanent absentee balloting increasingly available, it allows you to do the dirty deed with anonymity from your home while still proudly wearing a circle A on your jacket.

Whatever the result of the election is, political disaster could still lie ahead. In 1936, members of the CNT, the Spanish anarcho-syndicalist union, voted in large numbers to elect a liberal government to hold off the repressive policies of a rival right wing party. The results were tragic. The election of the left brought on a fascist revolt and victory leading to destruction of the left and anarchists alike under a 36-year dictatorship.

Many radicals in 1964 urged voting for a liberal Democratic presidential candidate because the Republican, they feared, would involve the U.S. in a land war in Southeast Asia. The Republican lost, but the Democrat, President Lyndon Johnson, brought about what they feared most.

In February this year, U.S. intelligence agencies reported to Congress that the Russian government was intervening in the coming presidential election in the manner they did in 2016 on behalf of then-candidate Trump. They did so out of national self-interest since the Obama administration, with Hillary Clinton as Secretary of State, had severely threatened Russia's territorial security by installing missile shields in Europe and sending U.S. tank and troop divisions close to its border.

Trump, whether in Putin's pocket, or showing uncharacteristic common sense, advocated peaceful relations with Russia. He was seen by the Kremlin as much less threatening than Clinton who expressed fealty to the Military/Industrial Complex by launching Cold War II.

It was also revealed that the Russian intelligence apparatus was aiding the candidacy of Bernie Sanders. They probably figured it was a win-win situation. Correctly or not, the Kremlin undoubtedly viewed the senator as the weakest candidate as did the Trump campaign. However, if the socialist had prevailed, they figured he would be the Democratic candidate least likely to initiate militarist moves towards Russia.

Sanders would perhaps have been less aggressive then some of the centrist candidates, but he would be an American president, the chief operating officer of the Empire in charge of defending it. If you think he would be of a different breed, a recent interview is instructive.

As if to signal to the war hawks that they needn't worry about him dismantling the imperial war machine if elected, Sanders, in an interview on CBS's "60 Minutes" in February, laid out the criteria under what circumstance he would deploy U.S. military forces.

He listed: "Threats against our allies. I believe in NATO," he told the interviewer.

NATO, a looming military threat to Russia, an alliance thousands of miles away from the U.S. that the Soviet Union was assured would be dismantled at the end of the Cold War. The progressive darling says, "I believe in NATO."

Sanders was asked if he would order military action if Taiwan came under attack from China, He replied, "Yeah. I mean, I think we have got to make it clear to countries around the world that we will not sit by and allow invasions to take place, absolutely."

"Yeah," he says, In other words, yeah, I'll start World War III. Absolutely.

What's the choice, though, More of the Trump regime and what that will unleash on the most at-risk people in this country and the environment? The most we can do is what the anarchist movement has done throughout our long history: organize for revolution.

The future could depend upon it.

Chapter 3
Culture

Will Marijuana Save World Capitalism?
Summer 1993

Review: *The Emperor Wears No Clothes: The Authoritative Historical Record of the Cannabis Plant, Marijuana Prohibition, & How Hemp Can Still Save the World*, Jack Herer, HEMP/Queen of Clubs Publishing, 1992 edition

Review: *Hemp: Lifeline to the Future*, Chris Conrad, Creative Xpressions Publishing, 1993

I have always loved getting high, starting with rip-roaring drunken weekends in my teens and college years of the late 1950s and early 1960s. Like many young people of my generation, my gang and I were always looking for new ways to get stoned in an era when little else other than booze was available.

Besides drinking, we experimented with nitrous oxide cartridges for model cars and futile attempts at rumored highs produced from such combinations as Coca Cola and aspirin in our quest for new mind-benders. When the 'Sixties hit, we smoked up, gobbled down, and snorted up whatever came around, imbuing much of our activity with a philosophical/spiritual/revolutionary quality which allowed us to look with great disdain upon those still imbibing alcohol.

We agreed with White Panther Party founder, Detroit poet (and one-time political prisoner), John Sinclair's essay, "The Marijuana Revolution," which held that pot and LSD intoxication dissolved the rigid thought patterns capitalism forced on us through the enculturating institutions of the family and school. It seemed very possible that psychedelic tripping and stoned states could aid in the subversive deconstruction of loyalty to capital's death culture, as we called it then.

Of course, capitalist society did not unravel, but the allegiance of a substantial number of young people to this society did, so looking back 25 or so years doesn't give me the sense of, "Oh, how young and silly we were." Rather, those experiences gave rise to an understanding that no single activity, and certainly no single substance, contains the unique power to create the conditions for revolution.

Rebels in that era did any number of things which those in authority found reprehensible besides drug use, some even as minor as growing long hair or wearing Levi's instead of slacks. Parents, priests, police, principals and politicians concentrated their ire on the outward symbols of a sub-culture which rejected the more important features of power than how one dressed (although the rejection of consumerism and the refusal to wear military-style haircuts is not to be minimized).

Besides conformist dress codes, rebellious youth also refused the dominance of militarism, political rule, sexual codes, and unquestioning submission to authority. It was these attitudes which were the real cause of such hostility to who were designated as hippies.

However, when the movement of the 'Sixties, based on white, middle-class youth, found it had reached the limits of its constituency, it began to disintegrate as the 1970s commenced. It was then that capital easily integrated much of the youth culture into its fashion machine as it also recuperated music, art, and even the rhetoric of social change itself. (Prior to then, no advertiser would have thought to label its hair coloring product as "revolutionary"!) Drugs, too, became largely another consumer indulgence.

All intoxicants exhibit a strange presence in a society where use is disconnected from a ceremonial context, and mainly function as a palliative for jangled nerves, a social lubricant, or as a diversion from emotional angst (none of which is bad, by the way, in and of itself). The desire of the rulers to keep people drinking rather than using drugs has less to do with ingrained puritanical attitudes (although fear of the deep powers of drugs is certainly a background consideration), and more with how it coincides with larger economic interests.

Booze is one of those anomalies of capitalist society like assault weapons and cigarettes, which, while being a major commodity, also wreaks havoc. Booze, as is well known by all, creates an enormous number of costly social problems and is often a factor in events such as rebellions among the poor (or even unruly college students on winter vacation in Florida!) which are distinctly unwelcome by the rulers. Eventually, all of the social costs are just factored in as the price of doing business.

The negative power ascribed to drugs also has a distinctly political component. Many activists in both the black and white radical communities believe the government, specifically the Central Intelligence Agency, has used the importation of heroin, and later cocaine, to stupefy and stagnate the threat of growing radical movements. This seems to me an entirely baseless theory, although the introduction of those drugs has had a debilitating effect on many activists, and certainly poor communities.

The involvement of the CIA in heroin and cocaine trafficking is undeniable (see *The Politics of Heroin: CIA Complicity in the Global Drug Trade* by Alfred W. McCoy), but came as a result of U.S. government agency alliances with drug lords in southeast Asia in the '60s and Central America in the '80s, not as conscious policy to destroy a movement.

Drugs obviously have a dark side evident in the social wreckage resulting from misuse and abuse, and it is on this aspect that the government and its stooges base their propaganda. It should be noted that although almost all the crime and violence associated with drugs would quickly end if their prohibition were to be lifted, there still remains the millions of addictive personalities created by a social system which fosters such mass anxiety that many people need a whole medicine chest of legal and illegal drugs to dull the pain of daily life.

That dark side was no stranger to my gang and extended

community as a number of friends and acquaintances fell victim to addictions, leaving behind a trail of misery and even death. It was increasingly easier to become disabused of the idea that drugs contained an inherent revolutionary quality as benign and beneficial substances such as weed and acid gave way to heroin, PCP, speed, cocaine, and finally crack.

Even marijuana, the alleged eradicator of the capitalist work and consumer ethos began to appear less potent as it became a regular feature alongside booze in the Detroit factories as a way to sedate the stress produced from noisy, strenuous, mechanized work. A roommate of mine was once getting ready for the first shift at the Warren, Mich. Dodge Truck Assembly plant at 5:30 am by rolling his day's supply of joints. I told him it amazed me how he could be high on the job since I was sure I couldn't work stoned. He replied that he couldn't work if he wasn't!

The benefits and problems with drugs aside, the government certainly has no right to ban any kind of drugs. They're our bodies and our minds, and we'll be responsible for our health and our brains, if you don't mind. However, a personal liberties approach has had little effect on the model citizen zombie who believes all the government propaganda about drugs, and there are but a scant few politicians committed to reform of the policy.

The commonly held prejudices against drugs, fostered by the official institutions of schools, churches, government, and media, represent the triumph of the puritanical, repressive side of American cultural traditions and form the bulwark against drug decriminalization. The social institutions that have a direct interest in the maintenance of drug prohibition are the liquor and tobacco industries, oil corporations (which would suffer direct competition from hemp products), and the growing anti-drug industry.

To win the stupidly labeled War on Drugs would eliminate hundreds of thousands of federal, state and local government jobs in enforcement and incarceration as well as thousands more in the private sector employed in testing, counseling, consulting, etc. As it stands, the equilibrium between offenders and the anti-drug apparatus is perfect to maintain that sector of the racket. As with most wars under capitalism, this one is good business.

The Herer and Conrad books are a good read for those interested in the beneficial commercial, medicinal, and environmental uses of marijuana. The history of the cultivation of hemp (agricultural grade marijuana) and its widespread use for a multitude of products down through the ages is necessary for a generation which associates its use only with getting stoned. Hemp was widely grown throughout the world for thousands of years and provided hundreds of products as diverse as paper and food; even non-oil-based plastic and fuel can be derived from it. So important was it to the economy of some nations that, according to Herer's account, the War of 1812 was fought with the hemp trade as a background cause.

Throughout the 19th century, in the U.S., cannabis was thought to possess a number of medicinal benefits, and a variety of over-the-counter remedies containing it were sold to the public. Also, World Fairs and International Expositions held from the 1860s through the early 1900s often featured a popular concession where Turkish hashish could be smoked. Although its industrial use had declined considerably due to lagging technology in the field and the continued introduction of oil-based products, hemp still was grown on American farms as it had been by Washington and Jefferson (a specific acreage of hemp cultivation was required by law for farmers in the American colonies), up until the 1930s.

By the early part of this century, its use as an intoxicant was mainly limited to people in the jazz scene, which meant American blacks and Hispanics, as Euro-Americans continued to drink alcohol as their drug of choice in until the 1960s. The racism contained in the campaign to criminalize marijuana was evident in the focus of the hysteria created by a compliant corporate press which gave sensationalized accounts of "reefer madness" at the behest of the newly-formed drug enforcement bureau headed by a personality as wacky as his counterpart at the FBI: one, Harry Anslinger.

The corporate press, particularly the vicious Hearst chain, churned out accounts of lurid sex scenes involving "crazed negroes" and Mexicans high on "marijuana" (the Sonora/Texas regional name for smokable hemp popularized by the Hearst papers) who were impervious to police bullets and clubs. So crazy was Anslinger that he hatched a plan in the 1930s to make a huge nation-wide sweep of hundreds of known marijuana-using jazz musicians, including Count Basie, Duke Ellington, and Cab Calloway. Fortunately, cooler heads prevailed and his plan was nixed by higher-ups.

Both books give a highly conspiratorial (and believable) account of how hemp came to be illegal through the Marijuana Tax Act of 1937 which ended legal hemp cultivation as well as dope smoking. Not so coincidentally, this was the same year the Dupont corporation patented rayon and which was creating numerous other petrochemical products that soon supplanted those previously available from hemp. The campaign to make it illegal took on the aspects of the hysteria associated with similar efforts such as the Red Scare of the 1950s, but its real focus was corporate imperatives not overt social or health concerns.

The Herer and Conrad volumes are part of a new wave of efforts to overturn the insanity of marijuana prohibition. They signal a switch in tactics from the civil libertarian demanding the right to get high to high-minded reformer trying to bring an environmentally sound and multi-purpose agricultural product into commercial use again.

Dope smoking revolutionaries were "all outlaws in the eyes of America," as the '60s Jefferson Airplane song went, and more than one person has emphasized that marijuana's illegality is part of its appeal. Pot use carries with it a certain willingness to accept risk and ignore authority's rules. Suddenly, dope smoking longhairs have begun reeling off a litany of the benefits hemp will provide and often end up sounding like a combination of Thomas Edison and the Chamber of Commerce. This new stance transforms hemp activists (as they like to call themselves) from outlaws into reformers and futurists.

Rather than advocating smoking down and tripping out for the pure joy of the experience, hemp activists are assuring us how everything from paint to cars to medicine can be produced and extracted from this wonderful weed, and with no environmental damage. What is lost in all this euphoria is any radical criticism of the commodities produced, the nature of work which goes into producing them, and the whole hierarchical nature of society.

When I read a news release from a drug reform publication, the *New Age Patriot*, which assures us that legal hemp will "... create new jobs and new wealth," and the "dignity" jobs produce, I know an anti-capital critique is not part of the author's program. It would take another article to examine the economic and social consequences of an industry which, while it might bring increased prosperity to a few aspiring entrepreneurs or already established chemical companies, would undoubtedly, like all industrial enterprises in the modern era, be defined by low wages, deadening and dangerous working conditions, and its own specific environmental problems.

The glowing promises of futurists rarely pan out, and the creation of jobs, new product creation, efficiency, etc., are the concerns of capital, not radicals. As it is, the U.S. Agriculture Dept. is currently experimenting with other plants which could serve as a biomass for the same products as hemp, thus cutting the ground out from under the hempsters.

Hopefully, none of the foregoing will be taken as an argument for continuing drug prohibition. I still cling to the seemingly outdated notion that drug-induced ecstatic states can be a component in destroying allegiance to this system and the world it creates.

Hence, it can be argued that decriminalization will aid that process in making drugs more widely available. Good, but let's argue for it on that basis and not with the logic of a good capitalist.

War on drugs? I can't even drive on drugs.

Surreal Life
Detroit Metro Times – January 5, 2005

Old rebels never die, they, well...just stick-up Toys "R" Us stores. Allen Van Newkirk, who played a seminal role in the 1960s radical and experimental cultural scene in Detroit, was arrested following a Dec. 12, 2005, robbery and subsequent shoot-out with Mounties in a Vancouver, British Columbia, suburb.

According to Constable Dave Babineau, media liaison for the Port Coquitlam section of the Royal Mounted Canadian Police, officers responded to a report of an armed holdup at the suburban toy store by a lone man who drove off in a van. Following a short chase, the vehicle and a police car collided, and the 64-year-old Van Newkirk exited from behind the wheel with gun blazing, Detroit-style.

Van Newkirk was wounded in the exchange of gunfire, and is charged with two counts of attempted murder, robbery and related offenses. Babineau described his wounds as "non-life threatening," and Jennifer Saltman, staff reporter for the twice-weekly *Coquitlam Now*, said the defendant was walking under his own power at a Dec. 28 court hearing. Neither provincial nor store officials would disclose the amount of the heist, but a store employee said it was thousands of dollars.

Many veterans of Detroit's 1960s scene remember Van Newkirk as a pistol-packing, motorcycle-riding early Detroit advocate of surrealist and Dadaist ideas. He published daily newspaper-sized posters titled *Guerrilla: Free Newspaper of the Streets*, featuring huge headlines proclaiming such provocations as, "Poetry Demands Unemployment."

John Sinclair, a founder of the Detroit Artists' Workshop in 1964 and originally a co-editor of *Guerrilla,* says, "The surrealists were his big inspiration, and if sticking up Toys 'R' Us isn't a surreal act, I don't know what is!"

He added, "I wonder what his message was. There has to be some subtext."

Sinclair, now based in Amsterdam, and Van Newkirk became roommates 40 years ago in a Detroit Cass Corridor apartment when they were both attending Wayne State University. "We were both trying to figure out a way," says Sinclair, "to bridge the previous era with the emerging thing that had to do with reaching illiterate teenage TV-watchers and pop radio listeners with art and political content through the media of marijuana, rock 'n' roll and LSD." The two of them were part of a scene responsible for an outpouring of poetry, publications, theater, art, experimental jazz and innovative rock that gave the Cass Corridor a far-reaching reputation.

Van Newkirk, at an imposing 6-foot-3, often made his opinions known by thundering down the aisle of radical gatherings denouncing proceedings as insufficiently revolutionary. His most notorious act occurred in 1969 during an appearance of the mainstream poet Kenneth Koch at an alternative New York reading space, St. Marks Church. Van Newkirk, incensed, ran toward the podium firing a pistol (filled with blanks, though the audience didn't know that), yelling, "Death to bourgeois poets."

Several confederates, including poet, author and NPR commentator Andrei Codrescu threw copies of the latest *Guerrilla* to startled spectators. According to Codrescu, "Kenneth responded, without flinching, 'Why don't you just grow up?' and goes on reading."

"I was wondering what mischief Van Newkirk has been into," Codrescu said on hearing of his old collaborator's arrest.

Van Newkirk also disrupted a 1969 Madison, Wis., conference of the Underground Press Syndicate, a federation of alternative newspapers. That time, he ran down the aisle, without the pistol, yelling, "All media are lies."

A collage he published in The Fifth Estate denounced the MC5 rock band as a commodity with a revolutionary veneer, outraging the band and Sinclair, then their manager. A confrontation with MC5 lead guitarist Wayne Kramer followed.

After publishing several editions of *Guerrilla,* Van Newkirk abruptly left Detroit in 1970 to set up the Geographic Foundation of the North Atlantic, an early radical ecological center located in Antigonish, Nova Scotia. There he put out broadsides and pamphlets under the name of *root, branch, and mammal.* He eventually was granted permanent resident status in Canada and moved to the Vancouver area.

Old friends say that from the early '70s through the '80s, they heard little of Van Newkirk's whereabouts and activities except for infrequent late-night calls or even less frequent visits to family members in the Detroit area. No one, it seems, had heard from him in almost 15 years.

Not surprisingly, he failed to turn up for the Artists' Workshop 40th anniversary in November, even though he had been on its board of directors.

Crossing the border might have proved difficult. At his last court hearing it came to light that he was on the lam from assault charges in Penticton, British Columbia. He had previous convictions in Washington state for felony larceny in 1990 and disorderly conduct and theft in 1994.

And while Van Newkirk faces robbery charges, old copies of his "free newspaper of the streets" sell for $130 each at an upscale San Francisco gallery.

Author Note: Allen Van Newkirk passed away in 2013 at age 73 in Chico, Calif. He spent five years in Canadian prisons after being convicted for the armed robbery.

I was at a New York City art gallery in 2019 where copies of *Guerilla* were offered at $2,000.

The Vegetarian Myth
Wheat is Murder
Spring 2011

Review: *The Vegetarian Myth: Food, Justice and Sustainability*, Lierre Keith, PM Press, 2009

Once, at a Tai Chi workshop I attended, an elderly Chinese master of the discipline suddenly stopped in the middle of the demonstration and asked, completely out of the blue, "Why do so many of you not eat meat?"

Since there were quite a few vegetarians among the eager students, the only response was an embarrassing silence and the soft shuffling of cotton-soled Tai Chi shoes.

"There's good ch'i in meat," he admonished us in his accented English, referring to the energy flow present in all living things that would enhance us by ingesting that of another being.

Someone, anticipating that the answer wasn't going to be well received, said weakly, "We don't want to kill to eat." "Why not?," asked the master. "Everything eats everything. One day worms eat us," he said roaring with laughter at his own comment. Faint smiles came from the assembled students who were thankful that the discussion went quickly back to the training at hand.

This is essentially Lierre Keith's argument in *The Vegetarian Myth*—everything eats everything. She views existence as a tightly interconnected circle of life and death encompassing all living beings and the earth itself, and that attempts to avoid or circumvent the process only brings the environmental, political, and health disasters she chronicles in her highly charged style.

The myth, referred to in the book's title, is one held by so many of us, that a non-meat diet can save the animals and the planet, and that a vegetable-based diet is essential for good health. Keith, a vegan for 20 years, denies each of these contentions with a fervor consistent with the manner of all apostates. Her book marshals an enormous amount of supportive evidence from social and medical sciences, and adds her own meatless history which she says almost destroyed her body.

Keith, now a vigorous flesh-eater, advocates a return to meat-eating as a way to heal ourselves and the planet, although she's sketchy on the details of what this would mean. She certainly doesn't advocate eating at MacDonald's.

You might think that an author who identifies herself as a radical feminist activist and who exhibits a driving concern for the damage being done to the environment would get a respectful hearing since her charges are so provocative and challenging not only to vegans and vegetarians, but to mainstream nutrition theories as well.

Instead, she and her book have touched off a firestorm of condemnation, denunciation, calumny, insults, and charges of bad faith against her. Her critics exhibit a fury in many on-line discussions of the book, calling her every name imaginable: a liar, a shill for the meat industry, an "animal holocaust denier," and a publicity hound, all of which culminated in a physical attack on her while she spoke at the March 2010 San Francisco Anarchist Book Fair.

Three men in masks and black hoodies ran up to her as she spoke and slammed a cayenne-laced pie into Keith's face, yelling, "Go Vegan." Several days later, she reported, "My eyes are still puffy and blurry, but the pain is definitely better. I think the worst part was hearing people cheer my assailants while I was being assaulted. I don't want to live in a world where people cheer while someone has cayenne rubbed into their eyes."

That act, the equivalent of macing someone, at an anarchist event should be condemned as cowardly and completely unacceptable, but instead has been defended by some. Like antiabortion terrorists, self-righteousness excuses violence. Most vegans, I'm sure find this act as reprehensible as any meat eater would.

By the way, there are numerous books in print that make the same nutritional assertions and criticism of vegans as hers, but perhaps the fact that it was an anarchist event spurred the assault.

The North American Animal Liberation Press Office released a statement praising the assailants who "made their statement very eloquently and succinctly on behalf of the billions of animals she advocates killing." Keith makes it clear that she opposes all factory farming and advocates restoration of forest and prairies in her book.

However, she must be aware, that cattle grazing has destroyed many of the prairies the author wants to re-establish.

I haven't eaten land animals in decades and most of my diet consists of grains, legumes, and vegetables, with some additional seafood and dairy products. My health is excellent. So is that of my veggie and vegan friends as well as that of the many famous people such as k.d. Lang, Moby, Morrissey, Rep. Dennis Kucinich, the late Coretta Scott King and Cesar Chavez, numerous professional sports stars including triathletes, body builders, and professional basketball players and baseball players, who adhere to a vegan diet. Yet, Keith says her vegan diet badly injured her body including causing a spinal deformation from which she'll never recover. She cites anecdotal evidence and studies demonstrating how the body cannot be sustained without ingesting animal fats and protein.

Many critics of her book (and, there are many!) take on her advocacy of meat consumption although much of the on-line rage stems from charges that her book incites "the murder of innocent non-human beings." To support her nutritional claims, Keith cites endless and seemingly legitimate medical studies affirming her carnivore point of view, many which confound current dietary recommendations including those published by the U.S. government, all which advise limiting meat consumption.

Contrary to what highly respected, independent groups like the Center for Science in the Public Interest advocate, Keith says that a heavy grain-based diet is the cause of what she identifies as the "diseases of civilization"–cancer, heart ailments, and other plagues of our era. Causal factors for disease and the impact of diet on health aren't as easy to discern as one would think. Am I healthy because of my diet and active lifestyle, or, because I'm a North American, white, middle-class man? How we live and what we eat greatly affect our health, but so does where we are situated in the class pyramid which often has determinative consequences.

Keith says she greatly respects the desire of non-meat eaters to live without killing, but asks them to look at the damage done by agriculture which she refers to (irrefutably, I'd say) as "bio-cide." The planet-wide swath of agricultural land with its mono-crop planting is really what has killed "billions of animals" that the pie-throwers say they care about.

Keith asks us to look at a piece of land with its thousands of inhabitants, not just its mega-fauna, and see the destruction and death necessary to raise corn for tortillas, wheat for pasta, or rice for biryani. Farming, especially the modern variety with its dependence on fossil fuel eliminates all vegetable and animal life other than the desired crop. When you eat vegetables, it too is on a mountain of corpses, big and small, when one counts the species that have been driven from the land for cultivation including the tiniest of living beings that are eradicated.

So, to eat grains, no less than meat, is to kill. Meat is murder? So is wheat. But, if you substitute the natural process of death for the loaded word, murder, a much different set of ethical standards arise. Keith realizes that systems of production have social consequences as well as environmental ones. The historical record is there. The accumulation of the surplus large-scale agriculture could produce was the first capital although shortsighted Marxists claim the system of capitalism itself didn't arise until thousands of years later.

With wealth that could be hoarded, a system of rulers established itself (the State), protected by armed men, created a division of labor, destroyed the matriarchy and implanted angry sky gods who ruled as men did on earth, grouped people into the squalor of cities, and began a relentless drive to conquer with its planetary system.

Annual grain production also allowed a population expansion

as more people could be fed, and as the number of people grew, so did the need for more land to be brought under cultivation, which produced more grain, which allowed for more people to be fed, which...

What emerges ultimately from her text is catastrophism, the long neglected Deep Ecology concept of Overshoot; the view that we've gone so far beyond the planet's resources, used up so much of what it could provide to a species in balance with nature, that we are headed for a planetary collapse. Keith, Deep Ecologists, and even many mainstream observers, state frighteningly that the march of agriculture has brought us to an untenable point as a species. We've overshot our carrying capacity with the destruction of forests, watersheds, seas, and the rapid disappearance of topsoil and now exist by drawing down on what's left.

This seems a much more potent question for the pie-throwers to confront rather than whether a human can exist on vegetables alone. If we're on a bullet train speeding along at 250 miles an hour with a washed-out trestle ahead, does it really matter what's on our plate in the dining car?

Nutritionists can argue forever about the claims and counter-claims about diet. That discussion is crucial to our individual health, but what do Keith's critics say to her central theses? Do those who want to live without killing deny that agriculture, which provides 80 percent of the world's diet, is murderous (in their terms) little different than the death created by meat eating? Keith states, the "foods the vegetarians say will save us are foods that destroy the world." Doesn't this necessitate conversation and debate rather than denunciation and violence?

Do Keith's critics deny that agriculture allowed the first rulers to arise and with them the State, patriarchy, and repressive religions? Or, that with the advent of agriculture, human and animal life became disvalued, and abstraction replaced real experience?

But, even if we agree with her, where does that leave the vegan, vegetarians, and others like me who eat a reduced animal diet? Maddeningly, Keith gives barely a hint. She certainly doesn't provide recipes; doesn't even suggest what proportion of meat properly belongs in a diet (although she offers the Innuits whose 80 percent meat and fat diet doesn't result in heart disease or cancer). She says diet ought to be appropriate to where you live.

Keith says the damage the planetary population will experience is unavoidable given the number of people on earth. She poses the question, are people going to attempt to manage what is unavoidable or will the blindly wielded scythe of Nature, neither cruel nor compassionate, do it for us?

Looking at Animals
Is There a Third Choice?
Summer 1997

Everyone knows the origin of meat, but few want to face the facts. Sue Coe's art and Alon Raab's review in this issue [Summer 1997] invite the reader to a "naked lunch," Beat author William Burrough's pungent phrase for that moment when everyone sees what's on the end of everyone else's fork. But at this meal, it's a bloody carcass of a being that lived a miserable life and suffered a horrendous death before ending up as a burger on your plate.

Animal rights as theory and animal liberation as action erupted quickly and mostly unchallenged during this decade in the anarchist and radical environmental milieu. Given the almost universal instrumental use of our fellow creatures, it seems necessary to examine the ethical foundation for opposition to animal slaughter. This seems particularly the case if there is an expectation of sympathy for what is essentially a new paradigm for relating to non-humans.

My own 26-year abstention from meat and poultry was based initially on dietary and health concerns, but I continued eating seafood since it is part of the macrobiotic/Japanese diet which first influenced me. Later, when considering the ethics of ingesting flesh, I justified my diet based on my willingness to participate directly in killing. Having fished at different times in my life, I've caught (suffocated), beheaded, cut open and eviscerated fish before cooking them up.

By this yardstick, I held supermarket shoppers in contempt for buying so-called steaks or chops (euphemisms for what Carolyn

Adams calls in her uneven *The Sexual Politics of Meat*, "the missing referent," i.e., the dead animal). Before dinner came in Styrofoam trays covered in plastic wrap, carnivores knew the slaughter process intimately. They didn't hide from their deed, nor did I. In this regard, hunters got off my ethical hook since they made the kill, saw the spark of life fade in their prey's eyes, and gutted the animal elbow deep in intestines and blood.

A demand today for meat eaters to conduct their own kill and butchering would undoubtedly create a massive jump in the number of vegetarians. Coe's art captures the horror of meat eating so dramatically that after seeing her graphic depictions one can only continue to eat meat by way of a process of tremendous denial.

Since the 1980s, however, my abstention from dead land creatures has been reinforced increasingly by a realization that the mass production of animals is a catastrophe for the environment. A simple bacon cheeseburger contains the wreckage of range lands in the West, pig shit-choked rivers in the south, and millions of unnecessary petrochemical drenched acres of crop land to provide feed for livestock.

Unfortunately, the seas are faring as poorly with factory fishing. Whole so-called fish stocks—salmon in all the entire North Pacific rim nations, cod and haddock in the Atlantic to name only a few— are disappearing from oceans and rivers at such a rate that we may be seeing the last of these wild creatures. Industrialized tuna fishing has been called "the last buffalo hunt." Modern fishing methods are so indiscriminate that often as much as 60 percent of a catch is categorized as waste, unwanted species that are discarded overboard. Habitat of non-targeted creatures is disrupted by fishing, threatening them as well.

Sea creatures produced in offshore fish farms are no less harmful for wildlife or the nearby environment. In the entrepreneurs' mad attempt to maximize profit by controlling everything from weight to color of their product, they introduce dyes and antibiotics, which when combined with massive concentrations of fish waste in coastal areas, gravely threaten native species and water flora.

The destruction/production is also bad for people. The nightmare slaughterhouses Coe describes have worsened in recent years—more unsanitary, more dangerous—as white, Midwestern union workers have been displaced by Laotian, Latino, and even Somalian immigrants only days off the boat from Africa. Wages have plummeted accordingly as the formerly privileged sector of the working class is kicked out along with their unions which, at least, defended minimal living standards and comparatively humane working conditions (for humans, that is). Now, it's not unusual to see Immigration and Naturalization Service (INS) agents, used to working the barrios of southern California, suddenly making a mass raid on an Iowa Beef Processors plant in Storm Lake, Iowa searching for undocumented laborers.

Any one of these issues—personal health, the environment, or labor ought to be enough to signal the end of meat eating by radicals or other people of conscience. Yet, for the most part, it doesn't. Maybe the reason is that we are omnivorous animals and meat eating has been deeply and irrevocably rooted in human societies since the Paleolithic Age.

But any attitude or custom can change, and animal rights theorists are asking (or demanding) that the respect and privileges conferred on humans be extended to other creatures. We are the only animals that act out of ethical considerations, hence, it is a uniquely human function to assign rights by virtue of popular perception—that is, how a human group (women, native people, minorities, etc.) or nonhuman entities (animals, trees, rivers, mountains, etc.) are considered by most people in a given area at a given time. Rights are a slippery proposition. They are granted either by custom or document and can be withdrawn as easily as they are assigned. You can be fully empowered with rights one minute and the next you're off to a reservation or death camp.

Anchoring rights as emanating from a god or as being inalienable only plays well if you can back it up. In a sense, all talk of rights is facile. What we want is what is enforceable in the real world. How we deal with animals is equally arbitrary. This culture says it's alright to kill and eat pigs (which are smarter than dogs), but kill Fido and you face jail time.

Some people argue it is ethically unacceptable to kill our fellow creatures since the avoidance of pain and the experiencing of pleasure is the measure of an act. However, most people are aware of but willfully ignore the "hogsqueal of the universe" (Upton Sinclair's vivid phrase describing the abattoir in his early 20th century book, *The Jungle*). Meat eaters prefer their pleasure over the animal's pain.

To those who believe animals are fully invested with rights equal to humans, their killing is by definition murder. But murder must have a perpetrator, as well as a victim. Does this mean people, including our friends and families, who unreflectingly eat meat or wear leather shoes have committed acts comparable to taking a human life? What about native people whose hunt is permeated with ritual and appreciation of the life given to the hunter? Dead is dead, it is argued, regardless of whether a steer is killed by a bolt gun to the head in a slaughterhouse or an antelope by an arrow in the forest by a hunter who sees the fallen creature as his relative.

Addressing the crucial question that humans should not eat the flesh of other animals, one argument suggests that although many animals besides humans are predators, we are the only species which can choose abstention. Is it here that the ethical imperative lies?

Animals are directed toward the kill by their genetic constitution, but why is the carnivorous predilection, so common in people, less natural than when practiced by instinctive impulse? If you oppose a human eating a bird, say a pigeon, should you be equally appalled when one is killed by a Peregrine falcon?

I've seen one of these magnificent birds swoop down on its flying prey at 80 miles per hour from atop a huge building, sending out an airborne spray of white feathers and blood before taking the catch back to its perch to be ripped apart by her and her brood. To say dead is dead allows for no distinction between rednecks at a pigeon shoot in Hegins, Pennsylvania, an endangered bird, or Amazonian Hoarani hunters. If life is undifferentiatedly sacred, does it matter if the act of taking an animal's is genetically driven or willful?

According to the absolutist argument, incantations mean little to the victim. But where does this leave the Inuits and Masai, tribes in which animal protein is crucial for their survival, and in the case of the former, absolutely without alternative? Are they murderers, as well? Can there be a mutuality between animals and people, without rights, so under the proper relationship, such as expressed by native people, a life is taken within an ethical context?

Ultimately, it is the absolutism contained in the sentiment about murder which worries me. How close does such an extreme formulation come to that of right-wingers who similarly charge abortion is murder? No one in the U.S. animal rights movement has yet gone to the lengths of the fanatics who bomb clinics or kill their personnel, but is the philosophical groundwork there?

Maybe there is a declarative statement that can be offered based on something other than our feelings. That is, you say animals shouldn't be for human use. Someone else says it's OK. Who's right? Is it possible to establish absolutes when there is no external or heavenly affirmation of either point of view?

A good starting point for a perspective that has the capacity for validation beyond our emotions is environmental philosopher Aldo Leopold's sense of holism. This is best articulated as a "land ethic" in his classic 1949 book of essays, *Sand County Almanac*. It says if we love our planet and its inhabitants, we must come to conclusions about what constitutes its biotic integrity.

A simple and seemingly adequate description of this state of affairs would be the condition which existed before the heavy hand of man (gender specific noun intentional) took a commanding role in the biosphere and began an instrumental redefinition of our relationship to flora, fauna, and things. Leopold states, "A thing is right when it tends to preserve the integrity, stability, and beauty of the biotic community. It is wrong when it tends otherwise."

But be advised: this formulation can leave domesticated animals destined for either burgers or coats without the ethical protection animal rights advocates demand. Domesticated animals, particularly in their modern form of production, are unacceptable when considered in terms of Leopold's precepts, but he had no objection to either hunting or meat eating when it was done within the context of sustainability.

The modern meat industry and its support requirements such as mass agriculture do monumental harm to biotic integrity. The reason to abstain from flesh in this culture seems much more firmly founded in protection of the earth than in animal suffering. All eating causes death, and some suffering. That's the "life economy" described by ecologists, recognized by primal animism and archaic traditions such as Buddhism.

Hence, farm animals aren't deserving of the protection we should afford wildlife since, not only is their existence usually inimical to their feral brethren, but also that they can only exist as human artifacts, literally animal machines functioning solely as adjuncts to their masters.

Unfortunately, there is nowhere to turn on the question of domesticated animals. The call by some animal rights activists to free the inhabitants of the pig pen, hen house, and stockyard would ensure their deaths no less than their current destination. In the few areas where domesticates are capable of surviving, such as feral pigs on Hawaii or wild cats in Australia, their presence constitutes another assault on fragile ecosystems.

Also, the land ethic would not, in many cases, afford absolute protection even to animals in the wild. For example, much is made of so-called hunt sabs, the organized interference with hunters by scaring away prey or bravely (or foolishly) standing in the line of fire. To be sure, disgusting spectacles like fox hunts by the English rich or the Hegins pigeon shoot makes me root for the disrupters, but can this protection be transformed into an absolute?

An island off the coast of Maine I've visited is overrun by deer, descendants of ones introduced 50 years ago to provide sustenance for the fishermen during the hard Atlantic winters. Now, with the same food available on the island as anywhere else, the deer are ignored and have multiplied to the point where they may be responsible for extirpating as many as a hundred native plant species and threaten the rare Fringed Gentian growing there in proliferation. What would the land ethic dictate? Simply that the deer should be eliminated given the harm they are causing to the biotic community. Cruel, but fair, as the line from Monty Python goes.

We are asked by people advocating full rights for animals to choose not to kill or accept the results of killing. But how far should this extend? Some people, evoke the criterion of sentience, the ability to think and cognitively, rather than reflexively, react to pain. This would eliminate flies and mosquitoes from protection, yet some East Indian religionists wear gauze masks to keep from inhaling unwary insects. Should we not kill at all? How about tomato worms or slugs eating our gardens?

I'm glad I'm asking these questions rather than attempting to answer them. It's a conundrum that in many ways can only be resolved with absolutist arguments. But even an absolute doesn't seem to resolve the issue. For instance, when I see a demonstration of 40 people outside of a furrier in a wealthy Detroit suburb, but only one of these same faces (an FE associate) at a protest to stop chemical dumping in the St. Clair River adjacent to a native people's island, it's hard for me to take their concern for minks seriously. Involvement in the latter would protect the environment, animals and people (us!). The other seems so narrowly focused as to be hardly worth the effort.

Though there are committed anarchists involved in both animal rights and radical environmental work, the above example seems to be more the rule than the exception. Everyone will do the political work their conscience directs them to, but it doesn't seem unreasonable to suggest at least some prioritization for a small, radical environmental and anarchist movement already marginalized by a utopian vision. In a culture where meat eating and animal usage is almost universally affirmed, trying to dictate diet on the basis of absolutist ethics seems like a hopeless undertaking, but, hey, I suppose one could argue no more so than advocating an anarchist revolution.

Getting Off the Road
Beats & A Sub-Culture of Resistance
August 1977

Review: *On the Road,* Jack Kerouac, Penguin Modern Classics, 1976

Review: *Naked Angels: The Lives and Literature of the Beat Generation,* John Tytell. McGraw Hill, 1977

Don't let anyone bullshit you, the 1950s were a terrible time to live through. On TV it was the Fonz and all of his friends having "Happy Days," but the reality frame was the American empire at its zenith. It was a world dominated by Eisenhower, Nixon, John Foster Dulles and other spokesmen for the American Century—the dominance of American military might abroad, and white, middle-class culture at home A time without rioting blacks, demonstrating students or Vietnamese in revolt to threaten the image.

Certainly, there were wildcat strikes, Elvis, James Dean, and Charlie Starkweather (who killed 11 people for kicks), but rebellion was easily contained because there was no outside at that time. Rebels were criminals, cranks or madmen. Rebels Without A Cause or, in the words of one of the j.d.'s (juvenile delinquents) in the 1955 film "Blackboard Jungle" when asked why he made so much trouble, "Like, I dunno, man."

Like, I didn't know either. I just knew I felt really uncomfortable in the world in which I found myself, but could never put my finger on the reason why. I mostly believed the authorities when they said something was wrong with me. After years of tortured run-ins with everyone in authority from my parents to the school and the police, I read Beat author Jack Kerouac's *On the Road* in 1959.

The message, as I read it at that time, hit me with the power of a religious conversion. It wasn't me after all, but a society that suffocated people, choked and reined them in at every step of the way, made them, in C. Wright Mills' potent phrase, "cheerful robots."

None of this was directly said, but the actions of the characters made it all obvious. Where the American '50s put its demand on moderation, Kerouac's central character, Dean Moriarty, and the rest were excessive at everything. Where the '50s dictated stability, Dean and his friends were always in motion. In fact, motion becomes the key to it all in *On the Road*. Motion comes to represent life and rebellion against stultification.

Dean and Sal Paradise speed across the U.S.—East to West and back, North to South and back—innumerable times.

"I wasn't frightened at all that night; it was perfectly legitimate to go 110 and talk and have all the Nebraska towns—Ogallala, Gothenburg, Kearney, Grand Island, Columbus—unreel with dreamlike rapidity as we roared ahead and talked." Driving naked; the rush of conversation; sitting cross-legged on the bed facing each other talking all night trying to figure out what it was; the excitement of digging everything—and everybody. "What a crazy cat that was, whoo! Did I dig him!" Dean yells. Listening to bebop jazz. "Out we jumped in the warm, mad night, hearing a wild tenor man bawling horn across the way, going 'ee-yah! ee-yah!' and hands clapping to the beat and folks yelling, 'Go, go, go!' Dean was already racing across the street with his thumb in the air, yelling, 'Blow, man, blow!'"

Even the style of the narrative itself almost leaves you out of breath. In *Naked Angels*, John Tytell relates that Zen maniac Kerouac, finally grasping both his message and his method, sat down and wrote *On the Road* in two straight weeks on one continuous roll of Japanese rice paper raging through the typewriter in one paragraph with almost no punctuation.

Kerouac had come to believe what the Beat authors had

asserted, particularly William Burroughs, that all revisions and re-writes diminish the emotions felt at the time of writing and that all editing is simply done in terms of contemporary values and writing conventions. Written in 1951, the book was not published until six years later with its style altered to quite normal standards of fiction. Yet its energy is maintained.

The impact the book had on me and my Motor City friends was electrifying. We were bored to tears with endless evenings languishing on the corner of Dexter and Davison broken by equally dull daytime jaunts to Kensington Park to sun and swim. The idea of breaking out and finding real adventure thrilled us all and we became possessed with planning and finally executing travels to New York City, California, Mexico, South America and on. It gave us a frame of reference that stated quite emphatically that this, the society of the 19 50s, couldn't give us what we needed and that it was up to us to fashion something different.

Upon a second reading of the book 18 years later, I'm not so sure everything we saw in the book was actually there. The same sense of motion and energy is there, but this time it seems more frantic, and "holy Dean' more like a 1,000 speed freaks we've all run into over the years, who, for all of their enthusiasm, could never "dig all the gone" this-or-that for more than ten minutes at a time. Any more time than that, and the dreadful feeling of boredom and purposelessness returned.

At the end of *On the Road*, Dean is defeated. He just couldn't keep up the breakneck pace of all the riding and all the relationships. The character with all the vitality, "ragged in a moth-eaten overcoat he brought specially for the freezing temperatures of the East, walked off alone."

It was much in the manner of the White Rabbit in *Alice in Wonderland* who had to run twice as fast just to stay in the same place. All of these years—through the New Left and counterculture—we may have just been trying to outrun ourselves and suddenly there's just no longer any place to go in this society. For the project that the Beats unknowingly started in the '50s and what blossomed in the '60s as genuine attempts to base human association around new ways of relating, just ran out of space.

This society was much more resilient than we had suspected (we really thought that rock and roll, reefer and a few demonstrations would topple it) and the way we lived turned out to be much more marketable than we had realized.

We had gotten to the far wall of what Reich called "The Trap," and either for lack of numbers or lack of will (or both), the final assault was delayed and finally replaced by a wholesale retreat into the social forms of two decades previously. New Leftists and hippies toppled over one another trying to make peace with the society they once contested, often all the while continuing the rhetoric of rebellion. Others have affected a total capitulation and mouth the rationalizations of a society they once scorned.

The net result of the process is the diminishing ability of all of us who choose to live on the margins of Capital and contest it as much as possible, to continue to function without ourselves being re-absorbed. For what was once seen as a sub-culture of resistance, now has its major recognition in the media and commodities, with the remaining practitioners quickly being relegated to the categories of the '50s, as criminals, cranks and misfits.

The almost total absorption of the artifacts and lifestyles of what we felt made us different from the rest of this society has narrowed our options considerably. It makes all of our activities and projects that much more crucial in a period of quiescence as capital's vortex moves to silence our attempts at remaining human and make our activity part of its own. A sub-culture of resistance is no longer a matter of choice, as in the '60s but a matter of our survival.

R–E–V–O–L–T
How Do You Spell Relief?
Winter 1983

Mass murder, random killings and the like are nothing new in this country. Bruce Springsteen, in "Nebraska," his ballad about a 11-person killing spree in the late 1950s by Charlie Starkweather, sings, "Well, sir, I guess there's just a meanness in this world."

It seems someone blows their top, flips their lid almost daily. So, reports of a homophobic minister's son in New York City shooting into a crowd of gays, or a driver ramming her car into pedestrians packed onto a Las Vegas sidewalk, or a disgruntled client tossing gasoline bombs before him as he shoots his way through a crowded Detroit law office, or a bored Southern California school girl who calmly fires round after round into her school yard, become almost mundane, ordinary, such is their frequency. They are the small percentage of flip-outs, those whose rage has gotten out of control.

Initially, there's always shock—America's leading emotional commodity, eagerly milked by sensational media coverage—and then onto the next page or right back after the commercials for a report on the leading economic indicators. However, it's not as if passivity to this type of news is a completely inappropriate response. After all, how *does* one react to daily reports of random violence and mass murder?

The Tylenol murders of early October (their very name denotes an eerie, modern clinicalness) represent a watershed in the growing syndrome of seemingly senseless violence. Only seemingly senseless because all things have their causes and here the causes are too close for comfort, too rooted in the mass psychology of this culture.

We live in a world so plagued with violence, there is such a "meanness in this land," that the Chicago Tylenol killings and the subsequent copy-cat product poisonings are like the dam breaking loose releasing a torrent of pent-up, murderous rage. The rage is now generalized—all are potential victims. It is produced by a lifetime, by generations of frustrations, repression, disappointment, anger, failure, confusion, ambivalence—all concealed beneath a calm exterior. The potential is there in all of us. It breaks loose in only a few.

Usually, these highly charged emotions are skillfully manipulated to shape reactionary social views—the urge to punish others, the desire for executions, support for the police and military, for wars, racism, denying abortions to women and the like. But in some individuals, the fantasies of violence, for revenge for all of the hurt, cannot be contained within society's domain—it escapes to its logical conclusion, murder.

It's never a monster who suddenly kills, but "the guy next door"—and "he always seemed so nice." Sometimes a whole society rushes into madness and all of the murderous impulses are given free rein, so all of the nice guys next door clamor to become concentration camp guards, torturers. Their grisly fantasies no longer have to haunt them: they are officially approved.

The copy-cat adulterations of food and drugs which followed the Chicago poisonings certainly weren't socially approved, but they suddenly became socially available. The fact that perhaps only a hundred or so took advantage of the availability out of a population of millions does little to ease the creepy sensation that random violence lurks everywhere. A newsweekly referred to the poisonings as "a chilling reminder of everyone's vulnerability."

This new terror was added to a land already racked with fear of nuclear war, crime, and now, potential attack from your neighbor in any form. It's like your mother turning on you. Where we live should be a place of nurturing, a sanctuary, not a war zone. In wartime everything becomes unraveled; one's life, one's emotions. Destruction is everywhere; attack is always imminent. When this becomes a permanent definition of the culture, life becomes intolerable. Without any mass demand for a new life, individuals retreat, public life disappears. Even vestiges of ancient, public rituals like Halloween are over through the fear of sneak attack from one's neighbors.

Television, official messages and controlled environments—guarded shopping centers and workplaces—represent the only safety. Public life shrinks that much more towards its final collapse.

The Tylenol murders exposed another public secret. Americans are suffering an epidemic of daily pain. Johnson & Johnson, makers of the poisoned pain reliever, were raking in $3-400 million dollars a year and this only represented a little more than a third of the pain reliever market. It takes only a short trip to most of our own medicine cabinets or a quick look at TV commercials to know that we are plagued with chronic, daily aches and pains. An incredible array of headaches, digestive and elimination difficulties, tension and sleeplessness, to the point where all of this is taken for granted. Aren't such pains and problems natural? And similarly, isn't murderousness, this "meanness in this land," as well, the human condition?

In a word, no. Both malaises are powerful messages from our collective psyches and guts that something is dreadfully wrong in this land. The rage which permeates every fiber of this society stems from a culture eviscerated of its human qualities. One which had to destroy a virgin land to establish itself, slaughter its original inhabitants, enslave another population to build its economic foundation, fight war after war to expand and defend its empire, all to produce a nation of factories and offices.

This history is not lost on today's inhabitants no matter how little they actually perceive of it. In a land of slaves to industry and business, at best you get headaches, at worst you murder. In between, lie alcoholism, mental illness, suicide, crime, drug addiction—a whole range of social disintegration which is the price for our history.

The positioning of wage labor at the center of human activity completes the destruction begun by the emergence of the nation state of the tableau of previous ages which immersed the individual in a mythic, joyous and communal integration with nature and the people about him. In place of a mutually recognized human identity people are now known by their job categories ("Hi, what do you do?;" soon, THX-1138). The wilderness recedes from our sight and from our visions. We do the bidding of economics.

Work itself becomes the task master. Its routinized and universal presence creates the illusion of an eternal quality as if humans always labored day in and day out at the same tasks for a lifetime. The human body and spirit is eroded by this deadening process producing a disheartened and weakened people willing to submit to work's daily humiliation and subjugation.

The major physical difficulties produced by work are well known. Wretches not favored by the class system are forced to take dangerous and unhealthy jobs which constitute the backbone of this economy. (At Three Mile Island, a member of the crew sent in to clean up the 1979 radioactive spill was asked by a reporter, "Aren't you afraid to go in there?" "I'm more afraid not to have a job," was the reply.)

Now comes the news that almost every job has hidden lethal potentials within it. From working with computer terminals, paint, printer's ink, office machines, photography, endlessly providing a list of health-threatening diseases. Also, the human form is twisted out of its normal shape by the requirements of jobs whose activity is modeled on the motion of machines: sitting at typewriters, lying under cars, standing in front of machines, on ladders, at assembly lines, passing, holding, lifting objects repeatedly for an enforced period each day are all beyond the limit of the body's capacity.

What is created is a chronically sick population suffering from job-related injuries and illnesses characterized on the lowest scale by an epidemic of smaller ills from which we seek relief by gobbling down billions of Excederins, Tums, and Sominex. These are drugs for the modern wage slave. Labeling them medicine, the advertisements try to disguise their real function—masking the pain, drugging.

The mind reacts as well with emotions as mild as feelings of generalized dissatisfaction and disaffection, and as severe as psychosis, defining a population in various stages of immiseration so widespread are their occurrence. Prior to this current economic depression, psychologists clucked about "on-the-job stress. Now, their concerns are with the stress of un-employment. Where is the joy, the reward? Even the material affluence reaped by one section of the population barely seems worth what must be sacrificed.

We are allowed by this affluence (even the poor) to now consume items on a daily basis which were previously only enjoyed on special occasions. Unhealthy to consume in quantity, but now heralded by advertising as compensation for our long hours of work, meat, coffee, refined sugars, flours and grains, alcohol and tobacco are no longer for use at festivals or celebrations, but have been advanced to the category of necessities. What is produced by this daily, massive ingestion of celebration items which are now, for the first time in history available everywhere as commodities, is a further debilitation of the body and an addiction, not only to the wares of the seller, but also to his remedies.

All of this physical and emotional suffering is placed within the context of a society in which the dominant mode of association is that of the business place where each individual is to be seen as a potential sale or as a competitor. Again, this is more than the human psyche can withstand, and withdrawal becomes the norm furthering the process of social atomization. The periodic human explosions are just its indicators.

To be sure, this is the picture at its worst, but a characterization which can come to shape even those who resist dehumanization and try to retain a sense of humanity in their dealings with others. The social and cultural configurations of this society all exist as affirmation for the war of all against all, whereas the resistance exists in spite of them.

Right now, we can only hope to make that rebellion, that negation, stronger by consciously opposing this scourge by maintaining our commitment to our projects, by resisting the increasing privatization, by creating public expressions of our desire to live a human life. For some of us, perhaps even in personal matters such as deciding to live a healthy life will be important. Understanding the notion that instead of sustaining you, here, too, the culture attacks you. We should see that the effect of the excessive consumption of celebration commodities mentioned above is no different than politicians. They are both out to destroy you.

Beyond the personal, things get more difficult. Our groups are small and our projects fragile. For instance, the Grinning Duck Club, an attempt in Detroit to have a place where people could gather unmediated by commodity consumption, to just talk or perform our music, plays, or art is presently out of commission. Our lives are that much more reduced because of it and that much more like the other victims.

Perhaps talk of healthy diet and social clubs may sound a bit pallid to those desiring clarion calls for revolution, general strikes, and direct action, but this is not what this essay is about. Rather, I meant to write about the maintenance and extension of human values among ourselves; this small group of us who feel acutely aware of being awash in this sea of modernity. How can we be kinder to each other and to ourselves?

While waiting for the assault on the bastions of authority and domination, we would do well to have as a priority the development of social forms which will at once nurture us, sustain us in our commitment to libertarian values, act as a model for the society we desire and, finally, be the instrument of this society's destruction.

What A Day It Wasn't
The Media Creates a Crisis
March 1981

Author Note: On January 20, 1981, American hostages held in Iran for 444 days were released, and Ronald Reagan was sworn in as President the same day. It was later learned that Reagan operatives secretly negotiated with the Iranians to not release the hostages until after the 1980 presidential election and to do so on Inauguration Day.

"What a Day! Hostages Go Free; Reagan Sworn In"
Detroit Free Press Headline, January 21, 1981

"Kill the hostages; Turn them into sausages."
"Kill the Hostages," punk song by Benedict Arnold & the Traitors

"He gazed up at the enormous face. Forty years it had taken him to learn what kind of smile was hidden beneath the dark mustache. O cruel, needless misunderstanding! O stubborn, self-willed exile from the loving breast!...everything was all right, the struggle was finished. He had won the struggle over himself. He loved Big Brother."
   George Orwell, *1984*

DETROIT—The unexpected intensity of the patriotic outpouring surrounding the arrival home of the 52 hostages at the end of January, shocked us at the Fifth Estate to the point where we were considering producing an extra edition of this newspaper as a small way of combating the reigning hysteria. But almost as rapidly as the hoopla dissipates after a Superbowl game is played, so did the hostage issue quickly disappear from popular attention and daily life returned to its normal routine.

However, while it lasted, the politicians and their media stooges gloried in a limelight of induced importance long denied them by a mood of general cynicism and distrust among the American people. Cleverly (and expectedly) the event was presented as the capture by foreign barbarians of American innocents no different from you or me and as a calamity worthy of being elevated onto the plateau of "national concern."

Indeed, if the truth were generally known of the Iran embassy's role as a key outpost of U.S. global militarism and its personnel's responsibility in keeping a despicable despot in power, it is doubtful whether many would have been willing to shower the concern on the hostages they did. In fact, it would be naive to think it would take this particular moment for the politicians and their mouthpieces to suddenly come clean when such an opportunity for them presented itself. Through utilization of the worst brand of manipulation, a "crisis" was declared which, in any real terms, only concerned the captured spies and their bosses, but was inflated into one that millions came to believe affected us all.

This ability of rulers to turn their concerns into the concerns of the ruled is, of course, nothing new, but television's repetitious and pervasive nature allowed this incident to be hammered into people's consciousness in a manner no Hearst paper of yesteryear could ever have hoped to achieve. The incessant coverage of every aspect of the prolonged holding of the hostage spies on a nightly and sometimes hourly basis through the electronic media carved the impression of a matter of earth shaking proportions—"America Held Captive" and "Day 387—The Hostage Crisis," etc. All of this created a collective consciousness that defined reality in exactly the terms the rulers desired. Even if you didn't accept the official version of the incident or have sympathy with it, you still were made to realize that what was occurring had significance beyond the normal day's events, so powerful is the media in defining our reality. And it is that capacity which characterizes power itself—the ability to define reality and make it act in accordance with that definition.

It never really mattered exactly how many people actually bought the patriotic hysteria and to what degree. There were enough millions who did, and when the homecoming of "our" hostages happened, the media could represent the cheering crowds as being all of America with only the oddballs and cranks outside of the unity of a "joyous nation." Although millions of people were outside of the patriotic consensus and stood unmoved either through disgust or apathy, they never were presented coherently or as having any significant dimension. This meant that dissenters from the approved ideas, no matter what their total numbers, could only view themselves as one person pitted against a mass, coherent, socially sanctioned body of public opinion.

Once the media had established the context of the "new patriotism," it quickly received official support for the grand illusion it was creating. It was local governments and corporations which went on the heaviest yellow-ribbon-tying orgies and, for instance, to encourage a large turnout for the Jan. 30 New York City ticker tape parade (actually tape is no longer used in stock brokerages, so the hostages had reams of computer print-out pages rained down upon them), Wall Street businesses gave their employees extended lunch hours and the city high schools were given the day off to attend the parade. Also, in a city whose population is at least 50 percent Black and Latino, the crowd in attendance was overwhelmingly white.

Here in Detroit, where the population is 60 percent black within the city proper, it was like the event was not even occurring so sparse was the display of recognition. However, in the suburbs, local municipalities sent city employees out on ribbon-tying sprees, businesses distributed free ribbons, whole office buildings were swathed in yellow and cops cars had yellow bands tied to their antennae. These were the areas in which public sentiment took the hostage 'return as important.

This is not an attempt to underestimate the numbers who did succumb fully to the onslaught of the stage-managed patriotism.

How deep it was is another question, though. One friend suggested it had all of the depth of the "Who Shot J.R.?" question and most probably involved the same constituency. Certainly, the displays of affection coming from both the viewers of the TV serial and the hostage parade spectators seem to have similarities. Fans of the seemingly ordinary TV drama about a rich Texas family meet inquiries as to the show's immense popularity by stating that they feel like they know the "Dallas" Ewing family. Identical sentiments were expressed at the Jan. 20 New York City parade. CBS radio carried interviews from along the parade route with spectators, some near to tears, who said, "I feel like I know them (the hostages)," and "I feel like they are part of my family." These emotions expended on strangers in an era when people feel it difficult to express intimacy with those immediately around them testifies to the power of the spectacle and its ability to build a pseudo-community through television. But television is not an irresistible device (although it does have certain physical hypnotic features, see *Four Arguments for the Elimination of Television* by Jerry Mander); it necessitates a willingness on the part of the viewer to participate in the deception being perpetrated. The apparent ease with which the people seem to be willing to accept a whole variety of obvious delusions seems to point to an almost inherent desire/need that humans possess to participate in a collective identity and there are those who will accept even a pitifully false community when faced with the loneliness of none.

While we may stand in wonderment at how anyone could be moved to welcome a "nest of spies," Marsha Fishberg could stand with 200,000 others in West Point, New York, as the hostages arrived in the U.S. (fittingly at an Army facility), and say to ABC radio news, "This is the most important thing that's ever happened to me; I know this is going to be part of history."

In reality, of course, absolutely nothing happened to Marsha, but her participation in an officially ordained spectacle gave her the feeling that she experienced something of great worth—that she was connected to something that connected her with others. The process she actually was involved in stretches back in its origins to the creation of the nation state itself, but takes its modern spectacular dimension from the use of the electronic media. The phantom community Marsha feels allegiance to is one without a substance greater than the cathode rays behind her television screen and the little dots projected into her brain which coalesce to form the images and symbols to which she is beckoned to signal her allegiance.

There are no authentic bonds which tie Marsha to the released government operatives and the community she feels she shares in is one which was established and is maintained by men with guns who arbitrarily define geographic borders and a political structure. Once this is done, the administrators of the state—kings, presidents, commissars—erect symbols recognized by rulers for eight millennia as having the power to make masses of people submit to the project of the state and through it, their own subjugation. The uniforms, flags, state buildings, parades, adulation of leaders, the entire pomp of authority which it bestows upon itself, are the mechanisms nation-state dwellers internalize as part of their own character structure. When millions do this, a mass personality emerges which directs the ruled to identify the concerns of the rulers as their own and having a monumental quality, while their own concerns appear trivial by comparison.

To refuse this process is to rebel against the modern world and its political character. The Marshas of the world select the opposite course and fall all over themselves trying to signal their assent to the ruler's symbols. What she and her counterparts do not want to face is the thorough emptiness of the Detroit Free Press headline at the beginning of this article; it really wasn't "What A Day!," because almost all of us went to work at dull jobs, attended meaningless classes, or stood in the unemployment or welfare line, shopped at the supermarket or watched TV. No stupid inauguration or phony welcome-home can change that reality.

The real celebrations will commence with the liberation of this society, when we no longer need newspapers and TVs telling us what kind of day it was.

Chapter 4
Religion

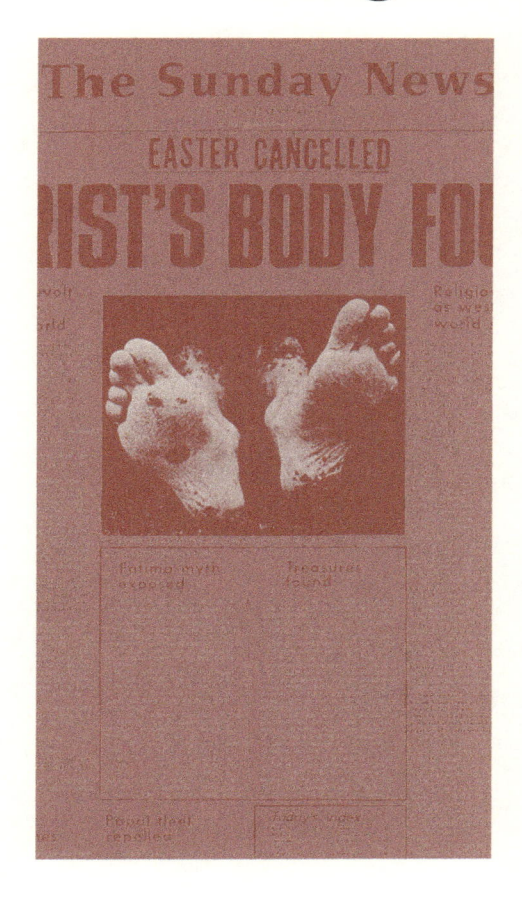

Easter Canceled
Christ's Body Found
April 1976

Author Note*:* The Fifth Estate staff produced a fake edition of a right-wing Detroit daily for Easter of that year. See next page. Copies were placed in *Detroit News* coin boxes around the city and several were posted on church doors to greet parishioners as they attended holiday services.

JERUSALEM–UPI– The Christian Faith lies in ruins today as the central myth of the world-wide religion–the Resurrection of Christ– was shattered by the discovery of a 2,000-year-old corpse and its positive identification as that of Jesus of Nazareth.

Western civilization has been rocked to its core by the revelation and although reports from Rome remain sketchy, several startling announcements have been made from the Vatican.

At 3:00 pm Rome time, the papal secretary announced the official canceling of the Easter holiday. "After all," said Monsignor Luigi Fasulli, "If you don't have a Resurrection and Ascension, you don't have much of an Easter, do you?"

Pasta also stated that the Pope and the College of Cardinals had resigned and that the Vatican's remaining skeleton staff was going about the dismantling of the Catholic Church.

Earlier in the day when mobs of disillusioned Christians stormed the Vatican they found the Pope's apartment bare, with the exception of an airline receipt for two tickets to Argentina.

Throughout the rest of Europe and North America, revolutionary

Weather
Cloudy
Details on Page 12A

The Sunday News

Today's Chuckle
Jesus is on the Cross &
His blood is dripping:
Get another nail,
His head is slipping.

THE HOME NEWSPAPER
Serving Capitalism from Detroit

102 YEAR NO. 178 — DETROIT, MARCH 30, 1976 40 CENTS

EASTER CANCELLED

CHRIST'S BODY FOUND

Workers revolt as anarchy sweeps world

WASHINGTON, D.C., LONDON, PARIS, BERLIN, MADRID, MOSCOW, WARSAW–UPI, AP– The future of governments, capitalist and socialist, remains in doubt today as waves of anti-authoritarian rebellion reverberate across Europe and North America.

Falling like dominoes in the wake of the news that Christianity was based on fraud, nine European governments have been toppled in the last 18 hours.

In Latin America and the United States uprisings in the major cities put the forces of tradition in grave jeopardy at this writing.

In every major European city, councils of armed workers have proclaimed the end of all authority of one group or class over another.

In the West, cries of "Down with capitalism," rang through the streets of Paris and London. In Prague and Moscow, hundreds of thousands marched for the first time shouting "No More Bureaucrats." In every city pledges to end wage labor, commodity production and the factory system brought joyous dancing in the streets as main intersections became the scenes of festive celebrations. How the wave of anti-Christian feeling rapidly developed into stronger anti-political sentiments was expressed by a Belgian office worker. "They had our minds mucked up with all that God and Jesus shit. We thought they were everything and we were nothing," he said. "When that went down the drain all those other people in control of our lives looked just as useless as the saints."

In Yugoslavia a Belgrade metal worker explained why uprisings had toppled bureaucratic state socialism: "We were all atheists before, but the example of our brothers and sisters in the West just set the example for us. Now we can set up real communism and get rid of all the "marxist" politicians."

Germany today is a place where no priest is safe from the diatribes of angered citizens. Portugal has become a no mans land where nuns are run out of town like so many beggars. To no one's memory even those weaned on World War II has there been anything to match the scorn and bitterness the average citizen feels towards those in power.

Political leaders of the surviving nations are barricaded at this hour in a swiss chalet, hurriedly mapping out plans for a last stand on the European continent. Men who once held such high positions as Prime Minister of England and Chancellor of Germany were seen being smuggled into the highly-guarded chalet by horsecart.

Anti-religious rebels, intoxicated by the unprecedented collapse of organised religion, have seized power in many areas. Rail and communication lines in most of the U.S. are said to be in the hands of atheists.

A first hand report by fleeing nuns in France indicates that local villagers have reacted to the news from Vatican City by seizing the churches and burning them.

Crowds estimated at over 500,000 swept through downtown Madrid today shouting revolutionary slogans and holding anti-religious demonstrations.

In one instance, throngs were seen pulling a makeshift trailer with a replica of a crude outhouse containing statues of Franco and Pope Paul IV.

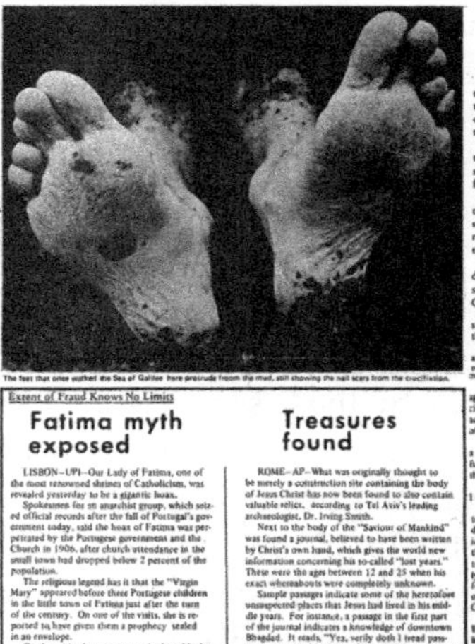

The feet that once walked the Sea of Galilee here protrude from the mud, still showing the nail scars from the crucifixion.

Extent of Fraud Knows No Limits

Fatima myth exposed

LISBON–UPI–Our Lady of Fatima, one of the most renowned shrines of Catholicism, was revealed yesterday to be a gigantic hoax.

Spokesmen for an anarchist group, which seized official records after the fall of Portugal's government today, said the hoax of Fatima was perpetrated by the Portugese government and the Church in 1906, after church attendance in the small town had dropped below 2 percent of the population.

The religious legend has it that the "Virgin Mary" appeared before three Portugese children in the little town of Fatima just after the turn of the century. On one of the visits, she is reported to have given them a prophecy sealed in an envelope.

On that visit, she, or someone looking like her, went to the townspeople to show them the power of faith. So awed were they by the sight that they built a shrine to her memory.

A crude candle-powered projector with a hand tinted slide showing Mary floating on a cloud was found yesterday in a cellar in Lisbon, raising anger at the Church to a new high. So great was the Parishoners' rage at being tricked that it is reported there is not one religious object left in all Portugal. Crucifixes are being used for paint stirrers in Oporto. Novena candles (cont. on p. 94)

Treasures found

ROME–AP–What was originally thought to be merely a construction site containing the body of Jesus Christ has now been found to also contain valuable relics, according to Tel Aviv's leading archaeologist, Dr. Irving Smith.

Next to the body of the "Saviour of Mankind" was found a journal, believed to have been written by Christ's own hand, which gives the world new information concerning his so-called "lost years." These were the ages between 12 and 25 when his exact whereabouts were completely unknown.

Sample passages indicate some of the heretofore unsuspected places that Jesus had lived in his middle years. For instance, a passage in the first part of the journal indicates a knowledge of downtown Bhagdad. It reads, "Yea, verily doth I tread passageways and hidden halls of the temples of pleasure, so too doth the fallen women follow in my footsteps out of Bhazghadian (Bhagdad) to my camp where we held lectures late into the night."

Further on is a description of an Egyptian banquet where Christ beseeches the noblemen. "So I say unto you, what good does it do a man to gain all the wealth of the world only to lose his soul? Thou must strip thyself of all worldly goods in order to enter the Kingdom of Heaven. For that purpose I have brought two chariots which thou can begin filling with thine unwanted luxuries."

Religion collapses as western world shaken

JERUSALEM–UPI– The Christian Faith lies in ruins today as the central myth of the world-wide religion– the Resurrection of Christ– was shattered by the discovery of a 2,000 year-old corpse and its positive identification as that of Jesus of Nazareth.

Western civilization has been rocked to its core by the revelation and although reports from Rome remain sketchy, several startling announcements have been made from the Vatican.

At 3:00 pm Rome time the papal secretary announced the official cancelling of the Easter holiday. "After all," said Monsignor Luigi Pasta, "If you don't have a Resurrection and Ascension, you don't have much of an Easter, do you?"

Pasta also stated that the Pope and the College of Cardinals had resigned and that the Vatican's remaining skeleton staff was going about the dismantling of the Catholic Church.

Earlier in the day when mobs of disillusioned Christians stormed the Vatican they found the Pope's apartment bare, with the exception of an airline receipt for two tickets to Argentina.

Throughout the rest of Europe and North America, revolutionary mobs have toppled government after government claiming that political states and religious beliefs had robbed them of their human potential. (See story on this page.)

The discovery that toppled Christianity began just two days ago several miles outside of this ancient and previously "holy" city. Fahkir Boumedium, an itinerant cymbal maker, stumbled across the centuries-old body while digging for brass at the site of an apartment-complex kibbutz under construction.

Digging by candle light in the early morning hours, he noticed a sandal-clad foot protruding from a drainage ditch and, digging further, Boumedium unearthed the cadaver's head still bearing the legendary Crown of Thorns.

Boumedium told UPI, "It's nothing to me, I'm a Moslem, but I thought others would like to know."

The anger of many ex-Christians stemmed from the obvious attempts of the Pope and others to first deny and then downplay the discovery. Even after medical, archaeological, religious and historical experts had confirmed that the half-decomposed body was that of Jesus, Pope Paul had insisted that to announce the bitter truth would be to bring havoc to the Christian world. Word finally leaked out from one of the panel of experts and the Vatican was forced to make the announcement admitting that the central tenet of their religion, the redemption of sin through the sacrifice of Christ, in their words, "was inoperative."

Worse yet was the report filed by Dr. Vera Similitude, of the United Nations medical team, who was one of the first to examine the body from a medical standpoint. In it she stated that Christ had not died from wounds inflicted by Roman Centurions, as reported in the Christian Bible, but rather had died from complications of an advanced stage of syphillis.

Speculation is high among informed sources that the entire New Testament was simply faked after the natural death of Jesus, who was one of many Hebrew religious fanatics preaching in Palestine during that period.

The truth concerning what took place between the time Pope Paul was informed of the devastating discovery in the Middle East at 4am Rome time and the time he finally relented and made the information public may never be known, but ashen-faced Romans arriving at St. Peter's in the early morning hours were greeted by a sight they will long remember: the historic shrine of Catholics everywhere and the base of Christian faith was boarded up and 'for sale' signs from an Argentine realtor dotted the huge plaza.

But as a small band of black-garbed, elderly Italians hopelessly said their rosaries in the muted night, radical Italians took other action.

Forming a loose coalition of leftists, atheists and cynical ex-Christians, they broke down the sealed doors of the Vatican and rushed into the former seat of Catholic power.

Untold millions of dollars worth of art objects and precious metals were literally stripped from from the walls in what must have been one of the fastest turnabouts in the otherwise quiet career of Pope Paul. So sudden was the departure that early arrivals at the once-sumptuous residence report a projector in the cinema room still running, endlessly repeating "King of Kings."

Coming on the eve of Christianity's holiest occasion, Easter, this betrayal by Vatican City has spurred repercussions unheard of in modern-day society. Howling mobs of Catholics stormed their churches in city after city only to find 'for sale' signs and announcements of car washes to be built on the sites of their former houses of prayer. As one Roman businessman put it, "This is a Watergate that dwarfs any other cover-up in the history of mankind."

That the "Jesus Christ Cover-up," as it is now being called in European capitals, is the most pervasive ever known goes without saying. Informed sources in Vatican City report that when the crowds broke through to the inner chambers of St. Peter's, radical groups were carting off literally tons of (cont. on p. 94)

World stock market crashes

GENEVA-UPI- World stock market prices plummeted today as billions in discounted stocks and securities found their way into an already shaky Eurodollar market.

The sudden abdication of the entire hierarchy of the Christian world had brought about an extremely volatile financial situation in a sensitive world capital market already wracked by double digit inflation and growing world-wide workers' revolutions.

When reports from Berne and Geneva indicated that huge amounts of blue chip stocks were being sold in random lots yesterday, speculation had it that the Middle East was ready to explode into war and the Sheiks were attempting to create havoc in the money capitals of Europe

The truth unfolded in the late evening when developements from Rome showed that the entire financial empire of the Holy Roman Catholic Church was being liquidated by unknown Lebanese brokers.

As one New York banker put it, "Sure we knew the Pope had a few bucks to throw around, but we had no idea it was this much."

Truly, an unprecedented amount of (cont. on p. 94)

Papal fleet repelled

PAGO, PAGO, American Samoa–AP–Much like the legendary man without a country, the papal fleet of Boeing 747's carrying the Vatican's major domos wander the globe searching for a place to call home. Refused landing clearance by the Pago-Pago islanders last night, the total number of countries to refuse them permission to land now stands at over 103.

Coming on the heels of a stunning aerial defeat at the hands of Wake Islanders, flying vintage WWII Japanese Zeroes, this was, as one observer called it, "like condemning them to Purgatory."

An informed source, on hand when the Pope received word of the defeat, reported that the Pontiff took it extremely well.

"What you gonna do?" The pope said philosophically. "I know I'm no Walt Disney in the hearts of the people but I was only trying to make a buck. Sure, once in a while I pulled their leg but it was all in good fun. We should let bygones be bygones."

Today's index

Accent	1-20D	Hobbies	6F
Art-Books	2B	Homes, Gardens	1-2K
Classified	1-20H, 14-16K	Horoscope	3C
Real Estate	4-14K	Lively Arts	1-10F
Contact 10	1B	Movie Guide	6F
Crossword	5C	Obituaries	19D
Editorial	8G	Death Notice	19D
Feature Page	7B	Outdoors	6E
Finance	1-10G	Sports	1-8E
		Travel	1-10I

Detroiters React to Destruction of their Religion, P. 12
Bishop Emrich's Last Column, P. 48
Lou Gordon Gloats, P. 19
Col. Heinl Assesses the Military Implications, P. 96
Local Religious Leaders Say Final Good-Bye, P. 23
Jane Lee Gives Advice to Ex-Christians, P. 48
Tigers Whip Bosox, P. 33

produced by the EAT THE RICH GANG

This page originally appeared as the March 27, 1976 Fifth Estate and was found throughout the city pasted on the doors of churches on Easter morning and stuffed in Detroit News boxes.

mobs have toppled government after government claiming that political states and religious beliefs had robbed them of their human potential.

The discovery that toppled Christianity began just two days ago several miles outside of this ancient and previously "holy" city. Fahkir Boumedium, an itinerant cymbal maker, stumbled across the centuries-old body while digging for brass at the site of an apartment-complex kibbutz under construction.

Digging by candlelight in the early morning hours, he noticed a sandal-clad foot protruding from a drainage ditch and, digging further, Boumedium unearthed the cadaver's head still bearing the legendary Gown of Thorns.

Boumedium told UPI, "It's nothing to me, I'm a Moslem, but I thought others would like to know."

The anger of many ex-Christians stemmed from the obvious attempts of the Pope and others to first deny and then downplay the discovery. Even after medical, archaeological, religious and historical experts had confirmed that the half-decomposed body was that of Jesus, Pope Paul had insisted that to announce the bitter truth would be to bring havoc to the Christian world. Word finally leaked out from one of the panel of experts and the Vatican was forced to make the announcement admitting that the central tenet of their religion, the redemption of sin through the sacrifice of Christ, in their words, "was inoperative."

Worse yet was the report filed by Dr. Vera Similitude, of the United Nations medical team, who was one of the first to examine the body from a medical standpoint. In it she stated that Christ had not died from wounds inflicted by Roman Centurions, as reported in the Christian Bible, but rather had died from complications of an advanced stage of syphilis.

Speculation is high among informed sources that the entire New Testament was simply faked after the natural death of Jesus, who was one of many Hebrew religious fanatics preaching in Palestine during that period.

The truth concerning what took place between the time Pope Paul was informed of the devastating discovery in the Middle East at 4:00am Rome time and the time he finally relented and made the information public may never be known, but ashen-faced Romans arriving at St. Peter's in the early morning hours were greeted by a sight they will long remember: the historic shrine of Catholics everywhere and the base of Christian faith was boarded up and For Sale signs from an Argentine realtor dotted the huge plaza.

But as a small band of black-garbed, elderly Italians hopelessly said their rosaries in the muted night, radical Italians took other action.

Forming a loose coalition of leftists, atheists and cynical ex-Christians, they broke down the sealed doors of the Vatican and rushed into the former seat of Catholic power.

Untold millions of dollars' worth of art objects and precious metals were literally stripped from the walls in what must have been one of the fastest turnabouts in the otherwise quiet career of Pope Paul. So sudden was the departure that early arrivals at the once-sumptuous residence report a projector in the cinema room still running, endlessly replaying the movie, "King of Kings."

Coming on the eve of Christianity's holiest occasion, Easter, this betrayal by Vatican City has spurred repercussions unheard of in modern-day society. Howling mobs of Catholics stormed their churches in city after city, only to find For Sale signs and announcements of car washes to be built on the sites of their former houses of prayer. As one Roman businessman put it, "This is a Watergate that dwarfs any other cover-up in the history of mankind."

That the "Jesus Christ Cover-up," as it is now being called in European capitals, is the most pervasive ever known goes without saying. Informed sources in Vatican City report that when the crowds broke through to the inner chambers of St. Peter's, radical groups were carting off literally tons of (cont. on p. 94)

Author Note: There was not a page 94.

Has George Bush Doomed Christianity?
Spring 2007

Perhaps the only positive result of the reign of the murderous moron in the White House as chieftain of the American empire is to what depths he has sunk the popular perception of Christianity.

The Bush mob's initial political approval following the 9/11 catastrophe he allowed to occur, utilized both the flag and Bible as its key iconography to fool the rubes. Although this is standard fare for craven politicians, the Republicans raised this cultural imaging to levels not seen in a hundred years. But, the unraveling of the reigning racket's lies, the exposure of their greed, corruption, and their hypocrisy and that of their most pious spokesmen, both in the Congress and the pulpit, have created an opening for atheism that would have seemed impossible even a short time ago.

In 2005, a national poll was taken showing atheists being held in such low regard that most respondents stated they'd rather have their daughter marry a Muslim than a non-believer. Now, books on atheism, such as Richard Dawkins' *The God Delusion* and *Letter to a Christian Nation* by Sam Harris, adorn *The New York Times* best seller list, and others of a similar nature are being rushed to market by publishers. They sense a boomlet.

The formal religions of the world—with their male sky gods, their blessing of temporal authority, their sexual repression, their authoritarian and hierarchal nature, their intertwining with the state, their misogyny and homophobia, and their horrific, bloody history of repression—are the implacable enemies of freedom. Oh, there are many in the reform movements who try to make the words of Jesus or other religious figures into instruments of justice, but the 2,000-year history of injustice caused by followers of these fictional figures requires not only a suspension of logic when faced with a preposterous proposition, but also a need to navigate around the mountain of corpses religion has produced.

As a small contribution to the struggle against this dangerous superstition, in 1976, the *Fifth Estate* published a fake edition of a Detroit daily newspaper announcing, "Christ's Body Found: Easter Cancelled"–if he didn't rise, there can't be a celebration of a resurrection. We stuffed the facsimiles into the paper's coin boxes and Pet-milked them on the doors of churches the night before Easter, all causing quite a scandal.

Now, life is imitating art.

According to an article in the February 27 *New York Times*, "A documentary shown recently by the Discovery Channel claims to provide evidence that a crypt unearthed 27 years ago in Jerusalem contains the bones of Jesus and that Jesus was married to Mary Magdalene, that the couple had a son, named Judah, and that all three were buried together.

"The Lost Tomb of Jesus," revisits a site discovered by archaeologists from the Israel Antiquities Authority in the East Talpiyot neighborhood of Jerusalem in 1980 when the area was being excavated for a building. The documentary's case rests in large part on the interpretation of the inscriptions which the film claims are Jesus, Mary, Mary Magdalene, Matthew, Joseph, and Judah."

Can you say, "Da Vinci Code?" In fact, this is more evidence that, as the widely read Dan Brown novel of that name states, "Christianity is the greatest story ever sold." So, cancel Easter; the basis of the myth has been rendered untenable.

It is even worse news for our religious friends who desperately try to make Christianity into a theology of liberation. Their task has always been a hopeless undertaking since their belief's basic story is a terrible message about us: we are all born, not with the potential for joy and fulfillment, but with a fatal flaw inherited from the mythical origins of the human race. Start off with that self-perception and anything is possible—Crusades, holocausts, ethnic cleansing of entire continents, world wars.

When the Christian myth, a Middle Eastern-centered spirituality, ceased being a messianic cult and cut a deal with the crumbling, corrupt, and decadent Roman Empire early on, it modeled its bureaucratic structure and territorial expansive ambitions in a manner identical to its new patron. Christianity established itself in Europe by extirpating the indigenous pagan and nature religions, and, in many cases, like Saint Patricius (meaning, member of the ruling class; or, Patrick), by exterminating their adherents. Christianity, like the civilization it sanctifies and which in return sponsors it, is a bloody sword.

Voltaire said in the 18th century, "Those who can make you believe absurdities can make you commit atrocities." It's time for the world to cast off the formal, hierarchal, patriarchal faiths, and find other venues for expressing one's spiritual connection with nature and its creatures.

Suggested reading:

God: The Most Unpleasant Character In All Fiction, Dan Barker, Prometheus Books, 2023

24 Reasons to Abandon Christianity, Charles Bufe, See Sharp Press, 2022

Godless
150 Years of Disbelief
Winter 2020

Review: *Godless: 150 Years of Disbelief* edited by Chaz Bufe, PM Press, 2019

More than a thousand years ago, a Chinese Zen master wrote: *"Magical power; marvelous action! Chopping wood; carrying water."*

The eleven essays assembled here by See Sharp Press publisher Chaz Bufe are effective diatribes against belief in gods that completely destroy every aspect and argument on which Christianity and other religions are based.

Although some of the texts are of recent vintage, all are rooted in the traditional notion on the left and among anarchists that religion is the "opiate of the masses," as has been famously said, and, hence, the distinct enemy of revolution.

In the opening essay, "The God Pestilence," late 19th century American anarchist Johann Most nails religion as "a reign of terror," a bloody sword that has brought death and destruction, torture and pillage to the faithful for thousands of years. Plus, the fog of religion, he insists, makes the believer incapable of independent thought. He acidly writes of the believer, "...once in the clutches of the priests, his intellect becomes barren—his intellectual functions cease to operate in a normal way, and instead religious maggots and divine worms wriggle through his brain." Whew!

What doesn't get addressed in any of the essays is why there is something in the religious spirit among the most devout that gives rise to such murderous impulses as we've seen in history and in contemporary slaughters among those with a slightly different take on a belief.

The faithful often answer this question with the "humans are flawed" argument, so that the blatant hypocrisy and violence associated with the faithful, it is claimed, doesn't invalidate the fundamental beliefs or institutions operating in the name of various gods. But this needs closer attention.

Almost all cultures across the globe, beginning at least in the Neolithic era 12,000 years ago, devised spiritual explanations for the fundamental questions of human existence. This occurrence was so universal that geneticist Dean Hamer recently suggested the physical presence of a so-called god gene within our human genetic composition.

Joseph Campbell, a 20th century academic who studied comparative mythology, similarly noted what he called a monomyth, one basic myth about existence expressed in a multitude of spiritualties world-wide that are but variations on a single great story.

And, perhaps one or both of these explanations for universal spiritual expression is correct. However, this in no way validates any or all religious beliefs. A better explanation can be found in the basic theory of evolution. Maybe within the social structures of early human bands there was a need for a mythical explanation of life's purpose and processes, an overarching narrative as adaptation for group cohesion and hence, survival.

The mytho-poetic spirituality that marked most pre-state social formations was a necessary component of their existence and can be illustrated by a circle within which all in a society held hands—the people, the flora, fauna, and the earth itself. All with an interconnected importance and purpose.

With the end of the Neolithic period 3,500 years ago and the rise of the state, this spiritual impulse is directed away from a circularity and replaced by a social pyramid where male sky gods replicate the newly formed hierarchical and patriarchal political structures and whose function is to sanctify the ruling order.

The intense hostility of revolutionaries to religion in the last

150 years chronicled in *Godless* is understandable since religion remained a central bulwark of the state in the modern era just as it was at its origin.

Christianity, for instance, never had a Golden Age before turning into a state-approved racket sanctifying the authority of the Roman emperor and subsequent ruling orders. Religion's role has lessened in recent years, but the most faithful still are the base of authoritarian political movements and states.

Spirituality, taking thousands of forms world-wide, are human-devised stories that obviously can't all be simultaneously true regardless of Joseph Campbell's theories of a single narrative expressed differently. In other words, spiritual beliefs are stories creatively rendered to meet the needs of a particular culture at a given time.

Some are worse than others. The Judeo-Christian story of a fall from grace and redemption through sacrifice is not particularly unique as several other Middle Eastern myths express this pattern, but the idea that we are born with sin as an inherent definition is a particularly pernicious and odious idea.

However, if we do have a god gene in us, and since churches by the thousands are thankfully closing across North America and Europe, maybe we need to make up one with better symbolism than a man being tortured because of our inherent corruption. Men (gender specific intended) invented the narrative fiction of the sky god religions to justify class rule and the suppression of women.

We can do better than that!

Let's devise a spiritual belief that honors the sacrifice of the exploding star that scattered its atoms across the universe until they congealed in this solar system and created the planets and stars and provided the building material for all its creatures including us. We can come together regularly to sing songs and have ceremonies in abandoned sky god houses of worship (no more worshipping!) about how everything is part of everything else and all deserve honor and protection. We can have lots of days off to recognize the sun (forget about the Son) and the moon and the stars and all the planets and ourselves and all the creatures and the rocks, rivers, and plants. No priests.

Or, if that's all too complicated or inconvenient, how about just everyone adhering to the Golden Rule?

I suspect most readers of this publication don't need convincing of the absurdity of religious belief systems, that they are a bulwark of political power, and lead to disunity rather than how they functioned 10,000 years ago within small band societies.

But, try this book out on your religious friends and family members. Maybe ask them to skip Most's vituperative essay where he calls religious people "brain defilers." However, it would be difficult for any of them to refute Sebastien Faure's essay, "Twelve Proofs of the Nonexistence of God," (proving non-existence is tough!) or editor Chaz Bufe's "'Twenty Reasons to Abandon Christianity." Early feminist Matilda Gage's 1893 "Woman, Church and State" makes clear the relationship of the latter to the suppression of the former.

Humor makes an appearance in Earl Lee's send up of *Dogspell,* a book urging Christians to have the same devotion to God as their pets do to them. Lee asks, does that mean being "on all fours, sniffing the crotch of God."

And, the epigram at the beginning? Chop wood, carry water, and the meaning of life becomes clear. It's what we do and what we choose every minute of the day that defines who we are and life's purpose.

No gods; no masters.

Chapter 5
Technology

We Get A Computer and Hate It!
The *Fifth Estate* Enters the 20th Century
Summer 1993

"Things are in the saddle and ride Man."
Ralph Waldo Emerson

After several years of discussing and debating the implications of a newspaper which criticizes technology obtaining computer equipment, we were finally forced into making the big leap, and now possess one. It may seem hypocritical to denounce computers while typesetting on one, but no less so than if I had arrived at our office by car with money in my pocket and began writing about the harm the internal combustion engine does to the environment and the need to abolish capitalism.

To paraphrase the opening lines of Jim Gustafson's poem, "The Idea of Detroit," our new computer just sits there like the head of a dog on a serving platter—a hideous object, but one too fascinating to turn away from. Actually, it's not a new machine, but used equipment we picked up from a lawyer friend—a Macintosh IIsi, it says on the front, and a LaserWriter Pro 600 printer, for those who are interested.

No one on our staff is particularly enthusiastic about our acquisition. We were happy with our quarter century old typesetter, our wax, press type, and Exacto knives. We liked doing layout manually and took pride in our proofreading skills. We are not pleased that much of these tasks are going to be taken over by a machine—one whose introduction has had a dramatically negative impact on the world.

Many of our computer-owning friends have assured us we will love it once we develop operating skills, and they have generously supplied us with all sorts of advice and instruction. We doubt, however, if we will ever love any machine, but the situation had come to the point where our old typesetter was so antiquated, it was no longer serviceable except by a firm in Seattle.

Thus, the coming of the computer hasn't proven our critique wrong. Rather, it has shown our argument to be correct that technological development bulldozes diversity and creates deepening dependencies—in our own case, painfully and infuriatingly so.

Until now, I've tried to avoid computers at all costs, but now having had this forced upon us, I've begun to consider what effect this will have on our publishing efforts and those of us who work on the paper. Upon beginning to learn their use, computers seem like fiendish apparatuses which order you about on their terms, not the reverse.

The labyrinth of programs within programs, windows within windows, macros within macros, reminds me of the infinitely descending portrait on the Morton Salt box. I'm sure the people who designed these machines would have been, in an earlier age, hobbyists who constructed large model battleships out of toothpicks.

We're always told what an advance computers have brought about in efficiency and accuracy, but where was the need crying to be met? Were the users of 3X5 cards—clerks, bank tellers, and secretaries—calling out to have their onerous work alleviated by electronic means? In fact, was any important, human-scale, human-oriented occupation or activity restricted by the absence of computers? Of course not.

Computers, like all technical/industrial inventions before them, came from stretching the capacity of human ingenuity beyond the immediate to produce a device theretofore unknown, to be presented for sale on the market, and create a need not previously there. Or, as anthropologist Marshall Sahlins puts it in his essay,

"The Original Affluent Society," "It was not until culture neared the height of its material achievements that it erected a shrine to the unattainable: Infinite Needs."

The capitalist world, defined by the religion of science and technology, has endlessly created what immediately becomes necessity. Just as today no one can imagine publishing a newspaper without computerized equipment, in twenty years (or twenty months!) we will be told that such machinery is hopelessly outmoded, too slow, inefficient, and only artificial intelligence which downloads thought direct to holograms can fulfill our needs to file recipes, plan wars, balance our checkbooks, manage production, etc.

A hundred years ago, anarchists printed weekly newspapers with handset type. None of them dreamed of desktop publishing systems to do on-screen composition. Instead, they dreamed about what the words in their paper desired: revolution, the elimination of capital and the state; a new world, not a new Pagemaker program.

A perhaps even more profound implication of technology is its connection with imperial domination. Most technological development, particularly in the modern era has allowed for the increased dissemination of empire both as a material and cultural force. For instance, the internal combustion engine not only extended capital's material base, but allowed it as well to define major aspects of culture from architecture to living patterns, while integrating its dynamic capacities to drive its weapons of war.

Another obvious example is television, which similarly became an important sector of the economy once it appeared on the market, but its real importance lies in its function as the medium for transmission of official messages, supplanting crumbling patriarchal, religious, and even state forms of authority.

Computers also play an enormous role as a commodity within the world economy, but their larger purpose, according to computer pioneer Joseph Weizenbaum, is to "conserve America's social and political institutions. It [the computer] buttressed them and immunized them…" Capital's world empire, following World War II, had developed to such a degree of complexity that it could no longer administer and coordinate its apparatus without the introduction of methods appropriate to its size, geography, and structure.

The stock market, the board room, and the Pentagon war room could not function without the sophisticated technology of computerization. The vertically and horizontally integrated superstate, capable of shaping planetary life is what social critic Lewis Mumford designated as the Mega-machine. Rather than fascism being defeated in World War II, it triumphed after WW2 with the victory of the U.S. and its allies (their enemies were cut in on the swag almost immediately). In other words, the Third Reich suffered only a momentary setback with the defeat of the Nazis. The totalitarian state triumphed and expanded throughout the world.

At the dawn of the Machine Age, people knew that the new devices being forced upon them would fundamentally alter their lives in a way they did not want and fought back against the use of power looms, the factoriums, and the work discipline which was demanded by them. This resistance to industrialization and mechanization has often been superficially criticized as being only a reaction to the job loss which was entailed in the shift from small craft shop to the new factories. But those involved sensed (quite correctly) that a new, much less human world was evolving, one which would destroy what decent aspects were left of an earlier age. In England, artisans and mechanics, peasants and craftsmen smashed machines, burned factories, and assassinated mill owners.

This early 19th century movement of British machine-breakers, the Luddites, was so successful in mobilizing the population against industrialism, that the destruction of equipment was declared a capital offense and often a dozen men were hung at once for the crime. In Lancastershire, power loom woolen production could only commence with the stationing of 20,000 British troops in the district. Contrary to the predictions of a glowing new era which the new machines would herald, the opponents of the new system were right. Industrialism ushered in an era of unmitigated misery for people and the destruction of the environment, an era which continues unabated throughout the world today.

Where are the exceptions that technology enthusiasts can show?

Which radical doubts that technology and industrialism must be centrally administered and requires a world-wide material and political grid to produce their splendors? Where is the utopian who has a vision of steel and concrete, plastic and computer chips, which does not require a robotized working class toiling at extraction and manufacturing, and whose effluent does not poison the earth and its inhabitants?

Show me the non-polluting, convivial, democratic, peaceful model in which industrialism and technology could exist after a revolution. I don't think it can be done.

Well, yeah, that's all true, they agree, but at least the computer will save us time, they assure us, in the production of our paper. Maybe it will, although we never thought we had a problem with slow techniques. As Thoreau and other critics of industrialism pointed out in the 19th century, we save time by killing eternity.

The Chicago anarchists of a century ago, who produced a weekly paper, depended on a mass movement to provide enough able hands to publish frequently. Now, one anarchist publisher told us, if it wasn't for computers, his paper wouldn't exist since so few people work on the project. The same is true with many single-person zines. It is debatable whether this is an argument for computers or a statement about the weakness of a movement.

That machines are the proper response to a movement's malaise brings to mind 17th century English philosopher John Locke's prescient statement, "There is no such thing as a labor-saving device." However, his idea usually needs explanation since the statement does not appear to be accurate on the face of it. For instance, it seems obvious that one can dig a ditch faster with a mechanized backhoe than with a hand shovel.

However, that equation is based on the social assumptions of technology which always neglect the totality of aggregate labor needed to excavate with a machine. Perhaps a better example would be the sewing machine which unquestionably is faster to sew with than hand stitching. Yet, when considering every aspect of production—mining, drilling, manufacturing, assembling, transportation, sales points, repairs—the whole world-wide technological grid needed to bring such a machine to market (and then have machine sewing arise as a labor-intensive industry)—a massive amount more total social time is spent in sewing than when it was done by hand.

Similarly with computers. Whereas some tasks may be reduced in time expended by certain individuals and job categories (almost exclusively in society's upper echelons), in general, computers link up increasingly more people into a dependency on the world-wide industrial grid for activity which was previously accomplished with paper and pencil. Again, aggregate labor has increased, not decreased. The production of computers creates a growth industry which utilizes toxic manufacturing processes and extends into Third World countries where women and children are employed as microchip assemblers under slave-like conditions.

Also, no workday has been shortened, and no worker's pay has been raised due to increased efficiency. In fact, computers preside over the acceleration of work, as more is expected in a shorter amount of time from workers who have their outputs monitored by bosses demanding increased production from these new miraculous machines and their human appendages. Workers are experiencing more stress, physical injury, pay reductions, and a further de-skilling of work as well as its accelerated pace.

This is the first edition we've produced solely with computers (although for at least four years friends have provided copy for us using them), so it is too early to evaluate what impact its use will have on the social process involved in publishing our paper. All of us look forward to working together and the most exciting period is always at the conclusion of an issue when our office is teeming with people doing last minute layout, proofreading, graphics, and re-writing.

To say the computer will have no effect is to misunderstand the nature of technological change, and to be ignorant of history. Obviously, the world has changed greatly because of expanding technology, but sometimes it can be demonstrated with little stories rather than repeating the well-known impact of larger technologies such as the changes the automobile has forced on society.

Very few would argue that ice boxes are superior to electric refrigerators, but the introduction of the latter in the early 20th century had a decided impact on rural communities. Across such regions as Michigan, Ontario, New York and the Northeastern states, ice cutting for the summer supply would always occur on the coldest day in January. Whole communities would gather. The men would hitch up teams of horses, go out to the frozen pond and cut great kegs of ice. These would be dragged to ice houses where they were stored in sawdust and often lasted until August providing what was needed to keep food cooled.

The women of these rural communities would assemble in the largest house, do quilting, trade the latest news, and prepare a large, sumptuous, communal meal followed by a social and dance. With the advent of electric refrigeration, all of this came to a halt and rural isolation was intensified. Today, whoever is left in farming communities sits in places like rural Iowa or Nebraska and watches hip-hop music videos on MTV

No one knew in 1898, when Henry Ford's horseless carriage chugged down Woodward Avenue in Detroit what profound changes the internal combustion engine would cause in human life and the health of the planet. However, people who have desires for a revolutionary transformation of the world have been forewarned about where the technology of computers is heading.

Its giddy proponents speak unashamedly about creating a "global computerized information network; one grand Communicopia" linked by a "seamless worldwide network" which will usher in an "Age of Information Transparency," as Arno Penzia of AT&T defines a new world dominated by a merged ultra-technology of computers, television, cable, and telephone systems.

The question is, will this benefit anyone other than the elites, the rich, and the supranational corporations? As the latinamericanization of society continues apace (20 percent affluent; 80 percent impoverished), this information age obviously isn't going to have everybody linked in. The average prole shouldn't expect to have a pocket fax machine and computer wristwatch. (In any event what would they need them for?) The technoid dream is of a world dominated by machines, transmitting the empty information of commerce and entertainment, with decreasing privacy and increasing speed, filled with ubiquitous screens, flashing digital displays, and constant machine beeps and noises.

Even though their dream is our nightmare, at least, they assure us, we'll be able to produce our paper faster. Beyond the fact that I'd be willing to have a John Henry-type contest between us doing manual composition and lay-out and a steam drill/computer, I'd like the cheery advocates of computers to consider the following: On June 13, 1993, *The New York Times* reported that three giant computer and entertainment corporations announced a merger to create the equivalent of software for cable television called Cablesoft. Such mergers and joint ventures dominate the news of late for communication corporations as they gear up for a new stage.

According to its salesmen, when it comes to fruition, this will mean "the transmission of coming generations of interactive programming." This is explained by James F. Moore, of Geopartners Research, Inc., as a process which will be "the gateway for popular culture" and "the substitute for newspapers and magazines and... gives it enormous economic potential for those who control the gateway."

In other words, boosters of computers, who have all assured us what an advance they will be for us, have set the context whereby our newspaper will soon become an antiquated medium, a picturesque Smithsonian Museum curio unrecognizable by any except those outside of capital and technology's net.

So, thanks, guys. For nothing!

Author Postscript: Just like The Clash or The Bobby Fuller Four singing "I Fought the Law and the Law Won," so it was with the *Fifth Estate* and computers. We fought computers and the computers won. Another essay is necessary for a retrospective on the impact computer technology has had on the production of issues and staff dynamics. Suffice it to say, computers dominate good portions of our work in producing the magazine, and our heads are stuck in front of screens little differently than most modern citizens.

Turn It Off!
Spring 1984

The call to turn off television or even to lessen viewing hours certainly should not be interpreted as an inherently radical suggestion, since it emanates constantly from educators, parents, psychologists, and others professing concern for the health and morals of the nation. Laying aside the fact that these well-meaning guardians undoubtedly are as hooked into extensive TV viewing as any other American, their pleas and advice should be seen as consistent with the continuing criticism television has experienced since its emergence as a mass medium 30 years ago.

Many, if not most viewers will agree that excessive viewing is harmful activity much in the same manner that abusers of alcohol will admit to drinking too much, all the while partaking. This recognition of television's pernicious effect could be seen in the early viewers' dubbing of themselves as "vidiots," and the object of their fascination as the "boob tube" and the "idiot box." Although these phrases faded as TV and extensive viewing became the accepted norm, even today no one complains of watching too little television, only that too much time is taken up with indiscriminate viewing.

When viewers complain about television, echoing the critics of TV, they most frequently mention television's irresistible capacity to dominate their thoughts, its hypnotic effect, how they continue watching long after their desire for entertainment has passed or how they continue viewing even when they want to stop.

With the recent announcement that the average TV viewing

per household had, for the first time, exceeded the seven hour per day mark, several affluent suburbs scattered across the nation reacted to the news by instituting "ban-the-tube" groups in which cooperating families go "cold turkey"—an immediate cessation of viewing—for periods of up to a month. (One may note that it is the slang of narcotics addiction which is employed.) Still, even with all of the high hopes of the anti-tube organizers, no one seriously believes that the one-month hiatus will do more than provide a momentary relief from the excessive viewing patterns which now predominate among all social strata of this culture.

However, one should not ignore class considerations which are a factor rarely if ever mentioned in analyses of why TV is watched as much as it is. The poor, the aged (who often are represented in the first category) and the unemployed (a new growth sector) are among those who log the highest viewing time in order to fill the hours normally comprised of society's other major compulsion—work. The middle- and upper-classes are apt to view TV somewhat less, partly due to employment, but also tend toward more selective viewing and will take time out for varied athletic, cultural, or social activities not pursued by the other sectors.

Still, all groups and all ages from all social classes speak distinctly of not viewing as deprivation, and a sense of real loss is expressed by those who have willfully forsaken television even for a short period of time. Artificial deprivation situations created by well-meaning parents in the "ban-the-tube" groups must seem analogous to fasting—participants will admit to the beneficial results of not taking in solid foods for a given period, but can't wait to get back to eating.

TV viewing is no longer thought of as an entertainment—as a desire—but as a human necessity. As so often occurs within commodity society, what once never existed as a need, takes on a sharply enhanced value through the modern techniques of marketing and advertising until suddenly no one can conceive of being without the particular item.

Television has become so commonplace that not to have a set in one's home marks the non-possessor as an oddball, a crank, comparable to someone who willingly foregoes electric lights or a refrigerator. It is this social perception which sets the stage wherein the medium becomes that which communicates with Americans more than their friends, family, teachers, classmates, or fellow workers. The mass act of viewing represents the shattered fragments of human communities regrouped into a pseudo-community of the spectacle—the reduction from reciprocal, face-to-face relationships which functioned within a setting of tradition and equality of participants to a situation of one-way communication directed by an elite of message senders to a mass of undifferentiated receptors.

All of the foregoing is yet another public secret since the social and psychological configurations of incessant TV viewing and what they produce are well known to almost everyone since almost everyone participates. A massive and pervasive culture has evolved around both television's less obvious feature, its form (more on this below), and its glaringly obvious content. In terms of the latter, almost the entire population over the age of two years is hooked into some segment of the viewing day and exhibits an intricate knowledge and a deeply felt affection for the characters of Sesame Street, through to the afternoon soaps, evening sitcoms, and ending with the jokes of Johnny Carson.

This personal involvement with fantasy characters (a trait once only expressed by children) has recently taken on an even more quirky quality as characters from commercials have arisen as objects of alienated affection (the "Where's the beef?" phenomenon). To be separate from all of this—to not know the latest machinations occurring in "Dynasty" (a weekly soap where mean rich people are featured) or to not know how "we" did in "the game" last night is to virtually stand-alone from one's fellow workers, family, classmates, and neighbors.

Jerry Mander, in *Four Arguments for the Elimination of Television*, describes what is produced within a culture whose population sits glued to TV sets passively absorbing images of what was once part of a directly lived human experience. This "mediation of experience"—Mander's apt phrase—comes as the modern epoch walls us off totally from the natural functioning of the planet and we are left to experience much of our world through the unified, centralized messages sent from our televisions.

Its power as a medium comes through its ability to transmit images, which no matter how arbitrary, are without reference points and contain the ability to define reality. This translates not just into the simplistic concept of power for a discernible ruling class (although it does do that), but describes, as well, an entire mode of living that maintains domination within it no matter who rules or even if there are no rulers at all.

In George Orwell's oft-cited *1984*, the Party enforced its tyrannical regime through utilizing omnipresent screens by which the citizenry was scrutinized for signs of deviation. However, in the present world, the situation is reversed. People passionately watch the rulers' messages and willingly accept the same type of twists and turns in politics, morals, consumer attitudes, etc. which the Party in the novel had to go to great lengths to enforce. 125,000,000 people all sitting in darkened rooms, all receiving the same message at the same time is something a dictator of yore could have scarcely dreamed of.

This colonization of experience—the creation of images and impressions of the world which meet the corporate needs of consumption and the political needs of passivity—is inherent not just in the direct social cues contained in television's content but even in its physical presence. The very existence of a set within one's house expresses an acquiescence to power—the TV is, in the old RCA ad slogan, "His Master's Voice"—and even before it is turned on, mere possession gives evidence of the owner's willingness to submit.

The assumption can be safely made that the majority of people reading this newspaper are among the many who feel at least a discomfort if not a hatred toward this society and have dreams of its alteration or destruction/replacement. Yet many of this same group maintain viewing patterns not dissimilar to those who feel at ease with the present state of affairs. It is foolish of us to contend that simply because we are infused with a desire for freedom and a critique of technology that we can remain impervious to television's reactionary content, its inherent biases or its peculiar physical properties.

Every message beamed to our brains through the 25,000-volt

cathode ray tube behind the shimmering, 300,000 dots which comprise the viewing screen are ones which make our vision of a new world that much more diminished. TV creates a totalized psychological environment for its viewers where the commodity reigns supreme and the tyranny of the fact announces that this is all there is, this is whatever can be and whatever will be. The absorption of images laden with dominant social cues is irresistible, whether contained within the 30,000 to 40,000 commercials a year the average American will view, or in the programming itself. The argument that one's intellect or radical values can distinguish between so-called neutral information and what the rulers wish placed in our heads fails to appreciate the function of both the brain and the machine.

The brain of a rebel soaks up the social cues contained in television images in a physical manner no less so than the model citizen who is longing for the messages. The images we despise, as well as ones we may find pleasant, reassuring, informative, or entertaining, pass through our brains with equal power.

As Mander puts it, "Once they are in your mind and stored, all images are equally valid. They are real whether they are toothpaste, Walter Cronkite, Kojak, President Carter...a Ford Cougar, a cougar....Once inside your head, they all become images that you continue to carry in memory. They become equally real and equally not real...(The images) remain permanently. We cannot tell, for sure, which images are ours and which came from distant places. Imagination and reality have merged. We have lost control of our images. We have lost control of our minds."

Television's role in the drive toward acceptance of a totally centralized, unification of thought gains much of its impetus from the inability of humans to live comfortably in exile — the ultimate punishment in many tribal societies who knew such censure was at the same time worse than, and the same as, death. Rebels who watch television experience an exile of sorts every minute they are viewing. Each message tells them: you are outside, you think differently, you dress, smell, look, and act differently. Come, join all the happy, smiling faces at the supermarket, in the bathroom, in the cars, in the bars — don't be out there alone. To be so is to suffer the fate of the Savage in Huxley's *Brave New World*—sanity in an insane world is always stood on its head.

The impulse to view comes from differing psychological sources within one's personality, the most obvious no doubt being that TV is a source of easy entertainment or pre-occupation for one's imagination. However, this seemingly uncomplicated desire is part of the process which further chokes off self-motivated autonomous activity as mundane as reading, gardening, sports, visiting, or self-entertainment, and strengthens the power of the television culture.

The turning on of the television as the first act upon arising or entering the home is a socially synchronized one that sets in motion one modality while excluding all others. All of what humanity once did since its inception to entertain itself around campfire, hearth or parlor, comes to appear as old-fashioned, or boring. It is only TV's constant dizzying pace which holds out the promise of entertainment once the old skills and joys are relinquished. There is something less compelling about an evening of folk singing with friends and neighbors than witnessing several of the 18,000 murders a child is treated to between the ages of six and eighteen.

TV's riotous, meaningless jumble of sights and sounds mirrors exactly the manic, compulsive obsessional quality of the wage labor which produces it. Those who see television viewing as a way to wind down or relax after a day on the job miss both the characteristics of work and TV. Through television, your mind does escape the obsessive thought patterns of your particular employment, but it is then quickly filled with the obsessive thought and images of someone else's job—those who create television. TV carries with it the paradigm of this culture—incessant consumption—with the mind rarely at rest, free of externally induced thoughts.

The viewing I've done in recent years has almost exclusively been centered around news shows which I hoped would add a visual dimension to the reported events of the day. But even this sort of discriminating viewing is problematic. Upon reflection it occurs to me that very little if anything was provided to my knowledge of the world through the selected clips chosen for broadcast. David Altheide in *Creating Reality: How TV News Distorts Events* writes that "...the organizational, practical and other mundane features of news work promote a way of looking at events which fundamentally distorts them…" Looking back I would say that I have learned the most about events from newspapers and magazines, some from radio and the least from television sources.

TV is best at transmitting images as cues for behavior and response and it is a mistake of the first magnitude to assume that the most sophisticated medium is at once the one most capable of imparting accurate information.

A personal example may serve to make my point: Last Fall, I eagerly watched much of television's coverage of the U.S. invasion of Grenada, often through to the bitter end of ABC's "Nightline" show, and found myself going to sleep each night depressed and despairing. Besides repeating every lie of the government uncritically, the medium itself oozed the even more insidious message, which was that everyone agreed with the invasion, and the proof was that it was being broadcast to millions uncritically. As circular as this reasoning may seem, it is TV's mass dimensions and the pseudo-immediacy of its counterfeit reality which nullify our own sense of reality. In effect, I was told nightly that I was an insignificant fragment who opposed what the vast approving masses had signaled their assent to.

Once away from the television, things appeared different. Detroit is a liberal, predominantly black city where the city administration and several U.S. Congressional Representatives had been sympathetic to the island's Bishop regime, and I circulate in a milieu where I met virtually no one who supported the American military action. Also, I attended several large anti-intervention rallies which served to buoy my spirits about the prospect of opposition to Reagan's policies. However, when I returned to TV at night, the feeling of isolation also returned, which is precisely the emotion TV is best at producing.

The Fifth Estate described the same process when Iran was holding U.S. embassy spies hostage several years ago (see FE March 18, 1981). In an article entitled, "What A Day It Wasn't," we stated, "…only the oddballs and cranks (stood) outside of the patriotic consensus and were unmoved either through disgust or apathy (and) were never presented coherently or as having any significant dimension. This meant that dissenters from the approved ideas, no matter what their total numbers, could only view themselves as one person pitted against a mass, coherent, socially sanctioned body of public opinion." It is ultimately this process which is TV's central function—our fragmentation and massified re-groupment for their messages—and even the realization of this is not in itself a defense against its power.

We should shut it off and get rid of our TVs for both the symbolic nature of the act—not having a set states eloquently that you are unwilling to permit liars in your home—and because of the actual damage it does to our minds. Television has moved to the foreground to join wage labor as the mighty discipliner of this society. Most other pillars of this culture cannot be avoided—work, commodity consumption, etc.—but in this case we are given the easy option of turning off their lies.

Author Postscript: I wrote this essay, but haven't completely taken my own advice. For years, my wife and I didn't own a television set, but like the beginning of drug addiction, the pusherman offered the first one for free, and from then on, we were hooked. However, not too badly. I only watch a little bit of cable news and sometimes a movie or a series. The critique, however, remains valid regardless of my choices or compromises.

Suggested reading:

Four Arguments for the Elimination of Television, Jerry Mander, William Morrow Publishers, 1978

Boxed In: The Culture of TV, Mark Crispin Miller, Northwestern University Press, 1988 [**Author note:** Miller's book contains the great line, "Big Brother is you, watching."]

Chapter 6
Direct Action

Occupy Confronts the Power of Money
The encampments as anarchy in action
Spring 2012

Author Note: The Occupy Movement was an international protest against wealth inequality that began as Occupy Wall Street in New York City in 2011.

"A specter is haunting [the world] — the specter of [the Occupy movement]. All the powers of [the world] have entered into a holy alliance to exorcise this specter."
  The Communist Manifesto — 1848, Karl Marx & Fredrick Engels
  [altered to reflect current reality]

One hundred and sixty-three years after the original words were written, the specter the rulers of Europe so feared (communism, the word altered in the above quote) appeared to have been successfully vanquished. But suddenly the Occupy movement went from 0 to 100 mph in a few weeks placing the question of the rule of money on the political agenda across the world, and, in the U.S. for the first time in a hundred years. Inspired by the Arab Spring, the Greek, Spanish, and English opposition to shifting the cost of repairing capitalism from bankers to the people, Occupy sites sprouted up in over a thousand U.S. cities almost overnight.

The dramatic events of September 17, when Occupy Wall Street launched, through December, brought the words that define the class system and its hierarchal rule to the point where its main phrases, "99%," "1%," and "Occupy," have entered the lexicon faster than any high school slang.

Criticism of Occupy, some of it from the left, that the movement is only a spasm of bottled-up anger without programmatic demands, and at worse, reformist, fails to realize that occupying the sites constituted a critique of capitalism and the culture it spawns. All of the contradictions and problems of the encampments notwithstanding, the taking of public space where capital's precepts are negated, a commitment to consensus decision making, the refusal of hierarchy, communal living, and confrontation with power, is anarchy in action.

Not anarchism, but, anarchy, the manner in which humans naturally associate to effectively and convivially live harmoniously. The politics of the people involved both as Occupiers and supporters were all over the left spectrum, but these anarchist processes were almost universally adhered to by all.

Even though Occupy immediately altered the political narrative, with even major media talking about corporate greed, the increasing poor, and the impact of austerity on most Americans, the idea of permanent centers of protest and even revolution, was more than the rulers could tolerate. Even supposedly liberal city administrations.

The coordinated militarized police assaults to remove encampments in cities across the country was reminiscent of the murderous attacks on workers in earlier periods of labor militancy. Although there was general outrage at the repressive manner in which police cleared Occupy sites using clubs and pepper spray, the most frightening police armament carried into these situations, automatic assault rifles, seems to have gone unnoticed.

The cops were ready to kill.

With the clearing of the outdoor sites, the hope among the powerful is that this specter has gone the way of communism now that the streets have been returned to commerce.

We'll see.

Much is still going on with the Occupy movement now quartered inside in many cities, and they continue to launch actions around a range of issues caused by the collapse of capitalism for large sections of the population. Still, the movement faces the daunting task of discerning what revolution means in the modern era.

The earliest concept of the revolutionary overthrow of capitalism posed by those who capitalism exploited and oppressed from its origins, was a straightforward proposition: The means of production (the economy) would be seized by the proletariat (the workers) who would eliminate the rule of the capitalist class and then administer society for the collective benefit of all. This is certainly a sensible and equitable solution to a horrid set of social circumstances that capitalism has always enforced upon society.

The main impediment to revolution is the political state which functions as the defense mechanism against attempts to eliminate capitalist property relationships. This socially constructed institution which arose thousands of years ago, hasn't altered its purpose of defending accumulated wealth and power since its inception.

The century-old illustration of the social pyramid from the anarcho-syndicalist union, the Industrial Workers of the World (IWW), illustrates the state apparatus contains more elements than just its repressive mechanism. The "We Fool You" sector, i.e., nationalist myths, militarism, religion, and the Spectacle, are the state and capital's first line of defense. Only after these cease to be effective, as is often the case, are the cops and army deployed.

There never was a Golden Age of the state or capitalism. Both were always a set of horrors from their beginnings, and although certain sectors of the world, and certain sectors within nations at different times achieve a degree of economic prosperity beyond just rewarding the owners, there is always a much greater number whose misery and penury is a key to the plenitude of the few.

The favorite form of governance of all ruling classes is absolutism. Their favorite class system is feudalism, but now with capitalist forms of ownership. This has overwhelmingly been the way human affairs have been administered in nation states since their emergence 6,000 years ago. Challenges to these arrangements have been few, relatively speaking, and met with suppressive force when they have occurred.

Political arrangements in the West have had some success with demands for rights and inclusion in decision making harkening back to England's 13th century Magna Carta, and culminating in the bourgeois revolutions of the modern era beginning in the 17th. What was gained in these revolutions, which installed the emerging capitalist classes in power, was usually a formal democratic system in which people had the status of citizens rather than subjects. What was lost was the ostensible reciprocity of feudal society where the peasants produced for the lords and in return were protected by them.

In the new capitalist societies, that social arrangement of mutual obligation evaporated, and the new class of workers were solely elements of production whose labor was purchased at the lowest price that could be leveraged by the emerging lords of manufacturing. Early revolts, such as those of the 19th century English Luddites, were suppressed by massive military force, demonstrating that without the iron hand of the state, capitalist production would not have lasted long.

Within capitalist countries of the West, movements arose around the inscription on the banner of the French Revolution, "Liberty, Fraternity, Equality." Taken to their full definitions, these words would proscribe capitalism and demand an anarchist socialism, so they mostly remain as pretty phrases trotted out on patriotic holidays in France.

For those who took them seriously, years of struggle ensued with numerous successes in terms of the conditions and rights of the common people. In this country, we know and celebrate the history of the abolitionists, suffragettes, the union and civil rights movements, and that of the women, gay, and disabilities rights struggles that have created a slow progress for inclusion within American society. None of these hard won victories should be diminished, but within the economic and political sphere, the same forces of greed and power continue to reign supreme all the while demonstrating a willingness (sometimes extremely begrudgingly) to allow some social equality; however, never economic.

To a large extent this is a conscious strategy on the part of the rulers to mollify challenges with the correct perception on their part that reforms extend and affirm the system. Once the personal prejudices of a white, male elite are brought to heel, the extension of some amount of inclusion works well for them. Color, gender, religion, sexual preferences, etc., doesn't matter if you are consuming, or if you are a company CEO.

The apex of this reform strategy, following some in the Progressive Era, was during the unionization movement of the 1930s which demanded a more equitable split of social wealth and other reforms to improve working and living conditions. This wasn't granted willingly by the rulers and came only after general strikes and class struggle so sharp that it resulted in the death of 300 unionists during the decade at the hands of the cops, national guard, and company goons.

The Roosevelt-era New Deal legislation that resulted, and the extension of the union movement's success, opened the way to the creation of a large, consumerist middle-class who saw themselves as having a stake in the system that had seemed near collapse just a few years previously. This is known as the Great Settlement which lasted approximately 35 years until the early 1970s.

The trade-off was no class strife initiated by the workers in return for a reduction in the rate of exploitation and a minimal share of social wealth. The latter provided for creation of a consumer class that the economy required as it went beyond producing basic industrial products. This vertical integration of classes under the aegis of the state, combined with mobilizing workers for the second inter-imperial war, could easily meet the classic definition of fascism.

The expectation that each successive generation would advance through the economic system was dubbed the American Dream, something that has significantly frayed in the last 40 years.

One of the slogans often heard in the Occupy movement is the plaintive call to "Restore the American Dream," uttered seemingly without recognition that the trajectory of capital world-wide has embarked on a massive reduction of economic and social gains made by the working class over the last 150 years.

If the capitalists have their way, and their forces and resources are many, there soon won't be a middle-class American Dream to which to return. The classic class formulation that all 19th century radicals tendered — capitalist and proletariat — will again become the norm.

The Dream, promulgated equally on the left and right, has always been a nightmare for other people here and abroad, and ignores that someone gets screwed somewhere, and badly, so we can shop at Whole Foods and buy iPhones.

The 35-year period which instilled the Dream myth in which anyone can "make it," and each generation does better economically than the prior one is now in terminal collapse in the popular imagination. And, myth is the operative word since upward mobility has always been fairly narrow within the American class system, it being, in reality, almost a caste system. Although some rise and a few falter, most people end up in the class to which they were born.

The great indignation among so many people contained in slogans such as, "The banks got bailed out; we got sold out," is both righteous and understandable. But the system isn't broken as is often suggested, but rather this is the way it works and always has. The attacks on what was once taken for granted as a middle-class standard of living are relentless with a recent survey showing that almost half of Americans are either poor or near poor. And, this in the richest country in the world.

The current trajectory of capital, the maximization of profit-taking, has as a model countries like Guatemala. This would mean for the U.S. that only about a third of the country would be well waged, and it is within that upper stratum where commodity consumption, financial transactions, and affluent lifestyles will continue in what we associate with middle-class living. Below that will be the vast majority, characterized by precarious labor, non-existent social services, deteriorating infrastructure, and general social insecurity.

A good illustration is the transformation of Detroit's Albert Kahn-designed Russell Industrial Center. During most of its existence since its opening in 1915, it operated in terms of its name, manufacturing automobile components for the city's many car companies. Now, its two million square-foot buildings, with industrial production long gone, is occupied by more than 150 creative tenants such as architects, painters, clothing designers, jewelry makers, photographers, musicians, filmmakers, bands, and art galleries.

Certainly, most of us would rather visit Russell as a vibrant center of creative talent than an industrial shop of grey men forced to work to the rhythm of relentless machines, but its transformation is indicative of how a waged workforce with defined benefits is replaced in the same location by its opposite. The former, the so-called American Dream; the latter, the new face of capitalism which is often marked by scuffling at the bottom, hoping for work or sales, as talented as many at Russell are.

So, what is to be fought for by the Occupy movement and an ideal of anarchy? Perhaps a vision is best encapsulated by the slogan — "Everything for everyone!" The question, however, becomes, what is "everything?" Do we demand that everyone on the planet have all the consumer junk the global productive machine can churn out? Surely, the world environment cannot sustain that.

What will it mean for the majority of us to be pushed out of a consumer-centered economy with much lower wages and no social safety net? At best, it can mean constructing a revolutionary society within the shell of the larger society based on the elements which sprung up spontaneously at the Occupy sites. At worst, most of the world could become a dystopian urban nightmare with a generalized Kingston, Rio, or Ciudad Juarez becoming the norm.

In Detroit and elsewhere, community gardens, shared housing, and local start-up businesses, many energized and connected to social justice groups, are often held up as the model for re-inventing daily life divorced from capital's mainstream. There's a great deal of enthusiasm for this as a new revolutionary paradigm by writers such as the late Grace Lee Boggs (see her *The Next American Revolution*) and publications like *Yes!* magazine. But, hey, guys, businesses are businesses, and capitalist.

Much of the activity and vision they chronicle, particularly with Boggs, is admirable and many anarchists are swept up in it. They see possibilities in what has historically been designated as a situation of dual power where revolutionary formations take the place of official ones.

The downside of this perspective seems to be an unintended cooperation with what capitalism already has in store for us — shedding off millions of people from its mainstream and having them fare for themselves. It probably isn't bad to be confused about which direction will bring about the changes in our lives. We hopefully are only at the beginning of a movement that confronts power.

Could it be that this time around, the system's capacity for co-optation has run out of space, leaving the future to be creatively re-invented?

Increasingly, it seems as though many people are ready for the challenge.

Recycling and Liberal Reform
Earth Day Special, 1990

It was perhaps an inappropriate time to ask a question since at that very moment two climbers from Greenpeace were struggling to unfurl a banner describing the pollution which would be emitted from Detroit's giant trash incinerator. Their problems were compounded by the fact that they were hanging in the girders of the Detroit-Windsor Ambassador Bridge some 150 feet from the water below.

I was on the ground anxiously watching the scene, but took a second to ask an equally concerned Greenpeace coordinator: If we were opposed to incineration, what then is the solution to the mountain of garbage piling up everywhere? He looked at me quickly, as if I had asked the dumbest question imaginable and said, "Recycling, what else?" and went back to the task at hand.

That was in 1987. This February, a local ecology federation, the Evergreen Alliance, held a spirited demonstration in downtown Detroit opposing proposed U.S. Environmental Protection Agency (EPA) regulations for incinerators. The almost 200 picketers expressed a range of political sentiments through street theater, chants and signs. While a majority of the posters focused on the immediate issue of the city's trash incinerator, several others called for "Reduce, Re-Use, Revolt," and "End Industrialism." However, 1 was struck by the sight of two leather-jacketed young guys holding a large, printed banner stating simply, "RE-CYCLE." Again, for them, the solution.

The above instances bring to mind the problematic tension

between reform and revolution that is always present for radicals during periods of mass social struggles. On the one hand, fighting solely for reforms has historically had the function of affirming and extending the system's power, while on the other, waiting only for the final revolutionary conflagration can dictate an isolated existence confined to issuing angry tracts denouncing everything.

Radicals have participated fully in the great reform movements of the last 60 years—labor, civil rights, anti-war and women—but despite their best intentions, a disappointing pattern emerges. Periods of intense social and political upheaval are followed by the granting of formal, usually legal concessions by the institutions being confronted. This signals the reform movement's effective dispersal as a radical challenge to power, which begins by purging the radicals involved and ends with the upper strata of the reformers being integrated into middle echelon power positions within the reformed apparatus.

This process of cooptation and dispersal occurred no matter how militantly the reforms were sought and regardless of the involvement of radicals. Defenders of these movements often argue that even in their surrender and acceptance of partial goals, they corrected wrongs, improved conditions, and changed the consciousness of the culture. Although this assertion is not without some validity, a long and complicated discussion would be necessary to analyze each of the above-mentioned movements and their accomplishments. Perhaps it will suffice to say here that even after years of the union and civil rights struggles, there is no resolution to the race or labor crises and that conditions for blacks in the U.S. continue to decline sharply as does the position of working people, even organized labor.

Like the social movements before it, the environmental movement contains the potential to unravel the totality of industrial capitalism, but how can radicals involved escape the twin dangers of cooptation and isolation? At a moment when the corporate and government institutions responsible for the ecological wreckage emerge as the gleeful sponsors of Earth Day, when *Vogue* and *Cosmopolitan* ooze fashions and fetishes expressing an "ecological concern," and when the media congratulates itself for inundating the public with environmental information, the cooptation appears to be 95 percent complete.

If this process is to be resisted, perhaps a good starting point is to re-emphasize the radical critiques of capitalism and industrialism that have appeared in these pages and elsewhere in the radical environmental movement and to keep these criticisms central to our activity. Keeping this in mind, a look at the calls for extensive recycling as a solution to many of the ecological problems we face may serve to illustrate the need to emphasize the radical over the reform.

Today, everyone in all sectors of the system twitters about pollution and ecology. Even the capitalists and political rulers realize by now that industrialism's incessant assault on nature cannot continue unabated. They realize, as we do, that they are "spoiling the nest" — what they see as their nest. At present, unlike capitalism's previous crises which have remained on economic, social or political terrains, the very legitimacy of its material basis is being challenged. The question is being posed even at the heart of the system itself: can industrialism exist harmoniously within an ecologically balanced world?

Since in the ruling circles it is taken as a given that the productive apparatus must never be significantly tampered with, recycling is posed as a universal panacea upon which all can agree and which can be realistically implemented.

Numerous municipalities across the U.S. are instituting mandatory recycling programs and more, if not all, will probably follow suit in the next few years as landfill space becomes less available and trash incineration is increasingly discredited. Many industries, seeing recycling as both a growth sector of the economy and as a public relations hedge against criticism of their products, have become big boosters of such efforts.

The former rationale is best seen in the pages of *The New York Times* Business Day section where articles abound like the one entitled, "Wringing Profits From Clean Air" (June 18, 1989). More recently, an article in the March 11, 1990 *Times* highlighting Browning-Ferris Industries (BFI), a waste disposal conglomerate, stated: "The waste disposal market is a barely tapped gold mine" and that "the nation's second largest waste handler is adored on Wall Street."

The public relations function is illustrated by ploys such as the recently announced McDonald's Corporation program to recycle plastic hamburger containers and other packaging which litter neighborhoods and add measurably to the toxicity of the waste stream. Styrofoam producers and big users, such as McDonald's, have created an industry front funded with millions of dollars called the National Polystyrene Recycling Coalition whose purpose is to blunt public criticism of plastic packaging. Even at McDonald's most optimistic estimates, only 6.5 percent of the one billion pounds of polystyrene used in all food packaging annually would be recycled in its East Coast facilities, yet it creates the image of corporate responsibility.

In any event, there is no real incentive for recycling all plastic restaurant waste since virgin Styrofoam costs less than what is recycled. Insidiously, McDonald's plans to install new "Archie McPuff" incinerators behind its restaurants, according to *Everyone's Backyard* magazine.

Also, to prop up their public image, the pages of the new crop of slick ecology magazines which have recently begun publishing, such as *Garbage* and *E: The Environmental Magazine,* are littered with ads from notorious polluters (and war profiteers, in the case of GE), all extolling the virtues of recycling.

This all said, let me state what I see as the numerous problems arising from a view that recycling contains the solution to any of the environmental crises the planet faces, but end by suggesting a role it could play in a human-scale, convivial society.

Problem No. 1: Recuperation

Through the structural integration of radical demands (recuperation), the social and economic forces which generated the garbage problem in the first place intend to transform our desire to stop despoiling the earth with landfills and incinerators into an extension of their power and wealth.

Thus, volunteer efforts of concerned individuals to create local recycling programs wind up functioning as pilot projects for waste haulers seeking municipal recycling contracts. Notorious trash disposal polluters such as Waste Management, Inc. and BFI have suddenly become concerned about the environment when lucrative city contracts become possibilities.

Another example is the EPA's recent directive requiring cities with incinerators to recycle 25 percent of their waste stream by 1992, hence, making recycling a component of the mad incineration schemes environmentalists thought their efforts were undermining. Cities like Detroit, whose incinerator demands an enormous and continuing flow of trash, may institute meaningless, happy-face recycling programs contending this legitimizes the remainder which is burned.

A sinister, rarely considered side to the mandatory recycling demanded by reformers is the increased power it delegates to the state and its repressive apparatus. The old anarchist adage that more laws mean more cops applies even in an arena as seemingly innocuous as garbage removal. Witness the situation in New York City where the October 19, 1989 *Brooklyn Paper* reports, "The persons being hired to enforce the city's mandatory curbside recycling program—Sanitation Recycling Police Officers—will be authorized to carry guns." This is not a gag article! The borough of Brooklyn has hired 177 armed cops to monitor its recycling program, so what starts as an effort in liberal reform, ends with more of our lives being policed by maniacs with guns.

The political state always seeks to extend its administrative control over those it rules, and now armed officials will be poking around in our garbage cans to make sure we've separated the green bottles from the brown ones. Any bets on how long it will take before someone gets shot by one of these cops for an anti-recycling offense?

Problem No. 2: A Narrow Focus

The demand for recycling creates too narrow a focus and carries with it a subtext that presents garbage disposal as the sum of the world's problems. All calls for reforms have a tendency to do this by sectoralizing the world into an endless list of causes without ever confronting the totality. While some ecological reformers have no interest in changing little other than environmental quality, single issue reform efforts such as opposition to the Detroit incinerator can potentially expand the immediate into the radical.

To many participants in that fight, the giant garbage burner is perceived as being emblematic of the entirety of industrial capitalism—the insane levels of production and consumption, the arrogance and insularity of power, the class structure and racism.

Although all reform efforts have a tendency to center mostly on immediate nuts and bolts considerations, an insistence on viewing the totality keeps a radicality in focus.

Problem No. 3: The Critique of Work

Demands for recycling can erode the radical critique of work which places the exploitation of wage labor at the cornerstone of capital's empire with human activity transformed into a commodity to be bought and sold. Most recycling advocates, wanting to provide realistic solutions (that is, ones within the current system's acceptable parameters), assure us or even celebrate the fact that recycling will create more jobs. Some, in their enthusiasm for recycling, show a woeful lack of awareness of the role class and race play in U.S. society such as in a 1987 Detroit talk by Lois Gibbs, a Love Canal victim and Director of the Citizen's Clearinghouse for Hazardous Waste (CCHW) which aggressively promotes recycling.

Gibbs emphasized to an attentive audience that job creation was an important part of recycling and could be presented to city officials as a selling point on that basis. She also asserted that such programs would help alleviate Detroit's crime problem by making minimum wage jobs at recycling centers available to inner-city youth. The racial and class implications of her suggestion that blacks will benefit from a job category that cities have traditionally doled out to minorities, often at the mentioned wage, that of garbage worker, are lost in this formulation.

Gibbs' remarks are not cited here to brand her as a racist or one who is unaware of the class nature of this society, but rather to point out that even the best-intentioned, most radical of reformers will wind up enmeshed in capital's logic—job and business expansion—if their starting point remains within the Machine.

The critique of work is further eroded thusly: As noted above, recycling as an economic growth sector has developed as corporations large and small realize that profits are to be made from what was once discarded. In a society where all human labor is measured as value-producing, the individual is thrust into the recycling process by expending unpaid labor in an extended workday through "voluntary" participation as waste sorter and garbage hauler for industrial capitalism's junk while others reap profits down the chain of exchange. We work during the day to produce commodities, and when we don't work we are busy consuming what other wage workers have created. Now, it is proposed that our duties include the addition of cleaning bottles, stacking and tying newspapers, and flattening cans for the recycling center.

Although many people express a willingness to take on the extra tasks as a contribution to a clean environment, this does not alter the nature of this activity within the political economy of capitalism. One could assume that in a post-revolutionary, post-industrial society there would be a drastic reduction in the level of junk produced and consumed with a corresponding drop in the hours spent at work. With wage work abolished as an institution and the dictates of the market and profit eliminated, people could decide communally how things are produced, distributed and discarded, free from the externally imposed needs of capital or the state. In a world which is technologically reduced and ecologically balanced, daily life's remaining tasks may very well be more labor intensive than previously, but as in the past, what is now done only through the coercion of wages will be replaced with efforts which are cooperative in character and beneficial to the general good of the community.

Problem No. 4: Affirming Consumption

Demands for recycling can function to affirm the overall mad level of consumption itself and the item being recycled, as well as obscuring what has been consumed. The only problem posed is how to dispose of what is left over—the trash—after consumption. For instance, there is joy in some quarters that 70 to 90 percent of the 875 million plastic bottles used annually in Michigan are made of PET or high-density polyethylene which can be recycled, and appropriate business ventures are establishing themselves for that purpose. [PW Note: Only a very small fraction of those bottles are ever recycled and some recycling centers refuse to accept them.] While not questioning why so many containers are produced in the first place, this view unwittingly further legitimizes plastics production and refuses to examine critically the off-the-shelf content of the recyclable containers. Besides milk, juices and other food products (most of which deserve critical appraisal themselves), much of what comes in these jugs, tubs and jars are, in themselves toxic to the environment—solvents, cleaners, lubricants, paints, poisons, waxes, etc.

In other circumstances as well, the content of recycled items or their very existence is never questioned, such as with newspapers. Recycling daily newspapers adds injury to insult with us doing the work. Papers such as the *Detroit News* and *Free Press* are cogs in the Big Lie machine which sanctify the core myths of this society and are key propaganda organs for commodity consumption. They specifically act to distort information about events and ideas which challenge the dominance of power, so it is beyond irony to recycle a paper like the *News* which first editorializes that the global warming trend is beneficial and then have it reappear with support for the criminal invasion of Panama.

Another illustration is the brag of the aluminum can industry that it has recycled one trillion soft drink containers since starting such programs, but with no mention of the nutritionless, sugared calories which make up the content of these cans when returned to the marketplace.

Problem No. 5: Industrial Production Ignored

The demand for recycling can overemphasize the wrong end of the problem, taking for granted the torrent of commodities spewed out by this society and concentrating only on disposing of its waste. Massive pollution takes place at the point of production and recycling can act as its ideological and even material justification if it can clean up the waste end of the process. Without a serious effort to reduce industrial production as a whole, recyclers become like jugglers who are given more and more balls to keep in the air as the productive apparatus continually seeks to expand.

There is no choice in the matter. It is the iron law of capitalism: expand or collapse. Conservative estimates by the EPA show 2.3 billion pounds of pollutants released into the air yearly through mining and manufacturing, and this figure ignores discharges into waterways and the earth which are also frighteningly high.

At any rate, there is no real political will for substantial recycling among the industrial and financial elite. As suggested above, industrial capitalism's internal logic does not permit the latitude necessary to change its mode of production and consumption into one which considers the needs of the planet. Corporate managers have no intention of allowing complete recycling or other ecologically-based production methods to prevail since the productive and extractive industries form the core of the U.S. economy.

For instance, the largest domestic industrial growth sector is the ethylene industry which produces the basis for plastics in plants that stretch hundreds of miles, from Beaumont, Texas to Shreveport, Louisiana, along the Sabine River. These horribly polluting, dangerous plants pump out a billion pounds of ethylene annually for a plastics industry whose products quadruple each year. So important are such economic concentrations that the U.S. was willing to risk World War III in the Persian Gulf in 1988 to assure that oil was kept flowing to these facilities.

Problem No. 6: Create Another Industry

When recycling becomes a permanent feature of the economy, it will probably be utilized mainly as a technique to deal with a significant portion of urban garbage, but in itself won't stop the destruction of the natural world. All the recycling efforts in the country can't stop the clear-cut logging of the remaining old growth forests of the U.S. Northwest when a conglomerate which bought out a logging firm with junk bonds needs quick cash to meet its debt service.

However, recycling is not a solution even to the limited problems of waste disposal its advocates seek to correct. Extensive recycling of the Mt. Everest of trash produced daily in this country would create another mass nightmare industry to parallel what exists now, one that could conceivably cause as much pollution. For instance, the Fort Howard Paper Company of Green Bay, Wisconsin which recycles "post-consumer wastepaper" is a major polluter of the Fox River and Green Bay with discharges of PCBs, dioxins, chlorinated organics, heavy metals and phosphorous into the water, plus emitting additional pollutants into the air. Its products are labeled "100% recycled."

Also, regardless of the enthusiasm of the plastics industry, a petroleum-based product is never really recycled even if it goes through a few generations and winds up as a park bench or parking strip. Eventually, it enters the environment as a toxic (having been produced in that manner) and remains there for a long time. The whole concept that plastic can be successfully recycled is more of the smoke and mirrors put forth by the industry to justify continuation of unrestrained production.

However, even if none of the foregoing was a problem, one only need look at the start-up picture for a massive recycling industry to realize that it would mean more factories, more machinery, more energy, more waste, refuse and garbage, more workers going to more work on more roads in more cars, with additional suppliers, on ad infinitum. Such is the nature of capitalist expansion.

The preceding picture may conjure up the bleak image presented earlier in this essay of the radical "issuing angry tracts denouncing everything." However, I would hope that this angry tract joins with others to create a thrust toward the radical rejection of capitalist society—the creation of a movement that undermines the historic confidence of the ruling order and challenges its basic concepts of progress and production realizing that both threaten life, liberty, and ecology. For now, our ideas and actions may only be a negation—opposition to petrochemical production, to any more growth, to wage work, to hierarchy, to the state, to the patriarchy; but from that opposition should come a material, geographically coherent community of resistance that refuses a vision that encompasses anything less than a free and green world.

A future based on the limited dreams of others will become our and the world's nightmare.

What about recycling? Can it play a role in this rejectionism or is it so inherently flawed as suggested above that one should avoid it? It would seem to me, that even with the attendant problems, as the central consumer culture we have a great responsibility to try to recycle as much of the horrid mess we create as possible. However, we should do this all the while realizing that a "good citizen" approach will remain only as a gesture unless linking up with other moves against the Megamachine. In Detroit's Cass Corridor area, a recycling project was created specifically as an adjunct to the opposition to the nearby trash incinerator. Although not free from the problems listed above and though only marginally cutting into the city's total waste stream, recycling here takes on the form of community resistance to the incinerator's operations—denying one's own trash as much as possible to that which will poison you.

For some, recycling may act as a perceptual gateway to understanding the deeper problem of production and consumption in this society, but this realization should only be a small step on a journey to a world in which there is virtually no waste to recycle.

In Defense of Self-Defense
Thoughts on Violence and Martial Arts
Fall 2017

THWACK! My fighting stick landed exactly where I aimed it—diagonally across the face of a fascist who was trying to rip down a banner a friend and I were holding, to which the stick was attached.

The blow struck him with such velocity that it snapped his head back while a rosette of blood gushed forth from his broken nose and split lips intermingled with a piece of a tooth and broken lenses from his glasses.

It wasn't a lucky blow. It was executed with intent and exact precision—waist and hips rotating, arms and shoulder following, right hand gripping the pole upwards, left hand down. I charitably did not bring the opposite end of the six-foot pole up into his crotch.

The blow was delivered during an environmental protest to protect myself and others around the banner from right wingers who had a long history of violent attacks against activists. In a larger melee that followed, two more rightists attacked me, and other demonstrators came to my defense. We suffered only a minor injury and no arrests.

Lest this sound like a recounting solely for purposes of violence porn (admit it; almost all of us like to hear tales of fascists getting their asses kicked like when white nationalist Richard Spencer got punched on Trump's Inauguration Day), we can look at the specifics of what is above and how it relates to questions of self-defense.

This article is only about repelling attacks and not about offensive actions against the right. Most organisms defend themselves reflexively. Pacifism is chosen behavior and can be effective in some situations and campaigns. A physical response to an attack has some genetically coded tripwires, but utilizing it effectively needs to be learned.

The key element here is training. I had practiced martial arts for years in which stick fighting was one component. It was done in classes that were specifically established for training us in defense against right wing attacks.

We began in a class taught by a high-ranking black belt, a Korean from Seoul who had been on his country's national police force, and who bragged to us about beating up protesting students, having no idea that we were American equivalents of his targets.

On the wall of his training room, he displayed crossed U.S. and South Korean flags to which he insisted we execute a bow of respect each time we entered his studio. We dealt with this by folding our hand in the crease of our bow which was giving a middle-finger salute. The class was taught very formally and rigorously, with achieving belts of rank a major goal.

We eventually decided to form our own class with a black belt friend as instructor and while most of the formalities were dropped, the rigor continued. Although we enjoyed the camaraderie and the building of martial skills very few of us previously possessed, our practice was not done with the intent of gaining individual self-defense skills, but rather building a collective community defense of our demonstrations and meetings.

Having an organized defense guard is nothing new to revolutionary or labor movements, particularly ones which anticipate armed assaults from either the government or right wing.

In Spain, the revolutionary anarchist labor union, the CNT, had its own militia and fielded armored vehicles during its fight against fascism in the 1930s. However, before the Revolution and Civil War broke out in 1936, CNT locals were often under assault from employers' associations who hired thugs to attack strikers and terrorize members.

The Spanish workers fought back with designated union members becoming *pistoleros,* armed men whose exclusive duty was to protect the other workers by force of arms. Their workmates pooled their wages to provide for the families of the ones who stood guard or exacted penalties against those who acted on behalf of the bosses.

The most well-known *pistoleros* were anarchists Buenaventura Durruti, who later led a militia unit, and Francisco Ascaso, who died on the barricades in Barcelona on the first day of the fight against the fascist uprising in July 1936. Although hundreds of other men served in this capacity to protect their comrades, the exploits of these two are particularly interesting.

Visible armaments, whether guns or fighting sticks, have the drawback of bringing the attention of the police who are increasingly less tolerant of armed antifa units as the demonization of antifascist forces is currently taking place. A contingent of black clad men and women carrying poles will probably not be considered well by the cops. Prior to demonstrations, police in many cities such as Seattle, have confiscated anarchist and antifa's sticks, signs, and other self-defense items while not subjecting rightists to the same enforcement.

Training is key to military dominance. Right wingers are heavily into martial arts, weightlifting, and weaponry. Many are ex-military, so the bravery of the antifa comrades in confronting them is particularly admirable, and often surprisingly successful. Acting as a disciplined cadre in a physical confrontation gives those involved, power beyond their numbers. Like a choral dance, training together builds solidarity and confidence.

There are many anarchists already proficient in martial arts and, in some cities, cooperative, non-hierarchal classes are available, but traditional schools will teach you the skills you need. Just don't tell them why you're there!

Training, even without a well-schooled teacher is possible although having a capable instructor is preferable. If there isn't a class available, there are training videos online giving instruction in open hand combat and various weapons.

Long poles, known as bo sticks or staffs (think Robin Hood and Little John), might not be the best option for each situation. However, you can easily obtain one at your local lumber yard by getting a 1 to 1-1/4-inch pine dowel used for a closet rod. You want one as long as you are tall.

Careful. You can do great damage to someone with this weapon, even kill them. Also, having a long shaft without knowledge of how to use it can mean your stick winds up in the hands of your opponent.

Remember, what you can do to someone else, can be done to you. Don't enter the realm of violence without the realization that you could become a casualty.

There are dangers inherent in martial training. Even people who desire non-hierarchical structures can find themselves and their group altered by the process of militarization. The tendency is for those who excel at physical prowess and exhibit the most bravery in combat to rise to leadership on the basis of this. They can become the decision makers since they are seen as the risk takers both by the group and themselves. As anarchists, we realize that armed force is the central definition of the state, and it can play the same pernicious role in our movement, something that must be resisted.

Writing this was disturbing. Most of us are people who don't feel good about hurting others, even those who mean to harm us. There is a long history of revolutionary violence in the struggle to eliminate the institutions of oppression and exploitation, and some of us may become part of it.

Although there can be pride in our victories, it is sad that we may be required to take such actions, no matter how necessary, which have no place in the world we envision.

Anarchists & Guns
Summer 2018

"Workingmen: Arm yourselves and appear in full force!"
1886 Haymarket leaflet

The initial clamor about controlling gun violence following the horrible mass shooting at Parkland, Fla. high school this February mostly subsided following huge demonstrations of students across the country in March and April. Young students appeared everywhere in the media advocating reforms, but no legislation has passed that will staunch the blood flow, and probably none will be forthcoming.

(As this was written, another high school massacre occurred in Santa Fe, Tex., followed by several other smaller ones that quickly disappeared from public attention.)

Timid, liberal policies will do little to stem gun violence, and right-wing proposals to arm everybody, led by the increasingly shrill National Rifle Association (NRA), only assures more killing.

Neither approach will successfully combat gun violence in a country steeped in a history of violence, where a third of the population owns 300 million firearms, and political limits constrain lawmakers to, at best, make tepid reforms.

While that mainstream debate continues, those who see the need for defense against a rising right wing current and perhaps for a revolution in a future period are involved in a parallel discussion about arms possession. If you oppose the political state what should be the stance toward legislation that would limit gun ownership and type of weaponry? Formal laws take the place of autonomous action in all spheres of life, providing both a protective and a repressive function. Armed might is the core of the political state. Without it protecting the ruling class and its economic and social arrangements, hierarchal systems from the first slave states to the current capitalist ones wouldn't have lasted long in the face of popular resistance.

However, the modern state mediates some of the worst abuses and natural consequences of an exploitative system. One can assume most anarchists, while opposing the state as an institution, are supportive of laws within the current system such as those governing the environment, product and workplace safety, discrimination, speed limits, and crimes against persons, all of which are enforced by the same tyrannical system of cops, judges, and courts which victimize the poor and people of color, and repress expressions of resistance.

It is certain that anarchists and other revolutionaries share a concern about the daily death toll the proliferation of firearms exacts, but the question to consider is, are arms a special and unique category different from air quality regulation or no left turn prohibitions?

Other than the United States, most Western countries have strict requirements regarding weaponry including ownership, type, usage, etc., resulting in gun death rates up to 90 percent less than that of this country.

All of the liberal proposals for background checks, mandatory gun locks and safes, prohibiting ownership by abusers, and banning semi-automatic assault rifles, if enacted, would probably reduce gun violence somewhat. However, even under that politically fanciful scenario, it would still leave a heavily armed population with a capacity to act out shootings against themselves and others.

When we move to a discussion on our end of things as to what position should be taken regarding gun ownership, a whole different set of concerns come into the equation. It takes place in a context far from the understandable liberal dismay at the repeated mass shootings, one that considers the consequences of a disarmed population unable to protect workers and minorities against a tyrannical government, racist or right-wing mobs, or the ability to defend a revolution.

Historically, anarchists have admired armed revolutionaries, on the European barricades of 1848, at the 1871 Paris Commune, the revolutionary resistance to the Bolsheviks by the Makhnovist movement and Kronstadt garrison, and the most frequently cited example, our comrades of the anarchist militias in Spain who fought both fascists and Stalinists in the defense of the revolution they created in the 1930s.

In the U.S., African Americans frequently employed armed resistance to white racist terror following the Civil War and into the 1960s. Workers in the coal fields of West Virginia and Kentucky fought cops, National Guard, and company goons to defend their unions or the right to organize in the 1920s. In 1886, anarchist labor leaders called upon their members to "Arm yourselves and appear in full force," at a rally in Chicago's Haymarket Square. Many did, but following a bomb blast and ensuing gunfire that left scores dead and wounded, four anarchists were hanged by the state of Illinois.

Huey Newton, chairman of the Black Panther Party in the 1960s, famously urged oppressed black people to, "Pick up the gun!" The specter of armed African Americans confronting brutal urban police forces led to a murderous campaign of repression against the party resulting in the deaths of dozens of Panthers in spectacular shoot-outs across the country, and an eclipse of their non-violent community-based programs.

The 1921 so-called Tulsa Race Riot was actually a white mob and police attack against a prosperous African American district. Black World War I veterans and members of the African Blood Brotherhood bravely built barricades to defend their neighborhoods against the marauders. The resistance against the mobs was so intense that white city officials aerial bombed the defenders, burning the black section to the ground, killing hundreds.

The third aerial bombing of the U.S. (the second being Pearl Harbor) came in 1985 when a Philadelphia police helicopter dropped an incendiary device on the communal living space of the

MOVE organization following a pitched gun battle with authorities trying to serve arrest warrants including ones for arms possession. The resulting fire killed eleven MOVE members including five children and destroyed 65 houses. Many of the black liberation group's members remain in prison serving long sentences.

All of these examples (hundreds more exist) were heroic struggles against oppression and exploitation, yet almost all of them were scenes of great bloodshed and usually defeat of the radical forces pitted against the ruling powers.

The Second Amendment to the U.S. Constitution was originally proposed by its Framers to guarantee states the right to raise militias to suppress slave uprisings and armed white revolts such as Bacon's and Shay's Rebellions. In recent years, its alleged ambiguity has morphed explicitly into a right of personal gun ownership, and increasingly advocated by the NRA to expand an armed population. However, the Framers also saw the necessity for having every white male armed in an era when they had a palpable fear of slave rebellions and Indian attacks. That siege mentality still exists among many whites, particularly ones who are armed.

The question here is what works for organizing defense of oneself and community and a revolution if that comes to pass. Just as in day-to-day organizing, we evaluate what works partly by examining the strategies and tactics of past campaigns so we don't repeat the same mistakes. What does this say about the efficacy of arming for revolution or for even community self-defense?

The first line of defense for capitalism and the political state once threatened is the police who are increasingly militarized. The cops of yore did damage enough when armed only a little better than their challengers, but now they possess military grade armaments including tanks and a variety of sophisticated weapons, surveillance, and command capacity.

Were the cops to fail in efforts to halt a mass-based movement demanding revolutionary change, the final level of protection of the state is its regular armed forces which could easily overcome any popular-based revolution or resistance. A modern revolution could only occur if sections of the military joined the revolution.

Regarding defense against fascist threats to our movements on a daily basis, let alone for revolution or even radical reform: We are currently way outgunned. There are ten million AR-15 assault rifles owned by Americans. How many can we estimate are in the hands of, in general, Trump supporters, or narrowing it to extreme rightists and open fascists compared to how many are possessed by anarchists or leftists? The math is not encouraging.

Employing increasingly strident, far right-wing rhetoric, the NRA with its five million armed members, could easily be transformed into fascist militias as happened after World War I when the German Freikorps, a right-wing para-military, was used by the government to suppress revolutionary upsurges.

Currently, on the left, there are small gun groups like Guerrilla Mainframe and the Huey P. Newton Gun Club, that oppose police brutality and advocate for the rights of black gun owners.

Also, there is Redneck Revolt, an anti-capitalist, anti-racist, and anti-fascist group which organizes white working-class people and has more than 33 local chapters, an offshoot of the John Brown Gun Clubs. They've appeared armed at Trump rallies in the manner rightists have elsewhere. Left groups are all under heavy police surveillance. The co-founder of the two black organizations, Rakem Balogun, was recently locked up for five months without bail on suspicion of domestic terrorism.

It's hard to say what this suggests doing. We are clearly outgunned both by the state and the right. Should historic defeats encourage us to submit without a struggle? Should we depend upon the state to protect us from rightist assault? The answers to these questions are obvious.

Harder questions are, should anarchists oppose any restrictions on gun ownership other than background checks, or even that? Should we see the Red Neck/John Brown Gun Clubs as a model of armed resistance against an increasingly crazed right wing which has no debate about the issue of guns?

In answering this, we should be aware that there will be 35,000 U.S. gun deaths in a given year with 100,000 people wounded. If anarchists were as armed as are current gun owners, would we be any safer from murdering one another, taking our own lives, and shooting others accidentally? Probably not.

However, revolution has always been an undertaking filled with risks and the future is uncertain as to what will occur as this country's politics get crazier. It's been said that we should have a big toolbox, one which includes a multitude of resources of which guns at a particular time could be useful ones.

Most revolutions are thought of as extremely violent events, but the act of revolution by itself, the wheel turning over the old society and bringing the new one to the top, is usually fairly non-violent. In Russia and Spain, for instance, revolutionary ideals supplanted the conventional norms of capitalism and the state as workers and peasants simply began life without bosses and cops. It was the defense of those new forms in which so many lives were lost.

No one from the Fifth Estate offers advice as to whether gun possession is appropriate or not, and certainly not this writer. The most appropriate tools are those which have always led towards revolution—organizing around greater freedom, protecting those most at risk from racism, sexism, homophobia, and xenophobia, supporting struggles in the workplace and the community, and subverting loyalty to the empire, its military, and its wars.

Once we see where this has brought us, it will be an organic process of deciding the best means of defense.

Anarchist Violence or State Violence
Winter 2013

The question of violence as a revolutionary tactic is neither new nor unfairly associated with anarchists, although debate has recently emerged over its use by Black Blocs during mass demonstrations, including Occupy events.

However, many are quick to insist that breaking bank windows or torching police cars doesn't constitute violence but rather should more precisely be described as property damage or political vandalism [Hey, the original Vandals carried out a final blow to a pretty nasty empire].

Violence is what the cops employ against not just Black Bloc participants, who are usually fleet of foot enough to escape it, but frequently in random attacks against people at demonstrations who are committing neither violence nor property damage. Or, provocateurs are employed to unleash the cops on protesters. Violence from the official protectors of property has been so severe that demonstrators have been severely injured and even killed.

Black Blocs at large demonstrations, such as at anti-war rallies or meetings of the imperial chieftains of the G20 countries, are usually comprised of young people who either cohere spontaneously and are drawn to one another, or with some prior planning, attack symbols of the state and/or capitalism.

Sometimes, the actions of the Black Bloc are only a footnote to larger marches, but on other occasions, such as the 1999 Seattle anti-WTO actions, it was a relatively small number breaking windows at Starbucks that thrust them into public consciousness and launched the most recent upsurge of militant tactics against the institutions of capitalism.

While Seattle set in motion dozens of subsequent actions by black-clad militants, it also allowed the creation of an official hysteria which is conveniently used as an excuse for the militarization of the police and justification for brutal tactics of suppression of even peaceful demonstrators where no Black Bloc is present.

At a demonstration in Detroit in 2000 protesting a meeting of the Organization of American States across the border in Windsor, Ontario, one thousand marchers were met by almost as many police who were ordered to wear long sleeved shirts in the June heat claiming they had received intelligence that demonstrators were preparing to splash acid on their arms. The local papers featured headlines howling that "anarchists from Seattle" were coming to Detroit to "burn the city down." All of the marches were peaceful.

During the 2003 anti-Free Trade Area of the Americas protests in Miami, the cops shuttered the entire downtown area for two weekdays and brought out armaments enough to fight off an army.

The bizarre scene, in one case, of union retirees, some in wheelchairs and others using walkers, marching by armored personnel carriers manned by battle-ready helmeted cops with.30 caliber machine guns at the ready was almost laughable if it wasn't for the fact that this has become an acceptable stance for the cops and their state and media approved violence. Over-reaction though it may be, store owners and bankers expect the police to keep their shop windows intact while those who want to bust them up have a different perspective on the sanctity of property.

Some in the Black Bloc enter the streets with a specific political perspective, while others may be just expressing rage at the way society is constructed and think "busting shit up" is a relatively reasonable response to those institutions which are responsible for the current state of affairs.

All societies are governed by rules set by the dominant class and regulate what is permissible behavior regarding terms of social alteration. A political thrust, such as anarchism, that has as a goal the elimination of the basic definitions of this society and who sets them is obviously considered illegitimate in the eyes of the rulers.

One strand of thought, sometimes implied or stated, is that if you dare to break one rule–such as breaking a window–the perpetrator is that much more likely to have fewer qualms about breaking the fundamental rules.

Organizers of what are designated as "peaceful, legal demonstrations" rage against the Black Bloc or others who won't abide by their definition. They charge that the militants "hijack" their events, distort their message, give the cops an excuse to attack marchers, and cause the media to only focus on political vandalism rather than their calls to end a war or protest against some economic or social outrage.

There's undoubtedly truth in their complaints, but without the Black Bloc actions many protest events would have gone unreported and unremembered.

Organizers of the Seattle anti-WTO demonstration complained that the vandalism of a handful of anarchists overshadowed the 60,000 trade unionists, environmentalists and other peace and social justice activists that participated in legal marches and non-violent civil disobedience. This is true and it's not.

Without the militant actions, it's doubtful whether the larger marches and actions would have even made the nightly news. Also, is corporate media coverage the ultimate goal? That somehow, if we appear on the corporate media for 20 seconds to present a usually garbled message of reform, let alone revolution, before the program goes to a commercial for vinyl replacement windows and the sportscaster returns with the scores, we will have had a successful demonstration?

Criticizing the Black Bloc or independent anarchist trashing will most probably be ignored by those most likely to carry it out. To them, to do so, only marks you as part of the timid left who lets the state define what is permissible. Complaining about the Black Bloc is like shaking your fist at the rain clouds which have ruined your picnic; it's beyond our control.

However, it seems that some questions need to be posed to those who want to go beyond the prescribed limits at large marches: Do those who alter the nature of a "legal, peaceful" event by their actions bear any responsibility to the organizers or others attending a demonstration?

Do those who initiate militant actions have a responsibility to those who are unaware that the tactics of a few may lead to a violent assault by the police? Is there a responsibility when ratcheting up the use of militant tactics that they may increase repressiveness in general?

Also, when the state repressive apparatus weighs in against those taking part in militant actions–the cops on the street and the judicial and prison system–what are the effects on those who run afoul of them and on the communities from which they come?

Should those choosing militant acts consider the consequences and responses required of friends, family, and comrades?

Should everyone be advised to never commit acts that could bring about detrimental results? This is certainly contrary to the advice revolutionaries across the ages have heeded.

Actually, everyone from store owners to the cops and the politicians ought to be thankful that the Black Bloc centers its actions on property wreckage. In eras gone by, anarchists took a much greater toll on the guardians and owners of property and capital. The current Black Bloc, however, comport themselves with a dedication to only damaging property.

Think of the 1886 Chicago Haymarket Square incident where those fighting for the 8-hour day, led by anarchists, were urged in a leaflet, "Workingmen, Arm Yourselves and Appear in Full Force!" And, they did, including someone, now widely considered to be an anarchist, threw a bomb into the midst of the Chicago police where the blast and subsequent gunfire from both sides resulted in the death of seven cops and four civilians with scores wounded.

Throughout Europe, from the 1870s through the 1930s, anarchists often participated in Propaganda by the Deed, so-called exemplary acts of violence against tyrants both for retaliatory and agitational purposes. Kings, czars, politicians (including a U.S. president), religious figures, and capitalists were the frequent targets, and fell at the hands of anarchist assassins. These acts led to a vivid association, aided by a sensationalist press, between anarchism and violence.

In the U.S., the image of a dark, bearded man, dressed in black hat and clothing, carrying a round bomb with a lit fuse resonated with a native population fearful of foreign anarchists bent on violence. And, this stereotype wasn't entirely born of invention.

Followers of Luigi Galleani, mostly Italian immigrants who read his *Cronaca Sovversiva,* in which he advocated direct action and armed resistance against the state, acted on his theories in a series of bombings between 1914 and 1933. Galleanists fostered numerous attacks against prominent American ruling class figures and police, killing and injuring many.

The culmination of an intense bombing campaign around World War I and its domestic repression came when Mario Buda, a Galleanist, in 1920, drove a wagon filled with explosives onto New York City's Wall Street which detonated killing 38 and wounding 148. Later, into the early 1930s, revenge was sought for the judicial murder of Galleanists Sacco and Vanzetti with attempts on the lives of the trial judge, police, and prison officials connected to the case.

It should be realized, however, that those who perpetrated violence against the rulers and their minions weren't the madmen portrayed in the capitalist press during that period. They acted within a context of state violence much greater than any toll exacted by the assassinations and bombings listed here.

Anarchist actions were minor when compared to the repression, massacres, wars, imprisonment and other outrages carried out by the state against the working class. The body count from all anarchist bombings would barely fill a hospital ward when compared to the inter-imperialist slaughter of World War I.

Anarchists were condemned by the press and politicians for advocating violence to achieve their ends. However, one finds calls for violent repression of strikers in headlines and in speeches quite common place, and which were acted upon by cops, troops, and goons.

None of this is meant as a justification of either violence or vandalism; every person will have to decide the efficacy of such acts themselves. However, the late British anarchist Vernon Richards put forth the ethical imperative in *Lessons of the Spanish Revolution* that an unarmed person should never be harmed.

Fifth Estate A-Gassed
August 15-18, 1967

Author Note: This account of a tear gas attack on the Fifth Estate office appeared in the paper's issue chronicling the 1967 Detroit Rebellion. A fictionalized version of the incident appeared in my novel, *Summer on Fire*, which is reprinted directly after the news story. The novel's portrayal is close to what occurred.

There is a Hebrew idiomatic expression, *k'ninah houra,* which was explained to me as being equivalent to saying knock on wood after telling of some good fortune you have incurred and you want it not to change.

I certainly should have said that phrase aloud after writing in our last issue that no harm had come to the Fifth Estate office, Mixed Media bookstore or Plum Street. For no sooner had our issue hit the streets than pellets were shot at the windows of Mixed Media causing total damage. The window was replaced with boards and a sign which read "Holy Smoke, Don't shoot—It's Love." Proprietor Barry Kramer assured us business will continue as usual.

Things went a little worse at the Fifth Estate office, however. We arrived at the office July 31 to find the interior of the building completely enveloped with tear gas fumes which attacked the eyes, nose and skin. It was abandon ship and the Fifth Estate really went underground for about a week as we set up our operations in the basement of the building.

Although there is no concrete proof as to who the villain was, circumstantial evidence does point to our guardians of law and order. First, the attack came at 1:30 a.m. several hours after the curfew when no one was out but the law. Second, the gas device used was of military origin and, with assistance from the overground press, the National Guard admitted that the Army had these devices and had used them in several East Side stores to flush out non-existent snipers. Third, Emil Bacilla and Tom Mitchell, who were upstairs above the office in the White Panther Party space, saw a jeepload of Guardsmen out on the street approximately ten minutes before the gas grenade exploded. So, circumstantial, but...

Things appear to be back to normal and running smoothly — *k'ninah houra*.

Excerpt from *Summer on Fire: A Detroit Novel*

Paul walked up to the door of the Fifth Estate storefront office with its boarded-up front window that was smashed months earlier by a Breakthrough brick with a note wrapped around it bearing a death threat to "Red Rats." The glass in the office of the adjacent anti-war office met the same fate via a brick with a similar message.

At the Fifth Estate office, this left only a smaller side window intact to which someone from the inside affixed a sign announcing, "Soul Brother," a supposedly magical phrase that would ward off Black looters. Paul figured it must have been one of the White Panthers from upstairs who had access to the office through the internal passages of the building. Cool.

But, fuck! There was a softball-size hole in the upper part of the window he hadn't noticed when first surveying the scene. Damn. That glass allowed the only outside light in the office. He hated fluorescents.

Paul opened the door with his key, walked in and the door closed behind him. At first Paul thought he had been struck from behind. Something knocked him to the floor. It wasn't a blow, but noxious fumes in the office filling his eyes, nose, and lungs. He tried to breathe, but could only choke. His eyes burned, blinding him. He rushed back out of the door, tumbling onto the Warren

Avenue sidewalk.

Gasping for air, his eyes stinging, Paul realized what was in the office.

Tear gas!

He sat on the sidewalk choking and coughing, his vision badly blurred. Cars whizzed by and a couple of pedestrians walked around him, none of whom stopped to ask if there was a problem.

Paul's normal breathing began to return, but his vision was still distorted and his eyes were burning. He staggered around the corner to the Lodge Freeway service drive reaching the door to the upstairs apartments, got rung in, staggered up the stairs guided by the railing, and was let in by a confused David Forbes, the White Panther Minister of Defense.

"What happened to you?"

"Fucking tear gas. Gotta rinse my eyes out," as Paul made it to the sink where he flushed his eyes with cold water.

Four more Panthers ran into the kitchen of the communal apartment and party headquarters and listened to a much-recovered Paul tell what just happened.

"Fuck," said Terry Aldrich, a 17-year-old runaway from Centerline, a Detroit suburb. "Last night I was up on the roof watching the fires about 2 a.m., and I saw a National Guard jeep filled with four soldiers pull up in front of the building and get out. I didn't want them to see me, so I ducked down, but I heard glass crash and they pulled off. I went down later when everything was quiet, but didn't see any damage."

"Those motherfuckers must have used a grenade launcher to blast one through the window. I'm surprised that the whole damn thing didn't come down," Paul said angrily.

Chapter 7
Music

No Dance; No Revo
What Did Emma Goldman Really Say?
Fall 2014

So famous is the quote (rendered in a variety of ways), "If I can't dance, I don't want to be in your revolution," that it is even emblazoned on a souvenir coffee cup peddled by the Berkeley, Calif.-based Emma Goldman Papers project, and attributed to the turn of the last century anarchist and free love advocate.

There's a problem with it, though. Two radical archivists with whom I checked couldn't find an authenticating citation for the quote anywhere in Goldman's voluminous writings and speeches, making its origins slightly suspect. But of all the words on thousands of pages written by Goldman about liberation and freedom, why does this perhaps fanciful quote remain the most prominent from her long career of fighting for anarchy?

Could it be that there is a human socio-biology that pulls us to the rhythms of dance, which even for a moment negate the straitjacket of authoritarian society with its thousands of rules meant to keep people within the rigid demands of the political state and capitalism?

In a decades old essay, "The Decline of the Choral Dance," Paul Halmos describes how pre-capitalist people danced together as a community at ceremonies marking life's significant events, and often just for its joy. Such dancing disappeared as social activity with the rise of capitalist society.

Halmos saw choral dancing as invoking a "rhythmic communal rapture," a state of being in which the body experiences a sense of freedom and solidarity with everybody and perhaps, everything around us. This emotional ecstasy prefigures the desire for revolution, and hence, is feared by rulers everywhere.

So, let's dance!

Dancing for Our Lives
Summer 2003

An obscure 1952 essay, "The Decline of the Choral Dance," by Paul Halmos couldn't have entered my consciousness at a better time. It was 1962, and I had spent my late teens and early twenties reading intensely in an attempt to discover the fundamental qualities of existence.

Reality seemed pretty bleak. Rigid conformity, compulsory patriotism, fear of atomic annihilation, and a cultural wasteland of bad movies and boring music predominated in 1950s mainstream society.

However, on the margins existed counter-critiques: Beat fiction and poetry, black artistry producing jazz and rhythm and blues, classic left and anarchist writings of bygone eras, and a bulk of literature spanning the previous 80 years which suggested that something other than what American novelist Henry Miller dubbed an "air-conditioned nightmare" was possible.

Still, most of what I read wasn't particularly cheering and much of my sense of life was shaped by the fiction I was devouring. My view of the world as bleak, cold and devoid of meaning was reinforced by writing such as Thomas Wolfe's frontispiece to *You Can't Go Home Again,* where he wrote, "that all man's life was like a tiny spurt of flame that blazed out briefly in an illimitable and terrifying darkness..." or life as absurd as I went through Camus' *The Stranger,* Sartre's play, *No Exit,* or even, looking for a respite, Vonnegut's whimsical *Sirens of Titan.*

Rebellion, as the alternative to conformity, appeared admirable and ethical, but seemed always to end either in insanity ("I saw the best minds of my generation destroyed by madness...." in Allen Ginsberg's famous first verse in *Howl,*), death (as at the end of teen-gang fiction such as Harold Robbin's *A Stone for Danny Fisher* or Bud Shulman's *The Amboy Dukes*), or defeat ("He loved Big Brother," the final words of Orwell's *1984*). Decidedly gloomy choices: go crazy, get killed, or be vanquished.

Fortunately for me, in that same period, assaults on the structure and culture of the dominant society were emerging that brought much of what I had been reading into question. Rebels were marching and organizing for civil rights all over the American South and refusing to back down even when confronted with lynch mobs and the iron hand of the state.

The Beat critique of the 1950s "plastic culture" made more sense as artists began to poke their heads up after the stifling McCarthy Era. Watching all of this unfold from sit-ins at Southern lunch counters to listening to obscenity-laced attacks on censorship and frank onstage discussions of sexuality by comedian Lenny Bruce, suggested maybe there was something here other than the "maw of the all-engulfing night" (Thomas Wolfe).

It was at this point of dawning realization of other possibilities that I read Halmos' somewhat plodding academic essay about the ancient and universal tradition of the choral dance which jumped out at me from among the others collected in *Man Alone: Alienation in Modern Society* (Dell 1962).

The book includes a range of writings from Marx (his solid early work), James Baldwin, Lewis Mumford, Eric Fromm and others describing the human condition and what we have lost under capitalism and civilization. I was delighted. Not only were my feelings of dread and loathing about this society confirmed, but the authors all suggested that the emptiness (the "Horror," in Joseph Conrad's phrase) was not the innate human condition at all, but something socially imposed.

Halmos' description of primal people integrating the mysteries and passages of life through mass community dances filled with rich symbolism (or reality, as they assert) and their almost universal appearance throughout the world, suggests a socio-biology of emotion and bodily motion that had to be destroyed in order to make people willing to sit at desks or stand in front of machines for hours each day. The reflection of this urge, and the longing for it, can be seen in the maintenance of group peasant dances up to modern times where they increasingly only exist as memento.

But Halmos' prediction that communal dancing would be excluded entirely by "couple-istic formality" may have been somewhat premature. The free-form, mass, psychedelic dances of the 1960s spoke to the longing for ecstatic motion and community, but also functioned as resistance to the dominant culture which prescribed dancing in couples in set patterns. These same qualities exist in the rave culture among young people today, but no less so than in some punk scenes and even among those who attend performances of bands like Detroit's Layabouts which are more like community festivals than concerts.

I would urge a cautionary note here, however, that we do not allow ourselves to become too self-congratulatory over our gestures towards reassertion of communal dances. I say gestures, because contemporary communal dancing can easily devolve into commercial styles, devoid of any radical impulse such as some disco of the 1970s. (For example, what we called the Brownian Bump, the former word referring to the physics principle of the random collision of molecules and the Bump being a goofy, but fun dance where people, well, bumped butts).

Even the most superficial disco can be fun, but it's not the stuff of which Halmos writes. Our dancing will become imbued with more importance and deeper meaning the more we are part of the process of destroying the culture of death that now controls the planet. Casey Neill sings about "dancing on the ruins of multinational corporations," which sounds good enough as long as we are also building another world where we will all dance together.

Make it so.

Suggested reading:
Dancing In The Streets: A History Of Collective Joy, Barbara Ehrenreich, 2008

Will Success Spoil Chumbawamba?
How does an anarchist band from Leeds deal with being international pop stars?
Summer 1998

I arrived early at Clutch Cargo's, once an imposing church, but now a trendy rock joint in yuppified downtown Pontiac, a gritty, predominantly black, industrial Detroit suburb. The occasion was a concert by Chumbawamba, the anarchist pop group from Leeds, England, which has achieved international acclaim for their catchy hit, "Tubthumping."

The song is so ubiquitous—"I get knocked down, but I get up again; you're never going to keep me down"—that not only has it topped the charts in Europe, North America, and Asia with triple platinum sales, but is now played at sporting events worldwide, supplanting staples such as Queen's, "We Are The Champions." The song, featured on a promotional compilation for the new VW Beetle, was heard recently on cheesy TV shows like "Beverly Hills 90210," and "Veronica's Closet" and is also on the soundtrack of the Hollywood production of "Home Alone 3."

To most listeners, there's little more to Chumbawamba than a band with a pop hit featuring an infectious hook that everyone will probably be sick of by the time this is read. But Chumbawamba is an unlikely candidate for commercial stardom. Probably unknown to most of the group's newly acquired fans, the group has long been a favorite of the international anarchist community for their uncompromising songs challenging the political state and capitalism. The band's origins go back 15 years in the British punk movement, and its members define themselves as revolutionary anarchists.

Their recent limited edition, "Showtime," distributed by AK Press, an anarchist publisher, is a double-CD with a Noam Chomsky speech featured on the second disk. On it, the band plays a live performance before an enthusiastic crowd in a Leeds pub during a two-day benefit for the local Anti-Fascist Action organization. During the concerts, a defense guard was on hand to protect the venue from English neo-Nazis who had threatened to attack the event. During the night following the first performance, the pub's windows were smashed, but the second evening came off without incident.

Chumbawamba played Detroit in 1993 at 404, a small storefront anarchist club that held about 50 people comfortably. That August night, with temperatures in the 80s outside, about 75 sweaty people jammed into the space, many of them stripped to the waist, and danced wildly to the band's infectious music and cheered their explicit revolutionary anthems.

Alice Nutter, one of the band's vocalists, remembers the event. "Yeah, we had to put Boff's amp on the cooker [the stove]," she says, "and we had to stop every once in a while to ask if anyone wanted to go to the toilet." The place was so crowded that the musicians were blocking the entrance to the only bathroom.

Four years later, the band is at the pinnacle of international fame and many people in the anarchist milieu are wondering whether success will spoil Chumbawamba. How does a group that has been featured in every publication from *The New York Times* to *USA Today* deal with fame and still hang on to its anti-authoritarian principles?

When the doors to Clutch Cargo's opened, the first rush of patrons looked as though they had just been dropped off by their moms from a Saturday afternoon at a shopping mall. In ran a stream of hyper-enthusiastic 11-, 12- and 13-year-olds, followed by their parents, many who decidedly looked like they had been dragged to a concert they didn't want to attend. Eventually, the audience was mainly comprised of adults, but a friend told me later, as if to emphasize Chumbawamba's popularity with pre-teens, "Yeah, They're my eight-year-old's favorite group."

I was there with several striking Detroit newspaper workers

at the invitation of Nutter whom I had interviewed for Detroit's weekly *Metro Times*. Several days after I spoke with her, I wondered whether she was aware of the almost three-year strike against the two local dailies, fearing one of the scab papers might try to get an interview with members of the band. My call was too late. Alice had already talked to a scab reporter and was anguished. She hadn't known of the boycott. She offered to let the strikers speak from the stage before their performance and set up a literature table in the lobby along with one from the local chapter of Anti-Racist Action (ARA).

Given all the kids in the audience, we didn't know what the reaction would be to a labor message, but when Barbara Ingalls, a locked-out printer, took the stage she got a rousing hand. Later, during the performance, Danbert Nobacon, another of the vocalists, dedicated a song to the strikers and took a newspaper boycott sign on stage with him.

So far, so good. But Chumbawamba's latest album, "Tubthumper," was a mystery of sorts to many of their long-time U.S. admirers. It was released in the U.S. on Universal, a major corporate label, and gone were the explicit anarchist lyrics denouncing oppression. Although tubthumping is the old name for radical street corner speaking, the latest lyrics are a gentler, more ambiguous set with nothing in them to directly suggest their core politics. Their big hit, a corny tribute to indomitability also celebrates the male culture of drinking at sporting events — "He drinks a whisky drink; he drinks a vodka drink; he drinks a lager drink."

The answer to our curiosity as to whether we were going to see a domesticated Chumbawamba came with the first song-one of their old ones — "Give the Anarchist a Cigarette" — "Nothing burns down by itself, every fire needs a little help." And, as if to assure the audience this was a band whose commitment remains intact, the next tune was another oldie, "Mouthful of Shit," which the band dedicated to British Prime Minister Tony Blair and U.S. President Bill Clinton.

Although many of the tunes they played were from their latest album, others were clearly anarchist and anti-religious. It was impossible to determine what the soccer moms and their kids thought while sitting through this, but when the band finally sang "Tubthumping," the whole place exploded. Everyone was on their feet singing the chorus in unison, throwing their fists in the air, and then it was over. An encore? Sure. They did an *a cappella* version of their earlier "Homophobia" just so the words, which are sometimes lost in their English Midlands accents, were perfectly clear—"Homophobia, the worst disease; love how you want and love who you please."

Following the performance, Nutter told us how two days earlier the band had taped a performance of "Tubthumping" for TV's David Letterman Show. In the middle of the song, they began chanting, "Free Mumia Abu-Jamal," before going back to the famous chorus. The show's producers went apoplectic saying they believed Mumia was innocent, but that he was a "convicted cop killer" and the band would have to do the segment again or it wouldn't air. After a short conference, the group members refused and left the studio.

Much to their surprise, the segment ran as recorded, but Nutter commented afterward, "I don't think we'll be invited back."

After the band appeared January 20 on ABC-TV's "Politically Incorrect" with Bill Maher and repeated the shoplifting advice her band often gives in interviews, twelve Virgin Records megastores in Los Angeles took "Tubthumper" off their shelves and put it behind the counter. Nutter said she believed it was just fine for poor people to shoplift records from chains.

"We were dismayed by her saying this kind of thing," whined Christos Garkinos, Virgin marketing vice-president. "Especially since we were one of the band's early supporters."

Nutter said it was Maher who singled out Virgin as a possible target, and she attempted to change the topic to "why people can't afford records and feel the need to shoplift in an unequal world."

Nutter defends the less confrontational character of the band's new lyrical direction and insists that their intent remains unchanged. "We don't want to just get our pop music into people's homes," she says. "We want to get anarchist ideas along with it."

Although there is little on their current album to overtly suggest this perspective, band members say this wasn't a marketing strategy. They had completed the album a year before signing with EMI in Britain after being dumped by their independent label which advised the band to "Take a year off and write stronger songs."

Pointing to an earlier recording, Nutter says, "If you look at our album, 'Pictures of Starving Children,' the way those songs are written, they're just theses. Each song has at least 32 lines, none of them repeated, and no chorus, because we were trying to get in as many words as possible." She says they wanted to do music with "choruses and hook lines, and were constructed like ordinary pop songs." Nutter says the band decided if they wanted to "really touch people," they had to "put the 'theses' somewhere else."

Unfortunately, with the U.S. release of "Tubthumper" on Universal, only half of their equation worked. They've got their top-of-the-charts music on MTV, on karaoke machines and at sporting events, but most people, like the prepubescent kids at Clutch Cargo's, were clueless as to the "theses" that ultimately animate Chumbawamba. An ad for a record chain in a local Detroit paper informed potential buyers that "this was the group's eighth album. Previously known for their politically charged lyrics, they toned down the social commentary just a bit on this album."

The "somewhere else" for the theses mentioned above was supposed to be the latest album's liner notes. The band spent months finding quotes from historic and contemporary radical figures that would give an anarchist spin to words which in themselves don't directly convey that message. These were contained in a thick booklet accompanying the CD in its European and Asian release. However, Universal's American lawyers threw up a roadblock-demanding a clearance on each quote. This would have delayed the debut of the album for months and left the band in an untenable position—a further wait for its release or an expurgated version. They chose the latter.

"Maybe we could understand about a quote from Orwell," Nutter says angrily, "but do you have to get clearance on ownership of anonymous graffiti taken from a wall in Paris in 1968?" She expresses frustration about how the album appears without the liner notes: "People in Europe and Asia got the album we wanted;

in America they didn't. The last thing in the world we are is lap liberals. We're anarchists."

Following the lyrics of each song in the truncated booklet that appears with the American release, is an invitation for people to write or e-mail the band for the missing quotes.

The debate about what constitutes "selling-out" is a complicated one, and hardly new to rock and roll. Obvious examples, from the early 1970s include Detroit's seminal rock band, the MC5, and folksinger/anti-war activist Phil Ochs, whose efforts to reach wider audiences with a reduced social message failed miserably. Although groups such as The Clash and Gang of Four achieved mainstream success through innocuous hit songs, they soon self-destructed over the dilemma of how to keep radical politics intact.

The band's milder lyrics, instant fame, and decision to sign with a major label aren't without critics in the radical movement from where Chumbawamba sprang. Class War, a militant British anarchist organization and newspaper denounced the band on their web site for Chumbawamba's decision to sign with EMI, a multinational media conglomerate and military contractor.

Commenting on bands signing with major labels prior to her group's contract with EMI, *Class War* quotes Nutter as saying in an interview, "I've too often heard rebel bands excuse their participation with big business by saying 'we'll get across to more people.' I'd be interested to discover exactly what they'll get across and to whom. Turning rebellion into cash so dilutes the content of what they're saying that I no longer think that they're saying anything."

There are obvious contradictions between a band that aspires to revolution and a corporation which seeks advantage in the international capitalist marketplace. AK Press pressed 7000 copies of Chumba's "Showtime" CD, but "Tubthumper" will probably top out at quadruple platinum and only a corporation can do the worldwide distribution necessary for this sort of demand.

Musically there's not much to distinguish "Tubthumper" from their recent albums, but lyrics needing supporting quotes or explanations to achieve the radical thrust the group desires suggest an inherent weakness. Although the band sees the new album's songs as threaded together, the themes by themselves don't seem to portray more than a protest against the anonymity and falseness of modern society. "One by One," does indict bureaucratic labor leaders and "Scapegoat" criticizes blaming others, but as the band laments, they could easily come off as "lap liberals" when the music stands by itself.

Nutter's criticism of their previous music seems curious. Many of their older tunes such as "Never Do What You Are Told," "That's How Grateful We Are," and "Homophobia," had the hooks and choruses she mentions approvingly. Their "I Never Gave Up" is an earlier "Tubthumping," with a similar theme—"I crawled in the mud, but I never gave up"—not stated quite as elegantly, but certainly with a memorable chorus.

To their credit, the band seems intent on using their fame to promote anarchist ideas. After a U.S. tour in late 1997, they headed back to England to do a series of benefits for several rape crisis centers and anti-fascist groups. "We were influenced by bands like Crass with the idea pop music could be intensely political," Nutter recalls. "They introduced us to the idea that songs didn't have to be about love, and they called themselves anarchist. Chumbawamba doesn't want to be just a pop group. We also want to be part of a radical community away from music because real life is more exciting than a rock and roll circus."

As to the question of success affecting them, she says, "As soon as it starts to spoil us, we have to give up what we're doing." Asked about the band's future plans, "To be in 'Home Alone 4,'" Nutter laughed.

Chapter 8
War

All Wars are Lies!
Spring 2006

"War! Uh!
What is it good for?
Absolutely nothing!"
    Edwin Starr, "War"

The Motown great Edwin Starr asked and answered this question in his 1970 song that became a best-selling record and the anthem of another in a series of long, hot summers.

By then, tens of millions of people around the world had come to a similar conclusion about the U.S. empire's brutal war in Vietnam that already had taken the lives of at least two million Indochinese and tens of thousands of those of the invaders. There was widespread realization that not only did America's Asian war have nothing to do with freedom, but was about imperial domination of a region far from its shores.

Starr's lyrics, unfortunately, are not entirely accurate. Although they are for the majority of people who want to live simple lives of peace and security, war serves very distinct core functions for the modern, imperial nation state.

The first purpose is key: An external threat, usually contrived, allows the creation of a permanent war state. The economy is rooted in massive transfers by the state of private wealth produced by workers and confiscated through taxation. Rather than returned in services to the populace from which the involuntary tribute was taken, it is used to sustain a massive war preparation system that ultimately drives the economy. It's been that way in the U.S. since the first quarter of 1942 when the nation, having turned its industrial sector completely over to war production, finally left the bad times of the 1930s Great Depression behind.

World War II provided an enemy necessitating huge expenditures of public wealth, becoming the first time where such outlays, before or since, were actually required by an authentic threat. Previous perils were manufactured to justify America's wars of expansion and to protect its looting of other regions. Following WWII, it was necessary to create a new enemy, the Soviet Union, which never represented a military threat to the U.S. When it disappeared, the bogeyman of terrorism was elevated to a status of permanent enemy, like Emmanuel Goldstein, Big Brother's enemy in George Orwell's *1984*, justifying the perpetual war machine.

It is heartening to see Americans catching on a little quicker than usual during this current war. Most people have figured out that it's not about a War on Terror, but rather, that it has to do with the decision made years before 9/11 to dominate an area containing great oil reserves and to secure bases where U.S. military power can be quickly extended in the Middle East and to those countries close at hand in Asia.

The neocons who devised this strategy in the late 1990s had an unusually clear vision of what will be developing in the coming decades. Oil production is peaking at a time when competition for increasingly scarce sources from growing economies like China's is heightening. If the U.S. isn't strategically situated, they reasoned, it risks being at a distinct disadvantage in coming economic and even military conflicts based on the need for fossil fuels.

The official rationale for the Iraq war came unraveled so quickly for two reasons. First, the Bush administration lies about weapons of mass destruction and a 9/11/Iraq connection were so transparently false. Plus, they were peddled by inept and arrogant flacks used to saying anything and neither being challenged nor ever paying the consequences for previous failures, who didn't even bother to do a sophisticated job of salesmanship.

The second reason relates to the first. The liars lied to themselves. They bought their own bullshit about liberating Iraq from a dictator (one who several in the administration had previously supported), fighting a war on the cheap, and being hailed by a grateful population.

Had there been an easy win for the U.S. invaders and occupiers, Bush probably would have been hailed as a great hero. But GI deaths mount as the situation in Iraq deteriorates. The corruption of Vice President Dick Cheney's Halliburton no-bid contracts and outright swindling of reconstruction funds with absolutely no results is exposed, increasing the realization that billions are going to another country while the U.S. infrastructure crumbles. That, all combined, has turned the tide of popular opinion against the Bush criminals and their war.

Only a few percentage points above the hard-core fascist third of the population still support the conflict, but these twisted souls would probably remain loyal to Bush even if they saw films of him participating in cannibalism. Over 50 percent of Americans now agree that Bush should be impeached if he lied about WMDs as the basis for invading, and most people agree that he did.

There should be scandal that the murderous gang of politicians in Washington lied to justify a war for oil and geo-political hegemony, but what U.S. war has been any different? Or, for that matter, any war ever fought between nation states?

It's worth going through a few U.S. wars, minus the patriotic cant, as a reminder.

The Mexican War (1846 to 1848) was solely for territorial expansion which gobbled up good portions of Mexico's north territories, including Texas, California, Arizona, and New Mexico. Some still refer to those states as "Occupied Mexico."

The Spanish-American war (1898 to 1902) was based on the lie that the Spanish blew up the battleship USS Maine in the Havana, Cuba harbor. Research done 100 years later shows the ship blew from the inside out, suggesting a munitions explosion. The Hearst newspapers beat the war drums to arouse a sleepy population into a patriotic frenzy, and soon America had the empire it sought as a way to enrich itself at a time when economic conditions were so bad that the rulers feared revolution. The war booty included the Philippines, Puerto Rico, several Pacific islands, and control of

Cuba. The U.S. had to fight guerrilla resistance in the Philippines, committing similar atrocities as it did in Vietnam, to stop a massive insurgency against the American occupiers.

From 1902 through to the invasion of Panama in 1989, U.S. Marines intervened over a hundred times in Latin America whenever American corporate interests were threatened.

U.S. Marine General Smedley Butler's oft-used quote is enough to make the point: "I spent most of my time being a high-class muscle man for Big Business, for Wall Street and for the bankers. In short, I was a racketeer for capitalism....I helped make Mexico, especially Tampico, safe for American oil interests in 1914. I helped make Haiti and Cuba a decent place for the National City Bank boys to collect revenues in. I helped in the raping of half a dozen Central American republics for the benefit of Wall Street. The record of racketeering is long. I helped purify Nicaragua for the international banking house of Brown Brothers in 1909 to 1912. I brought light to the Dominican Republic for American sugar interests in 1916. In China, I helped to see to it that Standard Oil went its way unmolested."

The U.S. entered World War I (1917 to 1918) only toward its end, but ask anyone why America intervened after three years of a European conflict and they usually return a blank stare. The official reason was the Germans had sunk an unarmed English passenger ship with great loss of life including Americans. As it turned out, the ship was secretly carrying munitions to Britain from the U.S. in violation of its Neutrality Act. That and a few inconsequential other items were the excuse the U.S. used to involve itself in an inter-imperial slaughter on the side of the Allies. The real reasons, beyond the rhetoric of making the world safe for democracy, were to insure war loans made to the Allies, particularly England, were secure and to begin functioning as a new imperial power that could dictate policy on a global basis.

Wars provide the opportunity for governments to police internal threats, as well, so, the U.S. used the conflict virtually no one initially wanted to ruthlessly stamp out the mass-based domestic socialist, anarchist, and radical trade union movements which were challenging the system at that time.

World War II (1941 to 1945) is so mythologized that the real reasons it was fought and the nature of the geo-political machinations which left 30 million people as victims cannot be easily summarized. Although the conflict is often characterized by some radicals as the one time we fought anyone worse than us, most agree that the U.S. was genuinely at risk. This view certainly has elements of truth to it, but mostly it is portrayed in official memory as the Good War, expressed in triumphalist terms of good over evil. This completely ignores the war's abundant complexity.

WWII was 100 percent about markets, empire, and colonies, and zero percent about democracy and freedom. It was only about ending a threat from imperial rivals, not defeating fascism as an ideology.

Here are just two elements:

"Appeasing Hitler" has persisted as a metaphor into this era as what not to do about aggressive dictators. The British are portrayed as spinelessly giving in to the German dictator at Munich at a time when they should have confronted his demands. Hence, they only forestalled World War II, but emboldened Hitler, making the conflict more certain rather than less. Eventually, goes the argument, it took U.S. entry into the war to save the day.

British diplomacy wasn't based on timidity, but rather predicated upon a cynical strategy of giving Hitler what he wanted in Central Europe by calculating, incorrectly, that his next military move would be against the Soviet Union. The British, no less than the Nazis, saw Russian communism as the main enemy of the West. U.S. President Franklin Roosevelt was in agreement with this policy as was corporate America, the latter which enthusiastically aided the construction of the Nazi war machine and continued surreptitiously trading with the enemy during the war.

Henry Ford received a German Iron Cross medal in 1938 in Detroit from a Nazi emissary. Hitler was a great admirer of the anti-Semitic Ford, an early enthusiast of the Nazi party, and kept a photo of the auto magnate on the walls of his Berlin bunker even in his last days. General Motors, IBM, and the Ethyl Corporation were many among other corporate enthusiasts who rebuilt the German war machine during the 1930s.

After the Wehrmacht invasion of Russia in 1941 (essentially fueled by Standard Oil diesel), then-Senator Harry S Truman expressed a view of many in the ruling circles when he said on the U.S. Senate floor that he hoped each of the belligerents would do maximum damage to one another, foreshadowing the internecine Iraq-Iran war that the U.S. encouraged in the 1980s.

However, as more and more goods were sold to Britain in 1940 through 1941 under the so-called Lend-Lease program, corporate America, no less than the Roosevelt administration, realized that if their best customer and major debtor were to lose to Germany, it would be a financial disaster for their recovery from the Depression. Suddenly, sentiment changed, particularly among the capitalist elite, from being pro-Nazi to realizing that it was those cheeky Brits who were fighting for Democracy.

The war in Europe was stood on its head, however, with the surprise victory of the Soviet Red Army over the vaunted German Wehrmacht, leaving the Communists in control of Eastern Europe by 1945, the possibility most feared by the West. Essentially, it was the Russians who defeated the Nazis, having responsibility for 90 percent of German battlefield casualties while sustaining 13 million dead of their own. By contrast, American battle deaths in Europe total 100,000, the same figure the Russians suffered in the battle for Berlin alone. The conclusion of the European theatre conflict on the Allies' part, beginning with the June 1944 Normandy invasion and including war crimes such as the firebombing of Dresden, had little to do with defeating the Nazis, something the Russians were on the way to completing, and almost all about post-war considerations regarding stopping the Soviet Union from being in a geopolitical dominant position.

In the Far East, the U.S., and its imperial ally Britain, battled Japan for control of China and other Pacific rim European colonies. It ended with the militarily unnecessary war crime of the atom bombing of two defenseless Japanese cities in a country on the verge of surrender. This was seen by the Truman administration as the first shot of World War III; one with the Soviet Union.

After peace prevailed on all fronts in 1945, Soviet successes in Eastern Europe and the upsurge of anti-colonial movements in Africa and Asia, were quickly turned to the advantage of the Western economies which created a Cold War where no conflict existed. Stalin neither planned nor intended "world domination." However, the U.S. manufactured a fear of the "march of Communism" creating a seamless segue for the World War II war economy to continue unabated. At the same time, the Red Scare during McCarthy-era at home was used, as it had been during the first international conflict thirty years before, to stifle internal dissent, civil rights, and labor militancy.

The murky origins of the Korean War (1950 to 1953), only five years after the end of a horrific inter-imperial slaughter is still the subject of debate. Suffice it to say, the first war to "stop communism" wound up with one million dead civilians at the hands of the U.S. in a war that was driven by a pathological ideology connected to a mad economy.

Vietnam (1960 to 1975). America's longest war, began as an effort to support the French colonial masters who had been re-installed in Indochina by the U.S. after Japan's defeat and ended with the complete destruction of the country; three million civilian deaths, and almost 60,000 of the invaders.

The slaughter commenced in mass proportions following a contrived 1964 incident in the Gulf of Tonkin off the Vietnam coast where it was alleged that two U.S. destroyers were attacked by small North Vietnamese boats. No damage was done and no one ever asked, what were American warships doing 8,000 miles from home so provocatively and belligerently close to another nation's coastline? Can one imagine if the situation were reversed and North Vietnamese destroyers were just several miles off the coast of New York City?

Although left critics of U.S. war policy protested at the time that the attacks were a contrivance, almost all of the media and Congress dutifully bought the story, allowing the enormous escalation of a war that the U.S. rightfully lost. Forty-one years later, the National Security Agency released hundreds of pages of secret documents showing, indeed, the evidence of the Tonkin attack had been "deliberately skewed." A little too late for the mountain of corpses that the lie produced.

The taste of defeat in the mouths of Americans was strong enough during the 1970s that it looked like perhaps the era of U.S. overseas adventures would be curtailed. However, the Reagan and Bush I administrations found a couple of easy to win wars that were used to roll back the public distaste for continuing conflicts. The reversal of the so-called Vietnam Syndrome and the unchallenged ability of the U.S. to extend military force anywhere in the world was more at issue during the invasions of Grenada and Panama than the manufactured excuses.

Both were in violation of international law and both based on lies. The first, that American citizens were endangered by the chaos following the meltdown of Grenada government on the left-ruled island, and the second, that U.S. forces were only enforcing an arrest warrant on a former client state dictator. The latter is particularly egregious since the invasion of Panama and apprehension of CIA-asset President Manuel Noriega took upwards of 4,000 civilians lives in the poor districts surrounding the presidential palace. This would be like the cops coming to your community to arrest a dope dealer, and in the process, burning the area to the ground and killing your family along with hundreds of your neighbors.

The intervention in Central America during the 1980s produced a bloody decade with the U.S. backing death squad governments, torture states, and paid mercenaries resulting in the deaths of hundreds of thousands of civilians. The slaughter was based on numerous lies about communist subversion, destabilizing regimes, Cuban infiltration, etc. The perpetrators of them populate the current Bush regime.

The 1991 Gulf War was just what the imperialists were seeking. Another U.S. client, Saddam Hussein, seemingly went bad. His invasion of Kuwait sparked a U.S. response that dashed the Vietnam Syndrome with an easy win, but included the unnecessary slaughter of thousands of retreating Iraqi conscripts. This nasty little Crusader incursion was the start of long-range plans to directly control Middle East oil reserves rather than allow a series of unstable surrogates to do so. The Reagan administration had supported Saddam throughout the 1980s, but Bush I saw a golden opportunity to improve his sagging poll numbers and increase U.S.

Middle East presence when the Iraqi dictator fell into a brilliantly conceived trap.

In July 1990, a meeting between the U.S. ambassador and Saddam occurred that was reasonably interpreted by the Iraqi dictator as a go-ahead for his invasion plans. Middle East national borders were almost exclusively drawn by retreating European powers after the World Wars to facilitate neo-colonialism irrespective of what ethnic tensions they increased or arbitrary boundaries were established. Saddam never would have invaded Kuwait had he not seen it as being consistent with the support he received from his U.S. benefactors during the 1980s.

Iraq War (2003-????). The lies surrounding this invasion and occupation have been thoroughly exposed in the same media that so compliantly repeated all the Bush administration inventions during the run-up to the war. They don't need repeating here. Suffice it to say, a gullible and frightened public, whipped up by mendacious politicians through an uncritical media initially gave high approval ratings to the invasion, sold as a hedge against the threat of post-9/11 terrorism.

It's shocking that Americans are shocked that this administration lied about the reasons for the Iraq war since it is consistent with each of this nation's previous ones. One wonders why no lessons are learned and why each generation, and in some cases the same one, are able to be fooled each time the reigning politicians discover the next grave threat to the nation.

This is partly due to an infantilized mass character structure created by living within authoritarian nation states (even ones which feature ostensible democratic facades) that create an inability to think independently, and a fear of contradicting Big Father surrogates. Perhaps, most importantly, is the creation of a spectacularized collective consciousness in which the socially atomized individual is submerged into the state and believes he shares in its prowess and glory. This substitute isn't much, but it attempts to compensate for being stripped of any real sense of authentic worthiness and localized sense of community.

All of it, the economic necessity for war, the imperial drive for markets and hegemony, the mass psychology of submission to the leader, are intricate components of the political state and have been since its origin. So, peace is not patriotic. Opposing war is a struggle against the grotesque institution that generates both wars and homage to itself.

Hiroshima
First Shot of World War III
August 1977

The barbarity of the nation-state since its emergence 6,000 years ago has only been limited in its intensity by a lack of the technological means needed to perpetrate horrors upon humanity. By the advent of World War II, science and industry, joined together in wedlock by Capital, achieved the breakthrough in destructive methodology and allowed a carnage of a staggering 30,000,000 dead.

Although it had been only half-jokingly said that World War II was the only conflict in which the U.S. fought any nation worse than itself, the real nature of the war should never be disguised. It was pure and simply a war of contending empires—opposing factions of capital—with each side and its allies either trying to preserve or extend the area and people controlled by its sphere of domination. When the rubble and destruction were finally swept away, new contenders already were poised for the next conflagration, anxious to act out the capitalist cycle of prosperity, depression, war and reconstruction.

Escalating deaths on the battlefield (from 4,435 in the American Revolution to millions world-wide from 1939 through 1945) were matched by the wholesale slaughter of civilian populations such as the Nazi exterminations of Jews, the fire bombings of Dresden and Hamburg, and the atomic holocaust unleashed on two Japanese cities 32 years ago this month.

Although it may be foolish to attempt to distinguish between acts of such enormity, the militarily unnecessary use of nuclear weapons on a defeated, unarmed civilian population may take the award for the most appalling. All the other acts, no matter how monstrous, were related to the conflict at hand—the psychotic racial dreams of the Nazis or Churchill's carefully targeted German working class districts for the destruction of the Nazi productive mechanism and the elimination of the possibility of post-war revolution.

The atomic attack on Japan had nothing to do with that conflict, but with the future one with the Soviet Union. The people of Hiroshima on August 6, 1945 and those of Nagasaki three days later were the first sacrifices of World War III—300,000 of them.

The prevailing myth, one still peddled by many official historians, is that the Japanese were so fanatically devoted to their emperor that they would never surrender no matter how disastrous their military situation might become and that only a full-scale land invasion costing a million American casualties would end World War II. I believed that; didn't you?

In reality, Japan attacked the American empire in the East in its quest to wrest China and the Pacific rim countries from control of the Western powers. However, by late 1944, Japan's ruling politicians began to realize that their plans had fatally failed and began to discuss plans for surrender. In June of 1945, the Japanese Supreme War Council authorized Foreign Minister Togo to approach the Soviet Union about their desire to end the war by September.

A state of war had never been declared between the two countries, although Stalin had promised his Western allies that he would begin action against the Japanese three months after the defeat of the Nazis in Europe. This timetable would have brought the Russians into the Pacific war in early or mid-August. The impact of this was not lost on either the Japanese or the Americans, both of whom realized, as stated in intelligence reports from both countries, that Russia's entry would be the signal for the unconditional surrender of the Japanese with the Soviets playing a major role.

President Truman, the Joint Chiefs of Staff, and other policy makers knew they had several options for ending the war on terms favorable to the U.S. They ranged from an air and naval blockade favored by those branches of the Service with conventional bombardment, a non-military demonstration of the A-bomb, a warning that the U.S. possessed the bomb and would use it if a surrender was not forthcoming, a series of political and diplomatic moves, or the use of the bomb on a major population center.

Interestingly, almost the entire inner core of the U.S. war machine opposed use of the bomb, including Secretary of State Stettinius and Secretary of War Stimson, as did the military. Right-wing General Curtis LeMay later said, as quoted in "Why We Dropped the Bomb" by Gar Alperovitz, "even without the atomic bomb and the Russian entry into the war, Japan would have surrendered in two weeks....The atomic bomb had nothing to do with the end of the war." General Dwight Eisenhower thought that the bomb was "no longer mandatory as a measure to save American lives."

The decision to use the bomb has to be seen clearly as a political act, certainly not a military one, whose intent was to force Japan to surrender directly to the U.S. before the Russian entry into the war and to strengthen the hand of the Allies in dealing with the Soviets regarding the Eastern European territory they occupied. It was a clear and sharp warning to the Soviets that in the period to come, the Western Allies were ready to go to any lengths necessary to protect their sector of world capitalism. This act of hostility was understood as such by Stalin and was part of what shaped Russian foreign policy in the Cold War years to follow.

The final decision to use the bomb was made by a small group of advisors around Truman, all of whom were fully aware of the political impact it would have on Russia. The world entered the Nuclear Age at a dreadful price in human suffering, with high rates of cancer and birth defects existing even today in Japan—testimony to the lethal capacity of the bomb.

It becomes difficult to find words that can express sufficient horror, dismay, and revulsion toward men who would coldly order such an act as part of a grand game plan, but it's not like they are creatures from another age relegated to the history books.

The same politicians now inhabit the war rooms of an ever-growing number of nations, all of which have or will soon have the capability of beginning a war that could eliminate life on the planet. Just as the first developers of the A-bomb over 30 years ago never gave consideration to not using their new weapon, one knows the impossibility of not using those possessed today.

Wartime Wildcats Took On Union, Government
Winter 1980

Review: *Wartime Strikes: The Struggle Against the No-Strike Pledge in the UAW During World War II,* Martin Glaberman, 1980, Bewick Editions.

Martin Glaberman's account of auto worker militancy during the war years from the perspective of both an observer and a participant is essentially a tale of resistance to the orders of bosses—both union and government—to participate in the war mobilization under terms unfavorable to the workers.

The cover of the book itself announces its contents: pictured are hundreds of cheering, waving, smiling workers running out of the Detroit Chevrolet Gear and Axle plant at the beginning of a 1943 wildcat strike. The elation on their faces makes one almost forget that the U.S. was at a crucial juncture in a war and that almost all of the workers involved considered a victory over the Axis powers to be of utmost importance.

Glaberman shows that the overwhelming patriotism of the workers and the fact that each war year set new strike records for the century was not the contradiction it seemed. All of organized labor had been locked into a "voluntary" no-strike pledge since the opening of the war, but it became obvious immediately that there was not an equality of sacrifice on the part of the corporations. Workers faced bad working conditions, wage freezes and inflation, while their employers were profiting handily in a manner not enjoyed since before the Depression.

Wartime Strikes describes both the resistance and organization against the pledge and links it to the whole range of shop floor conditions and grievances that had been at the center of working-class discontent during the period of unionization. Unlike the 1930s, however, the unions were unable to even give the appearance of embodying those concerns and functioned along with the companies and government in repressing the strikes and harassing militants.

The outlawed wildcats that flared during the war years were the rekindling of the spontaneous rebellious actions that typified the early 1930s, but had been largely extinguished as a result of the successful union recognition struggles. Immediately upon signing the first labor contract, the union apparatus appropriated the weapon of the strike from the workers and established itself as its sole legal possessor. Having disarmed a militant working class, the unions strove to create an era of social peace in which not only did they mediate the sale of labor to the corporations and function as arbiters of all labor strife, they became an integral and important part of capitalism's ruling mechanism.

This transformation from the radical image union organizers had during the 1930s to their perception as "responsible labor statesmen" in just a period of a few years, became nowhere as evident as when war was declared in 1941 and the unions began an almost delirious voluntary pledging not to strike for the duration of the conflict. Led by militant CIO unions, these pledges were made without even the slightest consultation with any union membership and the reward was swiftly forthcoming.

Union leaders were absorbed onto a variety of government war production boards, joint labor-management committees, etc. that completed the sequence which began with class war at the beginning of the previous decade and ended ten years later with workers marching off to the front in an inter-imperialist war, and to work stripped of their right to strike The integration of the representatives of labor into the government structure further strengthened the unions' drive to take all power from the hands of the workers themselves and to be recognized as friends, not opponents, of capitalism.

Glaberman describes all of this in devastating terms and then proceeds to document the wide-spread wildcats that continued throughout the war with violations of the no-strike pledge being almost a daily occurrence. The companies, seeing a working class formally restricted from objecting to speed-ups, arbitrary work-rules and management, etc., wanted to use the war years as an opportunity to regain profits lost during the previous decade of low profitability. *Wartime Strikes*, however, demonstrates the unwillingness of workers to allow even the smallest grievance to pass without an organized walkout taking place.

Most of the action is set forth in the Detroit area, the "Arsenal of Democracy," with often times crucial war production being at issue. Glaberman observes, "The wildcat strikes were, in fact, political strikes because they were directed against the government." And although the military was used in several instances to end large-scale wildcats, the attempted suppression of day-to-day job actions were, in the main, left to the efforts of the unions. Glaberman cites the account of former-UAW president Leonard Woodcock, then an international representative of the union, bragging about his ability to squelch a series of strikes in Muskegon, Michigan as typifying the activity of the national UAW leadership in suppressing the growing wave of wildcats. Local after local which supported the actions of its members on strike were put in receivership by the International or had their officials suspended.

Even with all the efforts of the unions, the opposition to the no-strike pledge was so great that the UAW leadership finally submitted a referendum to the membership late in the war to determine whether to continue to support it. When the votes were in, fewer than 25 percent of the eligible workers even bothered to cast a ballot, but the majority of those responded to the patriotic wording of the proposal and it was re-affirmed as UAW policy. But the same year, 1944, over half of the union membership went on wildcat strike at one time or another. Glaberman cites this, again not as being representative of an unresolvable contradiction, but rather as a compartmentalization of needs—those of national patriotism on one hand and that of class on the other. A worker could, by vote or by voice, give support for the pledge as necessary for the war effort, but walk out of a defense plant ten minutes later over the actions of a foreman charging that it was the latter's actions which caused the work stoppage.

Glaberman presents the story of the wartime strikes as not just interesting events in working class history, but as representing a potential always present. He cites Hungary in 1956 and France in 1968, along with the wartime experiences, as periods when no one expected the outbreak of class struggle. The moment of greatest social quiet may be the harbinger of a revolutionary upsurge right around the corner.

The only real failing of the book comes in the author's unflagging allegiance to Marxism which, when presented, is immediately forced into a polemic with reality. Glaberman's recitation of the Marxist litany in his conclusion rates as barely a distraction, but when he attempts to impose it on the events of a world he has just so vividly described, he fails miserably, condemned by his own narrative.

In an important footnote, Glaberman cites the famous passage from *Capital* where Marx asserts that the more humans are forced into the proletariat, the greater becomes the potential for revolution. The quote reads, "(As) grows the mass of misery, oppression, slavery, degradation, exploitation; ...with this grows the revolt of the working class, a class always increasing in numbers, and disciplined, united, organized by the very mechanism of the process of capitalist production itself." Standard Marxist fare to be sure, but contradicted by Glaberman's own account throughout the book.

On the next page following the above quoted footnote, Glaberman states, "It is likely that those sections of the working class who were relatively new to the factories, such as the southerners and women, were least likely to accept the discipline of factory work and the discipline of the union." And, earlier in the book, "There was also the element, for many southern whites, of lack of union experience. As with women, while union leaders and management complained that this led to inefficiency and indiscipline, it nevertheless tended toward greater militancy.

It can't be both ways. It is either a newly proletarianized peasantry from the *mir* of Russia, from the villages of southern Italy, from the American South, or the English lowlands that have historically fought against being "disciplined, united and organized" by the factory system upon their entrance to it or one has to accept the Holy Writ of Marxism no matter how much it confounds reality. It is always the new workers unacculturated to the world of alarm clocks and time clocks that lead the struggles and contrary to Marx, the world of factories leads only to "a steadily more robotized, powerless, de-individualized proletariat" ("The Practical Marx: Life Against Theory," FE October 22, 1979).

However, this last question, though interesting and important, barely manages to mar Glaberman's otherwise excellent account of working-class struggle and imagination.

The Empire Exits Iraq
Spring 2012

When President Barack Obama announced on October 21 that the nine-year U.S. invasion and occupation of Iraq was ending, it didn't even make first spot on many news reports. Another imperial slaughter had ground to an end, with many liberal publications, such as *The Nation*, declaring it an "ignominious end to a shameful debacle."

There were no victory celebrations, no teary-eyed citizens at confetti-speckled parades waving little American flags as soldiers marched smartly past. No one has even thought of revering the last 33,000 battle troops coming out of Iraq as part of another WWII-type "Greatest Generation."

There's a temptation to invoke T.S. Eliot's over-used but apt phrase, "Not with a bang but a whimper," to describe the final hours of another conflict in the West's thousand-year war against the East. Although the end came without much ado in the U.S. media, the bang has been felt in Iraq for the preceding 20 years.

The total of what the U.S. architects of death have wrought in their wars is never accurately tabulated. Hundreds of thousands of civilians incinerated in Tokyo, Hiroshima and Nagasaki; perhaps 2.5 million during the Korean War; upwards of 3 million in Indochina.

These are all estimates. No one in the West counts the Asian dead, yet we are informed in exquisite detail how many perished among those who inflicted the mass death: 58,151 U.S. military deaths in Vietnam; 4,484 in Iraq. Each of the fallen is considered worthy of an engraving on a wall or a burial with honors. Those they killed wind up in mass graves, unnamed.

The wars in Iraq and Afghanistan are easily and accurately portrayed as wars for oil and for the larger purpose of fueling the military/industrial complex, the engine of the U.S. economy. At the economic level, it doesn't matter whether the U.S. continues to lose wars as it did in Vietnam, fight to somewhat of a draw in Iraq, or win minor ones such as the attacks on Grenada and Panama, if anyone remembers the latter two. (The citizens of Panama City, however, recall well the 1989 invasion to arrest the country's formerly U.S.-backed dictator, Manuel Noriega, which left 4,000 civilians dead in the slum surrounding the presidential palace).

Radical journalist Randolph Bourne famously and accurately wrote in 1914 that, "War is the health of the state." Since the first quarter of 1942, war has also been the health of the economy. Military Keynesianism now pumps a trillion taxpayer dollars a year through a massive wealth transfer from private hands through the government to what they called munitions makers in Bourne's time.

It is certainly a cause for outrage that almost every war in American history has been based on either contrived rationales (quickly: why did the U.S. enter World War I?), or outright lies (Spanish-American War, Vietnam, Grenada, Panama, Iraq), World War II being the one time a war was fought by the U.S. against a country worse than itself or for reasons less malign.

But, there is another overarching socio/historical explanation besides economic ones that is rooted in the mass psychology of a pathogenic culture stemming from its European origins and gives the U.S. a primary definition as a permanent warfare state.

In the 15th and 16th centuries, Europe, primarily through Spain, Portugal, England, Holland, and France, extended an economic system based on exploitation and conquest and a culture of cruelty, religious fanaticism, and environmental destruction to what they designated as the New World. Actually, it was an Old World the mad European navigators stumbled upon that suffered their invasion, occupation, looting, and genocide.

It was an ancient world encompassing the Old Ways that had

sustained people for millennia and was broken by the armored invaders, although mega-states in the Americas, the Aztecs and the Incas, for instance, exhibited the same characteristics as the nations across the waters.

Europe had destroyed its land, impoverishing not only the common people, but the rulers as well. It was a continent wracked with endless warfare (the latter often celebrated in Western literature). Their solution was fortuitously finding another continent to wreck by exporting a moribund system with every disastrous facet intact even though the original explorers and conquistadors met a face of humanity that could have solved their problems differently by adapting their ways.

Instead, "They will make excellent servants," wrote Columbus in his diary the first night after being discovered by Arawak people on Hispaniola. The rest is a well-known terrible history. Europe survived through a scourge of mass death and looting. Its economy and culture became the world-dominant system.

By the late 19th century, the descendants of those first adventurers had done damage to the North American continent identical to that which Europe had suffered. Although conquest and purchase had already greatly expanded U.S. national territory, the country's internal contradictions were bringing it close to collapse with deeper economic depressions, mass labor unrest, great environmental despoliation, and wide-spread poverty and misery among the population:

Men such as Indiana U.S. Senator Albert J. Beveridge, who said, in the late 1890s, "We must have markets abroad or revolution at home," knew it was time for a nation on an isolated continent to move beyond its geography as had his forebears. This, by the way, was one of the reasons for the U.S. entry into World War I, although the Spanish-American war, and incursions into Latin America preceded the Great War. Presaging Cold War liberals, Sen. Beveridge was a supporter of all of the Progressive Era reforms.

When we hear U.S. Presidents or Secretaries of State talk of "American interests" in a region far from its own metropole, it comes from an understanding that U.S. wealth, shared to differing degrees by sectors of the domestic population, depends on access to world-wide markets and trade, particularly oil. The socially pathological culture of militarism and delusional sense of American Exceptionalism are necessary to create a mass acceptance of its horrific dead end.

Horrific since battle totals and the grotesque phrase, collateral damage, need a rationalization for such slaughter. All the wars mentioned above were based on lies, many now blithely recognized as such but ones which possessed overwhelming social and political power at the time of the conflict.

Almost without exception, people now know there were no weapons of mass destruction in Iraq, that Bush lied, as did Cheney (who delights that he's called Darth Vader by his detractors), as did Rumsfeld, Condoleezza Rice, and the pathetic Colin Powell, butcher of the first Gulf War.

Everyone also knows that if there were a modicum of justice extracted from the powerful (there isn't and there won't be under present power relationships), all of those who lied us into the Iraq war would be in the docket of the International Criminal Court along with the likes of Slobodan Milosevic and the perpetrators of the Rwandan genocide. Instead, Bush and his gang of war criminals write self-serving memoirs where they brazenly admit to suborning torture, become even more enriched, and are touted as elder statesmen doing book tours and the lecture circuit for $50,000 a pop.

Henry Kissinger, a man who has so many pending international warrants out for his arrest because of crimes he participated in against Vietnam and Chile that he rarely travels outside of the U.S., has his writing featured on the front page of *The New York Times* book review section.

The 20-year war against Saddam Hussein, first, by Bush Sr.'s invasion, the Clinton era sanctions, and finally, Junior's Shock and Awe, has been catastrophic. Massive amounts of Iraqi blood was spilled; much of it directly by the huge U.S. war machine with additional amounts due to the internecine clashes set off by the destruction and collapse of that society. The Iraqi civilian casualty toll is staggering; iraqbodycount.org, which lists only documented deaths, pegs the figures at 113,127. The British medical journal, *The*

Lancet, gives a much larger figure of 654,965, counting only through 2006 calculating from household surveys and extrapolating "excess deaths."

As always, battle deaths and injuries of the American troops who caused the Iraqi casualties are only a fraction of what they inflicted. Much is made of returning U.S. troops suffering PTSD (Post Traumatic Stress Disorder). This is a serious and predictable consequence of war, and given what it has wreaked on American troops, one can only imagine what Iraqis must be suffering as the result of the war inflicted upon them. The Iraqi Red Crescent Organization has estimated that since Bush's "surge" in 2007, the number of people who have fled their homes and become refugees topped 1.1 million.

The U.S. has spent $800 billion dollars directly on the Iraq war, with long-range costs spiraling the figure upwards to $2.3 trillion. Billions were siphoned off to war contractors like Cheney's Halliburton firm, with billions more simply unaccounted for through blatant and widespread corruption. At times, skids filled with $20 bills were unloaded from C-17 transport planes and passed out like leaflets by U.S. troops attempting to buy off local resistance.

Hundreds of U.S. bases in Iraq now lie deserted, but what isn't going home is the U.S. embassy compound in Baghdad, the largest in the world, occupying one and a half square miles in area with a price tag of three quarters of a billion dollars to build. Although U.S. troops have left, American security personnel will swell to 16,000, not exactly a complete withdrawal.

Just as the Tehran embassy functioned prior to the overthrow of Iran's Shah in 1979, the Iraq embassy will be a forward base for U.S. military and commercial ventures. Similarly, as the Islamic Revolutionaries in Iran designated the seized American embassy in their capital, it will act as a "nest of spies" looking eastward to Russia and China, something not lost on either nation.

Where next for the Death Star? Apparently off to Uganda, and to Australia, where President Obama announced in November that a couple of thousand U.S. Marines will be stationed there indefinitely as a hedge against Chinese influence in the region. The fact that Beijing sees this as a threatening provocation apparently matters little to those manning the Empire's central command at the Pentagon.

It is imperial interest added to cultural psychosis that drives the U.S. relentlessly towards war, but this time it's messing with the big boys. Steadily advancing into the sphere of influence of a nuclear armed super-power is reminiscent of the Cold War and fraught with the same chances of annihilation that existed a generation ago.

David Swanson's excellent web site, warisacrime.org, reported on the anniversary of the Japanese attack in Hawaii 70 years ago on a similar military/political situation: "When President Franklin Roosevelt visited Pearl Harbor on July 28, 1934, seven years before the Japanese attack, the Japanese military expressed apprehension. General Kunishiga Tanaka wrote in the *Japan Advertiser* objecting to the build-up of the American fleet and the creation of additional bases in Alaska and the Aleutian Islands, 'Such insolent behavior makes us most suspicious. It makes us think a major disturbance is purposely being encouraged in the Pacific. This is greatly regretted.'"

Such madness is afoot once again. Their preparation for total war necessitates our total opposition.

Chapter 9
Wilhelm Reich

Sexual Repression & Authoritarianism
Control of Bodies Equals Control of Minds
March 1976

The juxtaposing of anti-sexual statements on this page (not shown here) by the Vatican and certain authoritarian leftist leaders and groups is not meant as an exercise in cynicism, but rather to illustrate in graphic terms the role sexual repression plays within all authoritarian systems.

The Church, for example, is easily identifiable as a repressive institution. Its power to regulate moral conduct grew as did the centrality of its wealth and authority within the feudal system of the Middle Ages. The Catholic Church was the international agent of feudalism, sanctifying its rigid social relationships on the one hand as God-ordained and being the largest single landowner on the other, holding a full one-third of the soil of Christendom.

Its religious ideology tied people to the structure of feudalism's political economy not just through investing it with divine characteristics, but also by developing a hold rooted in people's basic psyche that would chain them to hierarchical systems of domination and submission even when that particular form of economy based on land ownership had long been replaced by the rule of capitalism.

In all regions where religion flourishes, it functions as an important part of the control system and is heavily supported by the reigning political structure. Although the neurotic mystics who founded religions did not necessarily intend that their creed be used to entrench systems of domination, when the crippling power of religion became apparent, all rulers were quick to adopt and support it.

Denial of the flesh appears as a constant in the world's major religions and the importance of this mechanism of sexual repression can be seen as the key to the reason why people have been willing to passively accept the dehumanization of their lives since the rise of class society thousands of years ago.

Some explanation is needed as to why soldiers go enthusiastically into battle for purposes not their own; why workers slavishly labor to make others rich and powerful; and why all of us accept the entirety of what civilization is today: the denial of human community and the affirmation of the State, hierarchy, and the general blunting of life's potential.

Radical social psychologist Wilhelm Reich (1897-1957), suggested that the root of this emotional plague, as he labeled it, lay in the suppression of infant and adolescent sexuality–from harsh toilet training to punishing masturbation to teaching that sexual intercourse is bad and dirty.

The child adapts to the punishments, threats, and scolding by repressing his/her sexuality. Further attempts by the child to affirm its sexual desires become revolts against parental authority and are met by further condemnation and punishment. The punishment assures that forbidden activities are infused with guilt feelings and ultimately produce an adult in which sexual drives and all thoughts of rebellion against authority produce anxiety, feelings of guilt, unworthiness, and inadequacy.

In describing this process in *The Mass Psychology of Fascism*, Reich poses the central question. "For what sociological reasons is sexuality suppressed by the society and repressed by the individual?" His answer is:

"The interlacing of the socio-economic structure with the sexual structure of society and the structural reproduction of society takes place in the (child's) first four or five years and in the authoritarian family. The church only continues this function later. Thus, the authoritarian state gains an enormous interest in the authoritarian family: It becomes the factory in which the state's structure and ideology are molded."

What is produced is known to us all: passive, docile, fearful, dependent, obedient, malleable, respectful masses–in short, the civilized human being. Without the passive multitudes, the idea of the State, with its 8,000-year history of tyranny, ruling always in the interests of a few to the detriment of almost all, could not have lasted a single month.

The validation of Reich's analysis of the role of the family can be clearly recognized in crude advocates of the State such as Adolph Hitler who said that the family "is the smallest but most valuable unit in the complete structure of the state." (*Mein Programm*, 1932).

Also, the family is not just the training ground for the authoritarianism that benefits the State, but also its essentially undemocratic internal structure is a model for the State apparatus itself. At the head of the family stands its ultimate ruler in the form of the father mirrored in the political realm by the emperor, king, president or commissar.

The ruled or the "governed," both in the family and in the State, usually have nothing to say about the administration of things or, at best, are given some formal say (elections or family "discussions"), but ultimately all-important decisions are made by the father or the leader. The enormous fear, respect, and deference granted rulers through the ages mirrors that forced upon us within the authoritarian family.

Swords have not been at the neck or guns at the breast of us as we reproduce society after society that has dashed the living in us. "There is a gendarme inside every Frenchman" goes an old saying: in other words, the most powerful cops are inside of us.

Human families left to their own designs might have evolved to any possible form, including that of a non-authoritarian, non-patriarchal, democratic structure such as developed in isolated geographic regions like Polynesia or the Philippines.

Since such a family-type would not serve the needs of the reigning society, religion's function is to imbue its compulsive sex morality (Reich's phrase) with the quality of being above human affairs, pronounced from Heaven, existing before mortal humans and after.

It not only continues the process begun in the family and

maintained through education wherein the individual is taught to submit to authority, but also wraps the family in a mantle of sacredness which insures its perpetuation as a social institution of control from one generation to the next. Hence, the emotional plague.

Our reduction to child-like states of anxiety and dependence creates a craving for leaders, not a situation where they are foisted upon us. There have been many social upheavals, rebellions, and revolutions against leaders and social systems (too numerous to count, in fact), but each time, after the blood and carnage was washed away, the basic relationship of rulers and ruled has maintained itself.

What was at issue was that the old society and its leaders had become too denying, too brutal, too incapable of providing for daily survival. The society or leader had ceased to be a good father/provider and the masses began searching for a substitute.

Was there anything in 300 years of daily life under Czardom in Russia that did not call every day for a revolution; its autocratic rule, staggering poverty, serfdom, religious domination of social life? Yet the great masses of Russian people loved the Czars and worshipped them almost like deities.

It may be appropriate at this time to insert the important notion that there have been rebels and rebellions that have questioned all authority from the family to the State and for short periods of time, conditions of genuine liberation have held sway over large numbers of people.

In the 20th century, the activities of revolutionaries in Ukraine (1917-21), in Spain (1936-39), come quickest to mind. Their suppression in those cases was accomplished militarily at the hands of the Bolsheviks in the process of consolidating their political power in Russia, by Stalinists and fascist in Spain. The elimination of these revolutionary social movements was considered to be of exceptional importance since it was recognized by the new reigning political powers that people in the act of rebellion had slipped (if even momentarily) from the shackles of authority.

New rulers, who have just gained political power through a social rebellion, have as a priority, almost on a par with suppressing elements of the recently toppled regime, the suppression of those very elements of the rebellion that brought them to power.

It's a tricky situation for the new rulers since to stop it too short would mean a containment of the revolutionary energies they are banking on to thrust them into power, but to allow the rebellion to go too far would bring into question the legitimacy of the authority of the new rulers.

George Washington and V. I. Lenin needed the revolutionary activity of the American and Russian masses, but neither of them wanted to go as far as the Tom Paines, the Daniel Shays, or the Russian factory committees wanted to push their situations.

The role of religion within authority's Holy Trinity (the compulsive family, religion, and the State) with its blatant antisexual ideology and its historic record of service to totalitarianism is easily understood as an institution of repression and most revolutionaries quickly reject overt religious mysticism of all varieties.

What is at first surprising is that identical or even more reactionary pronouncements about sex leap from the mouths of those same leftists who claim to speak for liberation and revolution. However, an analysis which looks beyond the rhetoric designed for public consumption by both the Church and the authoritarian Left quickly understands the hidden purpose of their repressive sexual views: the reproduction of patriarchal, authoritarian society.

Throughout the so-called socialist world, the sexual ideology of the leader and the state plays the same role that Christianity plays in the West. Sexuality is discouraged in youth, homosexuals are persecuted, and authoritarian families are exalted. Even the structure is the same. In place of saints, leaders are venerated through omnipresent statues of Lenin, Mao, or Kim. In place of the Bible and prayer books, schools in socialist countries provide for compulsory reading of the teachings of the Leader. Good communists are thought to be those who have the greatest amount of the Leader's thoughts inscribed in their minds.

Reich described the process of inhibited sexual excitation being replaced by religious excitation exemplified by such occurrences as priests ejaculating during Mass or women reaching near-orgastic states during frenzied religious revivals. Extending that analysis to the political realm, it is hard to miss the religious mystical tenor of mass political rallies dominated by the revered leader and structured to produce child-like emotions of dependency in the person attending.

At Hitler's stage-managed Nuremberg rallies, or the anthill-like, choreographed mass demonstrations in Peking or Pyongyang, participants are reduced to insignificance by the giantism of the setting while their actualization as a person comes through the celebration of the Leader or the State. Also, the very content of the pronouncements by the Vatican and the authoritarian left on sex share a similarity beyond the fact that both are repressive, anti-sexual statements. Both carry with them a fall from grace by the offending individual ("You are not a good Catholic" or "You are not a good communist"), bringing the entire weight of the dominant social institution down on the head of the sinner/counter-revolutionary (condemned in the New Testament..." or against the Revolution...").

Individuals generally find it hard to buck the weight of such condemnation. To do so means to become a pariah, a rebel, and suffer all of the consequences such a decision implies. In normal times, when a society is functioning relatively smoothly, even a totalitarian one, few opt to take such a road. It is just too perilous, both physically and psychologically.

It is precisely this fear, this timidity, which has allowed every society its ability to continue functioning even though the vast majority of its members have no real, sensuous, human reason to reproduce it.

While Reich characterized this dismal view of human behavior with its willingness to submit to authority as the "emotional plague," he did not despair of altering the situation.

In *The Murder of Christ* (1953), he states:

"It is possible to get out of a trap. However, in order to break out of a prison, one first must confess to being in a prison. The trap is man's emotional structure." (One must assume he also included women in this formulation). It is, he argued, only persons structurally capable of liberation who could then begin a successful struggle to abolish authoritarian social structures.

Suggested reading:
The Mass Psychology of Fascism, Wilhelm Reich, Touchstone Books, 1946 edition
Listen, Little Man!, Wilhelm Reich, Touchstone Books, 1948

Sex Economy
Toward a Self-governing Character Structure
April, 1976

Coming to grips with the totality of Wilhelm Reich's anti-authoritarian social psychology is beyond the scope of any short article. Instead, this will be a brief summation of his notion of Sex-economy, which, along with Work-democracy constitute two of his major concepts. Reich's genius lay in his examination of how sexual repression generated in the reactionary family structure was anchored in the maintenance of the authoritarian state.

Reich argued that humans had become conditioned to be "structurally incapable of freedom", and unless freed, the human personality would always be a barrier to an authentic revolution.

In contrast to the compulsive, sex repressing, rigid, and dependent personality structure created by the authoritarian family, Reich proposed a "self-regulating character structure" or sex-economy. Reich defined the latter phrase thusly in the glossary of *The Mass Psychology of Fascism*:

"The term (sex-economy) refers to the manner of regulation of biological energy, or, what is the same thing, of the sexual energies of the individual. Sex-economy means the manner in which an individual handles his biological energy; how much of it he dams up and how much of it he discharges orgastically. The factors that influence this manner of regulation are of a sociological, psychological and biological nature."

In short, sex-economy is how we manage our sexual activity and energies. Reich was very specific about the role of sexuality.

In *The Sexual Revolution* he states, "The core of happiness in life is sexual happiness."

Without an affirmation of sexuality throughout one's life, a crippling effect occurs, human happiness becomes impossible and instead, repressed, dammed-up sexual energy comes out in docility, timidity and the desire for leaders on one hand, or in sadism and the desire for dominance and power on the other. Both of these states leave people neurotic, compulsive and lacking the ability to enjoy life fully.

Contrary to the claims of many of his critics, Reich understood the inter-relationship between the character structure (mental make-up) of individuals and the functioning of the political economy. His theories in this regard went farther than those of Marx whose analysis extended only to Western capitalist society. Reich traced his view back to the origins of civilization when the first categories of ruled and rulers were institutionalized.

Reich never reduced the human problem to one of psychology, but saw "man [sic] through the economy and the economy through the man." Societies are not split into the productive forces which reflect a particular mode, e.g., capitalism, and then groups of individuals who staff the social relationships that stem from them, but rather each society produces a mass character structure necessary to reproduce itself socially.

Reich formulated this concept in *The Sexual Revolution* thusly: "As soon as an ideology has taken hold of and molded human structure, it becomes a material, social power." Reich's key to sexual and hence, social health lay in the "experience of full orgastic pleasure." Orgasm to him was not what is experienced in the course of sexual intercourse between two armored personalities, but rather "orgastic potency is the capacity to surrender to the flow of biological energy, free of any inhibitions..." as he wrote in his 1927 *The Function of the Orgasm.*

Reich postulated that the overwhelming majority of men and women were incapable of achieving this state and that the damming up of biological energy in the organism "provides the source of energy for all kinds of biopathic (medical) symptoms and social irrationalism."

The inhibitions that block complete sexual surrender and release stem from the suppression of childhood and adolescent sexuality and they take numerous and varied forms in the armored adult. Instead of being a complete act in itself, sexual activity takes on numerous non-sexual functions and becomes an arena where childhood fantasies and compulsions are recreated in the adult.

Sex becomes an act of dominance, competition, sadism, masturbation guilt, approval-oriented performance, proof of love, acceptance or rejection and a host of more neurotic and destructive impulses. The extent of the sexual immiseration of the vast majority of people can be demonstrated perhaps most profoundly in the manifestation of its most alienated form–that of a commodity.

Sexual commodity sales in the form of literature, movies, sex manuals, gadgets; its use to sell everything from cigarettes to transmission repairs; its appearance everywhere in jokes, gossip and graffiti, all illustrate a society compulsively fixated on what it finds unobtainable–sexual gratification and happiness.

The ability to break with patterns established early in our childhood is immensely difficult; even Reich in his last years lost his early ebullience and felt the current generation was hopelessly lost; that our hope lay only in the next generation.

In a more optimistic period Reich stated: "A general capacity for freedom can be acquired only in the daily struggle for the free formation of life." This puts the burden of social responsibility for a decent future and personal happiness right where it belongs– squarely on the shoulders of each individual. No party, no doctrine, no leader can accomplish this for us.

Reich postulated that the creation of genitally healthy persons would, as a matter of course, oppose those social institutions which impede one's sexuality. So, a sexual person becomes the enemy of the authoritarian family, religion, the State, and with it the whole structure of hierarchical systems at work, in politics, and in personal relationships.

Reich never detailed what an "orgastically potent revolutionary" would do or act like and a checklist would probably be useless anyway, but often people need something to bounce their reactions off of. In other words, how do I confront the character armoring in myself? How do I move from being a sexually repressive, authoritarian personality into being a sexually gratified, democratic personality?

With the posing of these questions, it might make some sense for this article to end since the suggestion of any program in this area would imply a pretension on my part. All of us suffer from the same afflictions (some better; some worse), but since newspapers are about written ideas (as opposed to living them) some points can be made.

It would seem that the following principles, at a minimum, are necessary to the sexually healthy functioning of the individual:

The affirmation of our own sexuality as fundamentally good, healthy and important; the affirmation of child and adolescent sexuality free from adult interference; the withdrawal of moral condemnation from non-heterosexual sexuality such as homosexuality, masturbation, etc.

Also important is the rejection of attitudes of possessiveness, jealousy and competition in our love relationships; the refusal to accept roles of authority or domination over others in the family, at our jobs, in our love relationships, or wherever else they present themselves; a constant struggle against our own passivity when confronted by authority or those who attempt to dominate us.

All of these just scratch the surface of our dehumanization and necessitate our immediate attention if we are not to be gobbled alive by machines and machine people (some of whom may be our best friends). Total liberation and human community are impossible under capitalism, but the realization of the repressed in ourselves coupled with the demand for our psychic and material liberation can make us a horde of Vandals riding to sack Rome.

Chapter 10
Capitalism

Confronting Poverty and the Poor
Spring, 1993

Review: *Food Not Bombs: How to Feed the Hungry and Build Community,* C.T. Lawrence Butler and Keith McHenry, New Society Publishers, 1992

Review: *Street Lives: An Oral History of Homeless Americans,* Steven Vanderstaay, New Society Publishers, 1992

Review: *Hunger 1993: Uprooted People,* Bread for the World Institute & Development, Washington DC, 1993

Review: *The Art & Science of Dumpster Diving,* John Hoffman, Loompanics Unlimited, 1993

Review: *How to Steal Food from the Supermarket,* J. Andrew Anderson, Loompanics Unlimited, 1992

The mere listing of the above titles almost constitutes an essay in itself regarding the existence of extreme poverty in the midst of a nation which officially bills itself as the richest country in the world. However, since the inception of the political state 8,000 years ago, all critical observers have known that its cardinal function is the governance of unequal distribution of wealth in a given society.

The state has always been a mammoth racket constructed of armed men and cultural mystifications. The latter's purpose is to make those on the lower rungs believe the wealth/poverty duality is a natural occurrence in human affairs. Doesn't the torturous religious document of an armored people state, "The poor will always be with us?"

Nothing in the first three volumes reviewed here will surprise most Fifth Estate readers, but nevertheless, the statistics of misery compiled in the *Hunger 1993* volume are staggering. These figures come alive in the *Street Lives* book and one is heartened by the efforts of the Food Not Bombs feeding program.

Although a hungry person hardly has room to challenge the motivation of food providers for the poor and hungry, it is quite evident that most church, soup kitchen, hunger, and social welfare organizations participate in the institutionalization of the destitute by their programs of maintenance which never challenge the reasons for such abject misery amidst plenty.

In this regard, the Food Not Bombs group is commendable for combining an anarchistic structure with political activism in its feeding programs. Distribution of literature explaining the reasons for poverty accompany every meal set out for the hungry (though pamphlets should not be placed close to the soup kettle, their how-to-section warns).

The book is a manual for operating a Food Not Bombs feeding program and its perspective of connecting this to radical social criticism is not without difficulties. Once you move from an operating base of charity to one of activism, the authorities no longer look kindly on your humanitarian efforts. For example, the San Francisco Food Not Bombs group has been arrested repeatedly and often attacked by the police.

Street People's eloquent self-accounts give a human face to the homeless, and their stories make one aware of the incredible diversity among those who have literally wound up out in the cold. Here, in the relatively low cost-of-living Detroit area, four of five renters spend at least half their income on housing, making it easier each day to slip from society's margins and over the edge.

In the urban area surrounding the Fifth Estate office, there is a surfeit of homeless panhandlers who, having been kicked off the welfare rolls in 1991, find begging to be their last resort. More and more of the destitute prowl the streets in search of deposit bottles and the odd quarter obtained from passing strangers.

While *Street People* articulates the humanity of the poor, reality often presents more paradoxes and ambivalences when one is actually confronted with them. Most people find it somewhere between uncomfortable and frightening to be approached by beggars. The local food co-op, for instance, is hiring a security guard to shoo away the homeless from its entrance in the belief their presence deters shoppers.

Recently, as the Fall weather began to announce the harsh Winter to follow, I was leaving an area restaurant where I had consumed an inexpensive lunch of Middle-Eastern food. Upon entering the street, I was approached by beggars twice, but gave nothing and was walking away absorbed in thought. I heard a woman's voice ask for a quarter, but shook my head, no, without even looking up. I was startled to hear her growl, "You cold son-of-a-bitch!," as she turned away, child in arms. She was black and poor. In her estimation, I am white, rich and uncharitable.

I began to think about how a compassionate person deals with the differentials in income between us and the underclass. It often seems humiliating to either give or to refuse the poor. Practically, you can't give to everyone, so who receives your beneficence? Rough men who you suspect of drug or alcohol abuse are low on the giving list, women with children, the highest, but an individual can't accommodate everyone.

So, how do you choose to whom to give? Is there a standard that can be suggested? Perhaps a certain number of gifts per day or week, a set tithing to the poor or just situational decisions? However, even if one or all of these is involved, won't you still be a "cold son-of-a-bitch" to the person you refuse?

The remaining two books will probably be more of interest to those who choose a downward lifestyle than who have it forced upon them. Hoffman's book on dumpster diving is an amazing compendium of how-to, but also illustrates the immense amount of waste present in what Americans consider discardable. So much so that the author is able to "alley-pick" a livable life-style.

He describes the mountains of packing that clog our trash

receptacles, testimony to the power of advertising and public anxiety that demands a hyper-sterility surpassing any actual sanitary or health need. Also, the amount of food discarded in the U.S. (as in all countries of the world including Somalia and Ethiopia) would meet the needs of everyone if it was distributed fairly.

Hoffman's anecdotally-written text is presented humorously as he guides us through the alleys and trash bins in search of dumpster treasures. And, his techniques (lean into the bin; don't put your whole body inside) reap a surprising amount of re-usable items, some displayed in an array of trophy photos.

The book features illustrations by Ace Backwards, the cartoonist who is often featured in both left and right-wing publications. Hoffman's politics are right-wing libertarian which provide several good anti-government raves, but they suffer from an ideology of rugged individualism and naive confidence in the market that these silly folks usually express.

How to Steal Food from the Supermarket is all nuts and bolts (did you know most supermarket security cameras are fake?) so the publisher must assume the high price for such a small book will be made up by the saving realized by employing the techniques described. Shoplifting always seems real keen until the protective arm of the commodity appears.

World–Wide Crisis
Is the Recovery Really Here?
Summer, 1983

When an economic system produces 32 million unemployed in the industrialized nations, it would almost seem unnecessary to inveigh against its profound inadequacies. But several factors make it worthwhile to look at the present state of disarray in which world capitalism is currently mired.

Although some wag (either a queen, Marx or the Bible) once said that the poor have always been with us, most people know by now that this is a culture-bound observation and no more than a justification for the privilege of society's wealthy. However, the saying is nonetheless true for the modern world.

Since the advent of industrial capitalism 200 years ago, indeed, the poor and unemployed have been with us as permanent institutions, something realized under no previous social system. Capitalism has never worked in the sense that the majority of people under its rule have experienced a stable, happy and prosperous existence. Rather, its history is one of travail—cruel work when available, unforeseen economic collapses, each taking an immense human toll, wars, famine, psychological misery, and on into the modern epoch where its historic calamities are joined by the menace of ecological collapse and planet-wide nuclear holocaust.

Capitalism has maintained its life by force, its midwife at birth, but equally by habit—the substitution of its pervasive culture for the other modes of living it has smashed or ruined. Today, whatever the condition of its economy, it stands at the apex of its rule in a cultural sense by presiding over the tyranny of the fact.

Capitalism has evolved to a state in which its material and cultural structures appear to dominate the entire spectrum of possibilities. no matter how badly it functions, nothing else seems possible. Capital's traditional opposition, the workers' movement, went into eclipse some 40 years ago, and nothing, save small pockets of resistance, now exists to challenge its rule.

After four years of world-wide recession marked by high unemployment, runaway inflation, and staggering national debts, the capitalist nations have used the occasion of a slight upturn in the downward cycle to announce that a recovery is upon us. The media pundits have responded accordingly and cite dropping inflation, and a slight rise in the Gross National Product (GNP), real income, housing starts, etc. believing that the problem is in large part psychological or attitudinal—that is, if everyone believes there is a recovery, there will be one.

Well, bad news for everybody. The problems are world-wide and deeply systemic and the good news approach on one hand coupled with harsh austerity programs from the likes of Thatcher and Reagan on the other, do no more than shift the burden that much heavier on to the working class and the poor.

Certainly, inflation drops with tens of millions unemployed, but what we are looking at is a picture of permanent crisis for capitalism. Crisis is nothing new for capitalism which has been on a constant cycle of boom and bust since its inception, but by the late 1890s, the crises had begun to occur with such frequency and such severity that even the capitalists feared a complete collapse was at hand. The development of colonies and foreign markets staved off what seemed to be the inevitable at the turn of the century, but it was World War I and its aftermath which created the cycle that defines international capitalism in the modern epoch—that of crisis, war, reconstruction and crisis again.

After the prosperity of the 1920s, the cycle was realized again in the Great Depression (which actually was not as severe as those during the 1890s) followed by World War II. The resultant period of reconstruction in the 1950s and '60s produced the vibrant economies of that era, but now the chips of a system which constantly overproduces are being called in again with the economy suffering what in other periods has been a pre-war crisis. However, the nature of modern war makes the prospect of reconstruction after a nuclear exchange inviting only to madmen (which is not to say it is an impossibility) and perhaps ushering in an era of small conflicts.

Even the so-called eras of prosperity are an illusion unless you happen to be of the right color in the right country in the right region at the right time, for capitalism has never been able to support all under its dominion in fine style at the same time. Capitalism is a system whose success is judged by its ledger sheets and not by the human happiness or the lack of it which it engenders.

Capitalism always immiserates physically and financially one section of its population—either by class within a given country, within a region within a given country, or by country within the world's nation states. The most easily understood examples of such relationships are those of Third World countries to the industrial nations or the relative shift of affluence within this country from the industrial Northeast to the South and Southwest in recent years. The vagaries of capital, sort of a karmic wheel of misfortune, have come to be taken as normal as those of the weather, so a recession or a shift in area of prosperity is accepted much like a severe storm— not pleasant, but nothing much you can do about it either.

Is there a recovery? Of sorts, but not one which will extend to those hardest hit by the latest downward cycle. In many ways, the much-vaunted trickle-down theory of capitalist economics did function previously in such a way that the enormous wealth of the rulers would provide the working class of the Western sector of capital with a relatively high standard of living. That may no longer be possible, with wealth trickling down considerably less as value escapes to different regions of the world leaving a vast and permanent underclass in the West with a marginal status formerly associated with minorities and the lowest rung of the poor. Most economic forecasters see the current upturn in the U.S. (one which is the weakest following a recession since World War II) as mainly affecting investors, middle-income people with secure jobs, financial service industries, retail and wholesale merchants, and naturally, the major corporations.

The reason so many will be excluded from the New Recovery is that the old, so-called smokestack industries which formed the backbone of industrial America—auto, steel, rubber, glass—are a dead-letter compared to the levels of previous production and employment. A look at the industrial cities of Ohio, Pennsylvania, West Virginia, and Michigan gives an insight into the hopelessness of the situation for industrial workers.

In Detroit, the only booming industry is crime, up dramatically as the reality of poverty hits so many formerly waged workers. The city admits to 21 percent unemployment, but that represents only those registered on the state roles and ignores what is designated as discouraged workers (those whose benefits have run out) as well as the tens of thousands of youth who reach working age never to see a job and hence, are uncounted. This is a full-scale depression in Detroit where a third of the city's population is on welfare or food stamps, and seven-day-a-week food kitchens are needed to keep people from starving on the streets.

These statistics are echoed nation-wide with minorities and the already poor taking the brunt of both the down-turn and now having their meager existence being threatened or ended by government cutbacks in social services.

Since the 1930s, capitalism has sought to shore itself up by a massive and in some countries, a generalized statification of capital (the New Deal in the U.S., Stalinism in the Soviet Union, fascism in Germany, etc.). The theories of Keynesian economics adopted by the Roosevelt administration and practiced as government "pump-priming" measures for civilian programs proved to be a failure with only the advent of World War II and its massive arms production being what finally ended the Depression.

The realization came to the capitalists that a peacetime economy was no longer possible. Only war and its preparation would ensure a functioning and profitable system. Even Lord Keynes, whose theories formed the basis of the New Deal, recognized the necessity of this when he stated in 1940: "It seems politically impossible for a capitalistic democracy to organize expenditures on the scale necessary to make the grand experiment which would prove my case—except in war conditions."

And these "conditions" are the heart of advanced capitalism—production of war materiel with the creation of the Soviet Union as our perpetual enemy as its justification after the Nazis were defeated. When leftists and liberals call for "Jobs, Not War!," in their usual dim manner they fail to realize that under modern capitalism, jobs are war. Besides the fact that the call for the creation of wage work is capital's program, these pitiful reformers also ignore that of the new jobs created there will be a disproportionately high number in the defense sector, the private sector already glutted with overinvestment. Also, the danger always exists that a working class whose existence depends upon state financed military projects will become the most vocal proponents of war preparations.

The argument that liberal economist Seymour Milman and other peace advocates have put forth over the last two decades that defense production is actually dysfunctional for capitalism, being capital- rather than labor-intensive, hence, employing substantially less workers than civilian production, and generates less profit in the form of surplus value is irrelevant. The economy is geared for war and well-motivated schemes for conversion to production for peace have less chance now for realization than when they were first put forth twenty years ago.

The U.S. empire and its vassal states demand constant protecting from rival empires and from internal revolts, with armaments needed constantly to repress both. But even if the U.S. could make peace with its competitors and stop sponsoring the repression of peasants and workers around the world, the conversion to an economy which would meet domestic needs of the U.S. only holds positive prospects in the short run for a system which needs a constant influx of profits. Production for domestic consumer consumption—a rise in the standard of living for everyone—has always run into the roadblock of overproduction for capitalism. A situation of permanent warfare—a garrison state—is the only model which appears to offer the promise of continuing profits for capital.

Ever since the emergence of the political state thousands of years ago, its rationale has been the mobilization of mass projects beyond the scope of cooperating neighbors—immense irrigation systems, temple building, and war as an institution and on a vastly expanded scale. Today, the state plays no different a role, but now its central project of preparation for war has taken on a transcendent quality increasing its capacity for destruction to entire rival states or to the planet itself.

Today, no serious challenge to what threatens our humanity and our lives can be launched without a confrontation with the state. Schemes of the reformers who still hold out hope for persuading politicians or sections of the ruling circles to choose a more sensible or humane course, fail to understand what historical and economic forces are at work.

We must evoke in ourselves and in others a rejection of the categories of capital. There must be a conscious desire to no longer live as objects of capital—as workers or as wards of the state—but to become free human beings trying to create a new society.

I'm Sticking with the Union?
The Battle of Detroit
Spring, 1996

"Hey! What are you guys doing here? You hate unions!"
A strike supporter

The labor militant who aimed this question at us was surprised, almost shocked, to see a group whom she considers anarchists critical of unions, shoulder-to-shoulder with striking Teamsters and newspaper reporters, squaring off against the cops at a suburban Detroit printing plant late one-night last summer.

Actually, we don't "hate" unions at all, certainly not in the manner of the companies which operate the *Detroit News* and the *Detroit Free Press,* corporate rags that have been trying to smash their labor organizations since the Great Detroit Newspaper Strike began last July 13. What our friend sees as "hate" has been our effort over the last twenty years to create a radical understanding, free of leftist mystique, of the role unions have historically played within the political economy of capital.

[Full disclosure: I've been a member of American Federation of Television and Radio Artists/AFL-CIO for all of my professional career and currently receive retirement benefits from the union's pension fund.]

But the question she asked us is an important one, and in many ways expresses the contradictions and ambivalence we often feel when we transfer our theories to daily life experiences. If unions are nothing more than the institutional way capital purchases labor, why were we out there on Mound Road facing off 250 cops from 20 different suburban forces that balmy September night?

The cops were suiting up with shields, helmets, three-foot riot staves, and gas masks. Our main defenses were bandannas over our faces to ward off the pepper spray and some flimsy sticks from our picket signs. The cops were preparing to force approximately 750 strikers and supporters away from a blockade of the printing plant gate which company trucks had to pass through to distribute the Sunday paper produced with scab and replacement workers.

Initially, we had no reason to think this would be little other than a ritual strike, followed by negotiations and a return to work. Many of us were drawn to the side of the strikers by their refusal to knuckle under to the humiliation the company intended for them, and by our friendship with several members of the Newspaper Guild, the association of reporters.

The unions had made enormous concessions in previous contracts and the workers hadn't had a raise in six years. Although the papers made a handsome profit in 1994, they forced the strike at a point when the unions were neither anxious nor prepared for a strike. Besides the reporters, five other locals of Teamsters, Pressmen, and Lithographers walked out.

Unlike past work stoppages, the papers decided to print a joint issue during the strike and immediately hired several thousand replacement workers recruited from around the country. They also brought in a heavily armed 1,200-man corporate militia from the Vance Corporation, whose specialty is strike breaking and picket line violence. It soon became abundantly clear the intent of the management was not the negotiation of a new contract, but the elimination of its unions.

The unions were determined to stop the circulation of the paper by calling for a subscription boycott, to which up to 300,000 people responded, and to stop the papers from leaving the main printing plant or local distribution centers. Confrontations at the News' Sterling Heights, Mich. printing plant and distribution centers were extremely intense in August through October, with often up to 1,000 workers battling the cops, sometimes resulting in victories for the strikers. Even in the face of numerous arrests and vicious police attacks, the picket lines often held until late hours of the night, forcing company trucks to leave the plant 12 hours behind schedule.

After years of being pushed around at demonstrations, to watch 40 cops in full riot gear charge a blockade of determined pickets and be repulsed after a brief, but furious battle, was extremely heartening. That night, the police knew they needed a 200-man reinforcement to do the job since the strikers were not prepared to give an inch.

As soon as the strike began, it quickly took on a quality no one had expected, least of all the major belligerents. The papers expected resistance but nothing like what they encountered. Numerous local and international unions offered support in what soon became a city-wide effort unseen since the heyday of Detroit unionism in the 1930s. By December, the strikers were publishing a 325,000 circulation Sunday paper of their own. Solidarity and aid was sent from locals across the country. The feeling in the labor movement is that if unions can be defeated in Detroit, they can be defeated anywhere.

Although the union bureaucrats have a tight lock on overall strategy, rank-and-file self-organization has been an exceptional feature of the strike, particularly in highly coordinated late-night attacks against newspaper distribution centers where tens of thousands of dollars in damages were inflicted by trashing offices and dozens of cars belonging to scabs and the company.

Also, an incredible camaraderie has developed among middle-class reporters who remain on strike (50 percent have returned to work) and the more working-class, industrial staff (very few who have crossed the picket line). Benefits, parties, fund-raisers and other gatherings have become the sites of not only friendship and solidarity, but also of an increasingly radicalized view of the world of corporations, workers and cops.

The downside of the strike has been the increasing toll, financial and psychological, exacted from the strikers and their families as the dispute rolls through its seventh month. Time is on the side of management. More and more reporters have left town for other jobs, and the industrial workers face the necessity of finding other work as well.

Radicals have always faced the question of whether it is possible to struggle within capital without actually affirming and extending by going no further than demanding piecemeal reforms? In the case of unions, John and Paula Zerzan pointed out in these pages two decades ago that rather than a triumph of some sort, the establishment of the first labor organizations marked a crushing defeat for humanity. Unions arose only after the early 19th century machine-breaking Luddite movement had been subdued by the English army and legal system.

When the representatives of early workers' organizations accepted the duality of labor and capital, and formally agreed to bargain over the selling price of the commodity of human labor, they acquiesced in enshrining capital as a permanent and dominant institution.

From the first, unions became junior partners in the racket of capital, accepting the new economic system's definitions and rules as their own. This was, and is, particularly true in the area of labor discipline where unions act as the first line of defense against independent or radical thrusts within the working class.

When radical labor formations, like the IWW, violated the standards for conduct, they were quickly snuffed out by a combination of government repression and vigilante action, usually without a word of protest from the official labor movement (or, as in the case of the McCarthy era, with direct participation from the union bosses). Radical historians note that any militant labor struggle which went beyond the capital/labor compact found itself not only being confronted by the state and management, but the union hierarchy as well.[1]

But even conservative unions had to provide something tangible for their members or they would have been immediately discarded. Their major function has been to raise the average selling price of labor artificially—meaning if the price of labor were left to fall to its "fair market value," U.S. and European wage workers would be looking at pay scales similar to those of Mexico or Sri Lanka.

Capitalism is the only economic system humans have created in which a good crop is a curse. If you have an abundant harvest of potatoes, the price falls. The same is true with the sale of human labor. If there is a lot of it, and there is, the price plummets in a manner no different than if it were rutabagas for sale.

Within a strict, radical critique of capital, the struggle over hours, working conditions and wages is viewed as simply which sector of the system gains what portion of the wealth produced. But to those functioning within capitalism as wage workers (most of us), these questions often determine the misery quotient of our lives.

The current round of attacks on unions is part of a world-wide effort by capital to enforce austerity measures which began with workers and the poor, but has now extended to the middle-class as well. Seeing little resistance, corporations are emboldened to increase the rate of work and reduce the rate of pay, all of which means more profits for their stockholders.

Also, the tasks unions once fulfilled for capital have ceased to be as important in an era when revolutionary resistance to capital as a system has diminished to almost nothing. Now, work itself is the disciplinarian, and the globalization of capital has meant a similar process for labor, so increasingly the U.S. labor market is in direct competition with that of Sri Lanka or Mexico.

Struggles for better wages, hours and working conditions historically did extend and affirm capital to the point where most workers and their labor organizations became zealous defenders of the system which had offered them a handsome price for their labor. However, employers often resist even modest reforms until there has been a recognition on their part that their ability to rule in traditional ways is being threatened.

During the 1930s, police, the National Guard, private security forces and vigilantes killed 300 workers involved in union organizing and recognition battles. But capital works by the carrot as well as the stick.

By the Depression era, the progressive sector of the ruling class, led by President Franklin Roosevelt, was acknowledging the need to contain the increasing revolutionary tendencies among labor as seen in the Minneapolis, San Francisco, and Toledo general strikes. A 1935 National Recovery Administration report stated, "Unless something is done soon, they (the workers) intend to take things into their own hands." The "something" was unions. Labor organizing was quickly sanctioned by law and unions were established throughout the country by the end of the decade.

Despite the best intentions of rank-and-file militants, this period, with its admirable sit-down strikes, romanticized by the left as a Golden Age of labor militancy, was, in fact, a period of recuperation. The decade began with general strikes, but ended with workers marching dutifully off to the second inter-imperialist world war. Although fascism was an authentic threat, workers' interests in every country were submerged beneath those of the ruling class. While workers were sent off to die, world Capitalism emerged from the financial doldrums of the '30s significantly strengthened through the creation of enormous, permanent war economies. On the home front, this process was assisted by cooperative trade union discipline which enforced No Strike pledges on their workers during the war.[2]

Leftists term union activity as class struggle. They assert inter-class conflict is not only how the proletariat combats being looted by capitalists of the wealth workers create, but is also a central feature of revolutionary activity. Marxists view class struggle in a tight little schema as the motor force of humanity's historical stage driving toward the emergence of communism.

However, Jean Baudrillard, in *The Mirror of Production*, stood the Marxist theorem on its head, postulating that rather than the process of revolution being advanced by class struggle, capitalism innovates its forms of domination and rationalizes newer modes of production through class conflict. Activity in which working class battles are fought on capital's terrain for wages, etc., stays within the political economy of the system it opposes.

Jacques Camatte characterized class struggle as "gangs within capital" fighting over pieces of a fragmented world rather than leaving the one capital has created.[3]

To be sure, class struggle has led to a more equitable distribution of capitalist wealth than if the process had been left to the tender mercies of the ruling classes who intended to share almost nothing.

The revolutionary project with which we identify does not strive to share the loot industrial capital produces. Rather, it seeks to eliminate swag, created by the destruction of humans and nature, as the basis of societies. Radical desire does not want a fairer share of capitalist wealth to go to labor. It wants to leave all of this system and establish a new world, not reform the current one.

The socialist project, on the other hand, has no intention of eliminating, what P.M. calls in his book, *Bolo'bolo,* the "Planetary Work Machine," which necessitates labor as life's central feature and the maintenance of an immense, centrally administered, world-wide production/distribution grid regardless of what "class is in power."

But this all said, how do we respond to attacks from capitalism's greedy, rapacious elite? A war in the Persian Gulf, an incinerator in our neighborhood, the cutting of an old growth forest, or assaults on our standard of living demand a response. Such struggles may be reformist, but is the only option to wait for the final revolutionary conflagration?

Beyond a critical analysis of what constitutes revolutionary activity or reform, there rises in the human consciousness a sense of anger and refusal that in normal times is suppressed beneath the exterior of the model citizen. Often an individual or a group reaches the point where they refuse to be pushed around any longer, or sit idly by while humans or the wild world are being exterminated.

For many of the Detroit newspaper strikers, their fight against the corporations fits most readily into this category. The reporters who realized they had nothing financially to gain from the strike have gone back to work. The remainder are participating in a self-created culture of resistance where many readily admit they like life on strike better than life at work.

You hear repeated comments about how the strike is the most important thing that's ever happened to them, how it's transformed them, how "life is now an adventure," (almost echoing the situationist slogan). and how bad daily life at work was prior to the strike. This from middle-class professionals who, for the most part, had never been on a picket line before last July and who conceived of themselves as lone actors within a profession.

The industrial newspaper workers had long considered

themselves middle-class, often politically conservative, patriotic, suburban Americans, but now many express the same sentiments one hears from the reporters.

Since the strike, men and women, young, middle-aged, and elderly, have fought battles with the cops, tracked down and harassed scabs, replacement workers and management, participated in endless all-night vigils and blockades to stop distribution of the papers, and developed a network of friends and comrades any social movement could envy.

The problem is that the strikers have nowhere to go except back to work. The union chiefs still echo the refrain, "All we want to do is go back to work and produce a quality paper," but this is ringing hollower as time progresses.

I wonder how many strikers would now agree that the papers they produced were a "quality product." To us, they were always 60 percent ads and 40 percent lies. Like all corporate media, they usually are on the wrong side of every social question, support every war, lie about every protest movement, and apologize for every monstrous act this system commits.

The union chiefs are depending on subscription and ad boycotts and their alternate paper to break the corporate will. The company owners have already taken a $200 million loss, so it's an open question as to how much more money they are willing to lose in order to defeat the strikers.

The AFL-CIO, Teamster, and Newspaper Union bureaucrats are horrified at agitation among some rank-and-file and middle-level union officials for a one-day general strike, a national labor mobilization in Detroit, breaking a court injunction by mass picketing at the newspaper's central printing plant, and roving pickets to block distribution.

The union chiefs cut the ground out from under these proposals in mid-January by issuing a statement that they "emphatically disavow any and all physical violence, property destruction, criminal activity and physical blocking of ingress and egress." This declaration, which sounds as if it was issued from the company newspaper front office, makes the type of activity that galvanized initial widespread support more difficult.

Nevertheless, I think this is an important strike to win and that some resources of the radical community should be mobilized in its support. I say "some" since it is equally, and perhaps more important, that our small, tenuous, anti-authoritarian, projects be maintained and extended.

As I write in early February amidst bone-chilling winter cold, the resolve of the strikers seems unshakable. Their goal appears to be less and less concerned with the formal demands of the strike and more with not being defeated by the corporations.

Maybe we should, as *Extraphile* magazine suggests, cheer the collapse of unions as a way of clearing the decks for more radical forms to emerge. To me, that only sounds good on paper. Is fighting battles "on capital's terrain" always a retreat, an acquiescence to the call of asking the rulers to "not kill everything so fast?" Here's where the ambivalence lies. Given the current meagerness of radical alternatives to capital and the deepening levels of misery, almost any resistance to the ruling order these days is encouraging. If we don't start here, where is the place?

That September night in Sterling Heights, Mich. ended differently than one would have anticipated. The 250 cops were just about to charge when, like in the old labor song which goes, "Hold the fort for we are coming," an additional 2,000 unionists and supporters came marching down Mound Road to make our blockade impenetrable. The cops were ordered to take off their riot gear and surrender the field to the strikers.

At that point, a tremendous cheer of joy and celebration rose from the crowd. I'm glad I was there.

Notes:

1. It should be noted that in numerous countries, union activity refused the rules of capitalist activity and entered into a contestation based on the revolutionary dispossession of the bourgeoisie. The repression of the IWW in this country or the revolution by the anarcho-syndicalist CNT in Spain (1936-1939 are examples of ruling class reaction to such

effrontery.

2. Judith Allen, writing in Internationalism, #3 in 1975, said, "Among the tasks the CIO [the national union federation] undertook was to help the capitalists introduce speedups and other types of 'rationalization' into the process of production (increasing the rate of exploitation of the workers), to help introduce compulsory overtime (extension of the working day), and to facilitate the laying off of masses of workers. But the real nature of this so-called 'victory' is nowhere better seen than in the millions of dead and wounded workers whom the unions helped to mobilize for the second imperialist world war."

However, workers at home often resisted the sacrifices demanded of them on the job. See *Wartime Strikes* by Marty Glaberman.

3. Camatte's most serious indictment of the reactionary nature of the concept of class struggle comes in his observation that its main function in the 20th century has been to install the capitalist mode of production in areas of the world where Marx and Engels never dreamed it would exist, i.e., China, North Korea, etc.

"The feudal system, which preceded capitalism, had imbedded in its class structure a series of mutual obligations for ruled and rulers. By the time that system of lords and peasants became moribund, those requirements for the wealthy had all but become ignored. When a radical merchant class emerged during the bourgeois revolutions of the 17th, 18th and 19th centuries, the gulf between rich and poor, rulers and ruled was enormous. In their triumphal form at the dawn of an era, the new capitalists planned to keep it that way."

Suggested Reading:

Unions Against Revolution, Grandizio Munis, Black and Red (No longer in print, but available online)

Strike! 50th anniversary edition, Jeremy Brecher, South End Press 2020

Coffee Keeps Us Rolling
Into Work and Disease
Spring, 1981

"Pour myself a cup of ambition."
Dolly Parton, "9 to 5"

And, we pour cup after cup of coffee to the tune of almost 16 pounds per person a year for the 100 million coffee drinkers over the age of 18. This works out to a staggering consumption rate of 800 cups annually and that's only-the average. The *Statistical Abstract of the U.S.* shows that 40 percent of us (I'm drinking a cup while writing this) drink two to five cups a day while 11 percent get really whacked out on six or more per day.

Coffee is pervasive to the point where it seems available almost everywhere and many people cannot imagine rising in the morning without a cup or ending a meal minus the stuff. Many restaurants pour you a cup upon your arrival and when you finish your meal, the waitress universally inquires, "Coffee?"

Coffee cultivation goes back thousands of years and has often been associated by the ruling authorities with vice. It was banned, for instance, in Mecca during the 15th Century on religious grounds, and European coffee houses have always had a slightly unsavory reputation beginning with their establishment in the 17th Century.

To most of us, though, coffee has lost any of its exotic qualities associated with its origins and is just a-delicious, warming drink which possesses the added benefit of a slight (or not so slight dependent upon consumption level) "pick-me-up" feeling.

It enables us to get going when we feel we can't or keep going when we know we have to. It is this latter function that deserves discussion along with the physical conditions produced among coffee drinkers.

As children most of us were fascinated by the work-a-day world of our parents and thought it very exciting to watch our fathers go off to the factories or offices and couldn't wait until we were old enough to do the same. Although work presented itself with generally positive images, there were several laboring situations that appeared as quite unappealing such as slavery or prison labor.

There was one special image, though, that always made me wince; that of Bolivian Indians trudging through the thin atmosphere of the Andes mountains beneath the huge packs on their backs. The only way they could continue in this arduous toil, we were told, was through the constant chewing of coca leaves which provided the stimulation necessary for their task's completion.

The question even then arose in me, "What taskmaster could be so cruel as to force human beings into labor that required constant drugging?"

By now the analogy must be obvious, though I suspect it may appear as either silly or unimportant or both. But how important is our daily dosing of ourselves with the drug caffeine, and what is its social function and its medical effects?

Let's ignore for now the complex economics of coffee cultivation which amounts to millions of tons harvested annually in 3rd World countries and its appearance on the world market as a major trading commodity (a story in itself) and instead concentrate on what it does when it is consumed. Some of coffee's most deleterious effects are well known to most of us, particularly as it relates to insomnia, nervousness and, most importantly, to heart ailments. The latter problem has been directly linked to heavy coffee consumption, but much of what else coffee produces in us is unknown to the majority of its users.

The caffeine in coffee is legitimately considered a narcotic, being a member of the same alkaloid chemical group as morphine, nicotine, cocaine, and strychnine—all having addictive properties. Daily use creates a tolerance to its effects and our glands gradually come to lose their ability to act naturally. We literally need caffeine's stimulation to awaken fully or to eliminate (in the latter case it is caffeine that stimulates glandular secretion which in turn signals the bowels—without coffee, constipation sets in).

Coffee consumption can reduce Vitamin B1 levels in the body by as much as 50 percent and seriously cut into Vitamin C and thiamin retention. Coffee can unsuspectingly be the cause of a plethora of mild aches and pains, upset stomachs, rapid heartbeats, increased breathing rates, blood pressure and body temperatures as well as create nervousness, irritability, and other personality distortions, particularly in heavy users. Ignoring coffee as a potential culprit in the above ailments, most of us see them as part of the human condition which are to be endured along with the rest of life's problems.

Isn't everyone constipated, afflicted by headaches, stomach aches, tension, and insomnia, etc.? Just look at the ads for their remedies on TV.

Coffee also produces long range and insidious consequences such as the link of caffeine to cancer. Caffeine has been tied to bladder cancer because of its potential as a carcinogen since over-roasting of the bean produces a dangerous nitrosamine. Also, no country which grows coffee enforces any regulation on the type or amount of chemical pesticide that can be used on the coffee fields.

In fact, large U.$. chemical corporations which have had their products banned from use in domestic agriculture, ship surplus stocks of lethal pesticides to coffee-growing nations where it is used without restriction. Caffeine has also been indicated as responsible for miscarriages and problem pregnancies in women who are heavy coffee drinkers.

Hey, how about decaffeinated coffee? Sorry, but that might even turn out to be worse than what it replaces since it contains the chemical trichloroethylene, a solution used mainly as a degreasing agent in the metal industry and as a solvent and dry-cleaning agent in the clothing industry. It is a close chemical relative of vinyl chloride and is used to extract the caffeine from coffee. Its carcinogenic properties are highly suspected as a cause of liver cancer.

> "I like to sleep to ten each morning
> But it makes my boss so annoyed.
> Thanks to the good taste of Maxwell House,
> For getting me going, and keeping me employed."
> 1950s Coffee ad jingle

What does coffee do for us that makes its use so widespread despite its obvious negative features? It does taste good, and most of us would agree that a nice hot beverage is a pleasant way to finish a large meal. Still, the larger function of coffee consumption is not in its taste, but in its ability to relieve drowsiness, mask fatigue, and to create a general sense of well-being. The question then arises, apropos of the Bolivian Indians, what is the nature of our social and work life which requires these qualities to be induced rather than occurring as a result of joyful, creative labor and a society in tune with nature?

Obviously, neither of these states exist under modern capitalism and coffee is simply a chemical agent which becomes part of the process by which the animal is kicked out of us each day to be replaced by a modern citizen in tune with the rhythms of production rather than one's own body. Most of us accept the humiliation which comes with the ringing alarm clock each morning as if it was as natural as the sun rising, and although we may be tired and our bodies react negatively to being awakened on a schedule, the first cup of coffee quickly ends the body's revolt against being awakened when sleep is still desired.

At work, the monotonous routine of machines or the shuffle of paper for projects we have no interest in other than the weekly paycheck, bring an almost somnolence that often can only be relieved by a quick jolt of caffeine. One secretary told me, "I swear every morning that I'm not going to drink any coffee, but by mid-morning I'm afraid I'm going to fall asleep right in my chair while I'm typing; so, it's off to the coffee pot."

Coffee, in fact, is the one item universally available free in most workplaces and nothing can produce a crisis faster than running out of it. "I think capitalism would collapse if coffee disappeared. There's no way I could do my job without it," the same secretary said, "and I'm sure it's the same at most jobs."

Maybe it would collapse, who knows? In this epoch, humans spend more time at labor than in any other era previously and it seems clear from both biological and anthropological evidence that the body and its capacity for activity is geared both to certain periods of the day and to the seasons. In Paleolithic societies, only a few hours a day in most cultures were necessary for food collection and hunting, while much of the afternoons was spent sleeping or lolling about. Even agricultural society, with its labor-intensive nature, allowed whole seasons off from toil in the fields and most provided for long afternoon siestas and the like.

The collapse we begin to feel on our modern jobs is not some problem, but rather a natural reaction our bodies experience. It's hard to say what to do in this situation. It's not like television where one can simply shut the set off. Many of us are forced to work at the rhythms established by capital, so coffee addiction becomes part of our survival ability. We can't work without it and wage work is the only way we can survive at this moment.

None of us can live truly healthy or balanced lives in a society that poisons us at every level of our existence and makes social harmony impossible. Still, don't we have an obligation, as people committed to changing that state of affairs, not to be personalities dominated by addictions? The commodities of intellectual and physical illness—TV, junk food, cigarettes, alcohol, and coffee—are part of the larger mechanisms of control which keep all of us shouldering the pack up the Andes without complaint.

We have a responsibility to both our ideals and to ourselves to be as strong and healthy as possible. The dichotomy of health and strength versus illness and weakness is by no means always a determining factor, but it can either be part of the matrix of submission or part of your desire to be free.

Marxism:
Obscuring More Than It Reveals
Criticism & Critique of a Failed System
Spring 2015

"In my view, anarchism has no significant contribution to socialist theory to make."
    Eric Hobsbawm, "Reflections on Anarchism," 1969

Hobsbawm, the late British Marxist historian, in his snobbery, unintentionally poses the question as to the function of theory of any sort in revolutionary challenges to the present system. Marxists believe it is important to come to the confrontation armed with memorized critiques of capitalism and history, believing this provides them with the organizational and critical tools for overthrowing the system.

The late David Graeber, an American anarchist, in his 2003 article, "The Twilight of Vanguardism," asks in a different context, "… [I]f the role of revolutionary intellectuals is not to form an elite that can arrive at the correct strategic analyses and then lead the masses to follow, what precisely is it?" But, it's exactly that. Marxists make no disagreement that it is its purpose and utility.

The beauty and power of the voluminous anarchist writings through the years resides in their vision of a new world lived in circumstances when capitalism and state have been discarded. When a moment of revolution arrived historically, it wasn't because people in revolt had finally read enough analysis of their misery, but that they could no longer tolerate it.

The vision, for instance, posed by anarchism leading up to the late 1930s Spanish Revolution, came from a desire for freedom that had been nurtured for decades by writings and agitation. As the anarchists said at the time, they had "a new world in their hearts." They called this the quest for The Ideal in human affairs.

Marxists denounced this as romanticism; utopian, and destroyed the revolution, not only in Spain, but in Russia before it. With all of their analysis, the main contribution of Marxism has been the gulag; for anarchists it has been revolution.

A tiny sliver of revolutionary theorists contend that Marxism can be divorced from the authoritarian utilization of its theories and become part of a larger theory of liberation. On closer examination, however, this turns out to be impossible since Marxism only has its "world historical moment" when linked with the political forces of Leninism.

The most significant Marxist theorists, ones who brought the ideology into reality on a mass scale, are Stalin and Mao, who not only ruled in the name of Marx, but expounded on it as well. In other words, the hopes of radical intellectuals aside, Marxism only comes to power through the apparatus of the authoritarian political party with everything that implies.

The so-called libertarian variant of Marxism mostly remains confined to the university and exists with no efficacy in the real world. No one is interested in it except other intellectuals and ultimately, it, along with all of critical theory, becomes only the most interesting sector of sociology.

No longer "a spectre haunting Europe" or anywhere else, for that matter, defanged Marxist theory has become a huge intellectual market and growth industry within academia. Written in texts often so arcane that they can only be decoded by initiates, such that Marxism is no longer reviled except by the rabid right. Those who profess this ideology (literally, professors) are elevated to positions, for example, within the American Sociological Association as "Chair of the Section on Marxist Sociology," or prestigious teaching positions at universities.

The editors of the New York-based *Monthly Review*, which wept at Stalin's passing in 1953, are now trying to sell us the same old Marxist ideology they have peddled all these years as a supposedly ecologically purified version. However, it's like they can't help themselves. The cover of their 2014 catalog features a photo of Lenin. In an attempt to prove it has left its moribund past, the magazine features recent articles by its editor with titles such as, "Marx and the Rift in the Universal Metabolism of Nature." Undoubtedly, it will receive rave reviews from the Section on Marxist Sociology.

In their defense, these professors of Marxism often have a radicalizing effect on students, many of whom are and have been active on their campuses and beyond. However, to accept the basic tenets of this outmoded system of critique and analysis will lead them to the same ideological dead end as their mentors.

Another sector of the political spectrum advocating Marxism are the creepy, authoritarian Leninist cults with their alphabet soup acronyms featuring memberships so small they could probably have national conventions at a McDonald's and whose membership turns over faster than the restaurant's fast-food workers.

This essay examines how Marx and his epigones view humans, their function within capitalism, and how they reproduce the world which we inhabit.

Few would dispute the contention of Marx that the reigning ideas of a given society are those of the ruling class during any epoch. What has to be faced squarely, however, is not just that the Marxist concept of humans fails to transcend those of the ruling capitalist class, but that Marx's views and those of even his present-day advocates mesh exactly with those of the capitalist model.

To Marx and his followers, human beings are essentially producers and have never been anything else. The late anti-authoritarian Marxist, Seymour Faber, wrote in *Our Generation*, "One of the assumptions underlying Karl Marx's discussion of alienation was that production was not only a means of satisfying needs outside itself, but that which made man human."

The only reason this view appears to make sense is that it is the world-view of the prevailing capitalist society and when it is repeated by Marx, it sounds just as reasonable. Instead, if this productivist model of society is viewed within its historical context, it comes through clearly as the definition needed centuries ago by the ascendant bourgeoisie to marshal the entire world out of the lethargy of feudal society and into the torrent of industrialization, commodity production, and the accumulation of capital.

This self-perception of humans as a special category of producers was unknown in human history until the capitalist epoch. Marxism makes no break with this. Marx not only relishes the productivist model, he is its strongest advocate. Whatever develops the means of production is good, for the higher the degree of development of capitalism, the greater its contradictions, the more developed the proletariat, and the greater the material base for communism (or, so the theory goes). He is a prophet of production extolling its virtues and denigrating its detractors.

When the Luddites in England, workers at the dawn of capitalism, began an assault on the production system by breaking machines, burning factories, and assassinating their owners, understanding that they were being drawn into a system that would wreck their lives and livelihoods, Marx declared that it was the bourgeoisie who were the revolutionaries in this era, not the workers. It is no wonder then that the most enthusiastic exponents of Marxism were found in the state capitalist bureaucracies of the communist countries where they functioned as the ascendant bourgeoisie.

As a vision of the future, Marxism offers only more of what capitalism has already presented us with–a continuation of the development of the means of production. No matter that the entire productive apparatus remains an externality to the humans involved, it is assumed that the quantitative development of the means of production will lead to a revolution of social relations.

This is nonsense. Every material aspect of our lives is a thing of capital, a thing that was created only for the needs of capital and never for those of humans. Our jobs, workplaces, commodities, cities, transportation, schools, dwellings; all of it developed with humans fitting in as an afterthought if considered at all. The only thing Marxism advocates is to remove the capitalist class from this process.

But exactly what is missed here is that the means of production are capital themselves and their further development will only mean our further enslavement and capital's continued domination. The very nature of the technology of capital demands centralized political control and management, and only after its dismantling, when human affairs are based on decentralized, human-scale technology, can we begin to talk about a liberated future.

Those who envision a technocratic, self-managed future where automation and cybernation satisfy all of our desires, continue to push the productivist model for coordinated economic and political control where humans remain reduced to workers, an inherent category of alienation. But it's very possible that the people affected might not want to buy the program of the leftist politicians and planners. They may not want to continue massive auto or steel production even with a workers council in charge as management.

Marxists, with their fetish of production, shudder at such a possibility of the refusal of their hobby horse, but let's be through with them. If we are going to advocate anything, let it be a revolution of desire, one that really overturns everything and sweeps away the entirety of the muck of capitalism.

Marxism stands squarely as an ideology of capital; a rigid fetter on the mind that can only make us shrink from the real potential of a human existence.

Suggested reading:
Fifth Estate, Spring 2015 Special Antii-Marx Issue – fifthestate.org/archive/393-spring-2015

Isn't All Money Fake?
Winter, 1992

Review: *Counterfeit Currency: How To Really Make Money,*
M. Thomas Collins, Loompanics Unlimited, 1990

Money is a fairly curious substance. Its official function is to represent value, but once said, you can immediately challenge all the assumptions inherent in such a formulation: Value? Its representation? Since value itself is a representation of abstract worth, money operates within economies as a representation of a representation! No wonder its properties seem so inscrutable.

Unable to get a reasonable handle on what money is and how it functions gives rise to a host of whacky theories about it. For instance, to a whole section of the right-wing, money has a totemic quality somehow bound up with the basis of American liberties which began to unravel with the passage of the Federal Reserve Act in 1913.

Money, by its very nature, can only be successfully issued by a government, but once in circulation it seems to have a life of its own, uncontrolled by those who attempt administrative methods to affect its fluctuations. The money nuts say the latter problem stems from currency no longer being tied to a gold standard or other precious metal. This fails to realize that granting gold (in reality, only a pretty rock) a particular value is no less an arbitrary assignment of worth than what they ascribe to unbacked currency. In fact, the whole concept of value is itself an abstraction dependent upon human assignation.

In any event, we know those funny pieces of paper are what make the capitalist world go 'round and that their possession translates into political domination and social power. Wars are fought, people's lives made miserable, all for these scraps with pictures of dead politicians on them. We also know governments jealously guard their monopoly over the printing of money and few crimes are more assiduously pursued than counterfeiting.

The dreaded fear is that unauthorized printing of currency will erode the value of money and public confidence in it, concerns which are undoubtedly true. One startling assertion in *Counterfeit Currency* is that 20 percent of U.S. money is bogus, a dark secret kept from the population for the above reasons.

Collins' essay, though, is not a treatise on the perplexing qualities of money, but a how-to manual, a precise, step-by-step guide to producing and circulating counterfeit money. It's hard to imagine a great number of people will actually put the book's techniques into practice, but it is consistent with Loompanic's other wild manuals on the commission of illegal acts such as how to build your own atom bomb and a series on how to kill.

Loompanics' publisher, Michael Hoy, fashions himself an anarchist of sorts, more of a free market, individualist than is palatable to anti-capitalist, communal types, but it is clear from books like this and others in his catalog that he has little respect for government and polite society.

Is it radical for anarchists to print and circulate bad money? Is it destructive of the state or just an innovative way to partake in the circulation of commodities? Is eroding public confidence in the currency good? Does counterfeiting beat work or is it simply another job? Are the high risks worth the effort?

These are questions for the reader to ponder. The book is interesting as an unabashed manual of criminality and for its blatant nose thumbing at the law, but much of the text is devoted to the details of counterfeiting and probably of interest solely to those planning a career shift or desiring an income supplement.

Author Note: This review was printed as an Introduction in a subsequent edition of this book.

Chapter 11
On The Road

An Anarchist In Cuba
Socialism or Cell Phones
Summer, 2008

On February 2, I stepped off a plane that had left a frigid Toronto three and a half hours earlier and landed in the balmy sunshine of Holguin, Cuba. It was impossible to know then that I had arrived two weeks before the end of the island's Revolution as we know it.

On February 19, the Castro Monarchal Brotherhood passed the scepter of rule from Older Brother Fidel to Younger Brother Raul, initially signaling a continuity, not a rupture, of what had come before that date. From all reports, there was no commotion on the island about the change, no great objection, nor celebration. Things were expected to continue as they had.

The changes that signal an end to the Cuban Revolution (more below about what it actually consisted of), were, in fact, changes celebrated internationally as "reforms," "a loosening up," an "entry into the 21st century" — the announcement that a host of electronic toys (now thought to be almost necessities in most of the world) would be available on the island. Cell phones, DVDs, computers, and iPods can now be purchased and used. Other improvements (not exactly reforms, but badly needed) such as the purchase of a large number of Chinese buses to replace the crowded, uncomfortable ones that made travel such a problem for the average Cuban, were welcomed by all.

By virtue of being employed as a full-time journalist, a category protected by the U.S. First Amendment, I was able to travel legally to Cuba without violating the so-called Cuban Democracy Act, which among other things prohibits visits there by U.S. citizens.

This was my second trip, both times as part of an organized tour which has positive and negative aspects for one trying to make an assessment of the country being visited.

The tours were wonderfully organized and featured amazingly knowledgeable guides and translators. Most tourists, a large number of whom hail from Canada, are solely interested in beaching it in a warm climate and rarely leave their all-inclusive resorts where the only Cubans they come in contact with are in the service sector. The itineraries of the tours I traveled with were designed to acquaint us with the island's culture, history, and politics.

I was very aware of the history of the Soviet-American Friendship League tours of the 1930s, when U.S. communists were similarly brought to Stalin's USSR and came away declaring they had seen socialism being built. Being on a tour meant that we had little interaction with Cubans on the street although there was no attempt to restrict us from doing so. My Spanish is so pathetically weak that I doubt whether I would have been able to carry on much of a conversation about politics or the economy in any event. Also, I'm sure I could have found people who loved the Revolution as well as those who were waiting for its collapse.

Given many of the deprivations people experience and the repressive nature of the government, the dissatisfaction is understandable, but in a recent CBS poll taken in the U.S., 82 percent of those questioned said *this* country was on the wrong track. Cuba is a poor country whose economy has been terribly distorted by the U.S. embargo and probably from bureaucratic bungling as well, but still, it probably provides the best material conditions for the poor of any nation in the world, including the U.S.

For a police state, one doesn't see very many police or military as you travel about. However, less obvious to the visitor are the 135,000 Committees for the Defense of the Revolution, neighborhood organizations which are charged with monitoring their fellow citizens for "inappropriate behavior" including not only political offenses, but other forms of anti-social acts such as child or spousal abuse. The committees attempt to manage behavior at the community level by handing out warnings to citizens, which if not heeded, can lead to criminal charges. There is no organized political opposition, so most activity dealt with is of a social nature. They are also an apparatus for upward mobility through the Communist Party hierarchy.

Amnesty International estimates that Cuba has about 330 political prisoners at any given time, mostly civil rights campaigners, functioning in very small groups or as brave individuals confronting the state. All states are politically repressive to one degree or another; all maintain a system of police and prisons.

It is perhaps the height of hypocrisy for a country like the United States to criticize Cuba given this country's own terrible history of suppression of civil rights and liberties, its horrendous prison system, and current torture and detention centers abroad. Still, for those of us who desire the end of the political state, we hold to a standard that demands democracy as the key component at every level of decision making. One man at the head of a government for almost 50 years violates this concept, and any number of political prisoners is unacceptable.

There are perhaps four large categories of American thought which provide definitions of the fifty years of Castro rule:

The right-wing, which views the island as a totalitarian, communist police state where starving people live under daily repressive rule and the government is involved in drug trafficking and terrorism.

The center through to the liberal left which agrees, perhaps in the mode of Michael Moore's movie, *Sicko,* that the Revolution has provided good social services for the poor and resisted U.S. hegemony in the hemisphere, but needs to install more democracy and private investment.

The organized left which sees very little wrong with the island and views all criticism of it as aid to the U.S. empire.

The anarchist view which, indeed, sees the island as a police state needing a second revolution to install workers democracy, but has no use for calls for returning to private forms of ownership or foreign investment.

Political democracy and the overthrow of elite and police rule is always the goal of any authentic revolution, but so is creating

The author in John Lennon Park, Havana, Cuba, 2010. An inscription at the foot of the bench has lyrics from "Imagine" in Spanish, *"Dirás que soy un soñador pero no soy el único."* In English, "You may say I'm a dreamer, but I'm not the only one."

a society of economic and social equity; essentially, anarchist-communism: no government, no capitalism.

In states such as Cuba and the remaining countries that identify themselves as socialist, a ruling apparatus remains and practices what has traditionally been labeled, state capitalism, where the government replaced private entrepreneurs in developing Western capitalism. It hires wage labor, supervises investment, commodities are produced and exchanged for currency, etc. It's the manner in which formerly agricultural nations, from China to Russia, were able to build a modern economy and infrastructure.

Accompanying the state economic structures were draconian political apparatuses that declared, in the words of Fidel seen posted across the island, "With the Revolution, everything; against the Revolution, nothing." Of course, it is the government that gets to define what's inside and what is outside. Cuba, however, never has been able to build the industrial infrastructure created by other communist states and, hence, has a population restive for the commodities they see citizens of other nations purchasing.

The right-wing vision of what they refer to as "the return of democracy" to Cuba is a bad joke given its history, and, in fact, means the resurrection of its status as U.S. corporate investment target and playground for Western vacationers which it was before 1959. I've heard Cuban-Americans, ones who have never set foot on the island, tell me that until the Communists took over, Cuba "was a wonderful place" where "everyone was happy."

This is willful ignorance in the extreme. In fact, before Castro's takeover in 1959, Cuba was a dictatorship, a torture state that functioned as a whorehouse and gambling den for rich Americans, which allowed unrestrained corporate exploitation run by a corrupt domestic elite that enforced it all for the Mob and U.S. companies. If anything, the Revolution has vastly improved the lot of the common people of the island to the extent that there is a unique phenomenon in Cuba, unknown elsewhere among the poor and certainly poor nations, that everyone should have equal access to adequate goods and services. Most poor just assume they won't.

The advocates of what they call reform in Cuba would very quickly force the island into being another Jamaica with a return to deep class divisions, a dependency on tourism, its cities degenerating into crime-filled areas like Kingston, and little or no social services for the poor.

One wonders whether these democracy advocates think the poor, or anyone, would be happier in democratic Mexico, where farmers have been ruined by NAFTA and forced into the capital city already bursting at the seams, where *narcotraficantes* battle the cops with automatic weapons, where hundreds of women are murdered in the border regions each year, and the vast majority of people live without social services and as a pool of cheap labor for U.S. corporations, or, in totalitarian, commie Cuba, where the basic necessities of life are provided or subsidized, and violence and crime is minimal?

In every article about the recent brotherly transfer of power, it is always noted that the average Cuban receives $20 a month from the government in wages, that housing and transportation are major problems, and in right-wing accounts, that the people are starving (a total lie without basis; farmers markets are bursting at the seams with produce, although meat and poultry can be scarce).

The implication is that the Revolution is a failure for being able to provide so little in financial reward for a month's labor. Cuba is a poor country, made poorer by the U.S. embargo, and has always had an official ethos of equity, hence, the small amount of wealth the country possesses is distributed in the most equal manner possible, or such is the official account.

However, Cuban Communist Party bureaucrats and others in so-called sensitive sectors of the economy have always had a wage above the average and an availability of housing, cars, and commodities that most Cubans don't. Now, with an increasing number of joint tourist and industrial investment ventures with foreign companies, there is a growing strata of wage workers in those industries who similarly have an income significantly higher than the average Cuban.

It is not unusual to meet a college professor or doctor working as a guide or interpreter knowing that a week's work can bring them hundreds of Canadian dollars in a week. It will be those who have disposable income who will be able to purchase the newly offered DVDs, cell phones, and the rest of the technological junk that is so appealing. I realize calling it "junk" displays an individual bias. Most citizens of the modern world don't see such items as luxuries, but increasingly as necessities. I'm sure the proliferation of spontaneous music jams, for so long a feature of Cuban urban life, will soon be a quaint exercise performed for the throngs of tourists searching for the "real Cuba" while former street musicians will be listening to Korn on their iPod.

The sudden permission by Raul to allow purchase of 21st century technology gadgets appears to many as a grudging acceptance of a modernity that had been resisted by the geriatric leadership until now. There's delight in some quarters that the seemingly dour world of Cuban communism will see its Revolution unraveled with the introduction of DVDs, cell phones and video games. In this regard, those desiring Cuba to retake its proper place in the world capitalist order may be correct.

Even with its privileged bureaucracy, its police control, and centralized economy, there has been a communal, imaginative aspect to the Revolution, certainly including its vibrant culture, that occurs mostly at the local level such as in women's groups challenging traditional machismo, vast community organic gardens, a pride in having defeated and held off the imperialist monster of the north, its health care and education systems which provide a better infant mortality and literacy rate than the U.S., and other successes that have made Cuba a model of what can be done with little. (For instance, Detroit's infant mortality rate is 16 deaths per 1,000 live births; Cuba's is 6.)

A recent clandestine poll taken by an organization affiliated with the U.S. Republican Party, "found that more than half of [Cubans] interviewed considered their economic woes to be their chief concern while less than 10 percent listed lack of political freedom as the main problem facing the country," according to a June 5 *New York Times*. If accurate, this indicates widely held attitudes reflecting rising expectations based on an understandable level of dissatisfaction about crumbling infrastructure, inadequate housing, restrictions on mobility, poor transportation, and other shortages, but it also means, how are you going to keep them down on the socialist farm once they've seen capitalist commodities?

This desire for the latter items, Raul's reforms, suggests strongly that Cuban attitudes are changing in a direction contrary to Che's idea of creating Socialist Man. The so-called new freedoms may become the thin wedge of bringing back what *los barbudos* resisted for half a century. In the same study above, 80 percent of Cubans polled (remembering that this is from a right-wing group) stated they wanted a market economy, probably indicating, if the sampling is correct, the hope that a Western economy would provide more of what remains scarce.

Perhaps many Cubans dream of being able to shop like their Miami brethren, but, on this path lies only what other poor nations experience; poverty alongside wealth, limited or nonexistent health care and other subsidized government services, crime, and in Cuba's case, the island could return to being an alternative to the Dominican Republic for American tourists with all that accompanies such an economy. Allowing unbridled foreign investment again–corporate looting–suggests the model of Mexico where corporations flock to the country for its low wages and lack of labor problems. A glimpse of what could be expected is in the recent news of a Mexico City Ford Fiesta plant that announced the halving of wages to $2 an hour.

Riding on an air conditioned, European-produced tour bus, we easily made it along Cuban roads, some in excellent condition, particularly the 16-lane ones constructed by the Soviets that could double as landing strips, or, the scenic La Farola road that twists and dips through the Sierra del Purial from outside of Guantanamo City to Baracoa where Columbus visited on his second day in the New (to him) World. Other two-laners were pot-hole-filled, but going slowly through beautiful and historic countryside left no one wishing for a speedier journey.

My only real disappointment of the trip was that we had been promised a view of the overlook of the U.S. military and torture base at Guantanamo Bay. Although photographs of the facility are readily available on the U.S. Department of Defense web site, the American government made the ludicrous charge that the Cubans were allowing Al-Qaeda operatives to peer in at the base.

Signs of revolutionary exhortation proliferate everywhere as billboards and on buildings, including one which announced that this was "A Revolution with Energy,!" and displayed a fluorescent bulb of the type that has been installed everywhere on the island. Government workers went door-to-door trading them for the old incandescent ones. There's no way to estimate how the population relates to these signs or whether or not they have an impact on collective consciousness.

When we arrived at a destination, we always had first rate accommodations although curiously, our guides needed permission from the Ministry of Tourism to enter even though one was an officer in the Cuban army reserves and our tour bus and the hotel is administered by Gaviota Grupo, a section of the Cuban armed forces devoted to tourism. After a Raul edict in March, Cubans can now stay at tourist hotels, although they are priced way beyond the means of the average citizen. Still, Cubans found the prohibition insulting and were glad to see it ended.

As we drove through narrow city streets with our huge bus, we were aware of the shabby exteriors of most ordinary homes. Our guide said that people don't fix up the outside to avoid ostentatiousness, but that the insides are adequate. From what we could see through open doors, most floors are tiled; there is furniture and a TV. Still, the difference between our tourist accommodations and the average Cuban housing is striking. Our guide told us the country needs 100,000 new homes built each year, but nowhere near that is occurring.

In Santiago de Cuba, the southern city hailed as the home of the Revolution, we visited the Moncada Barracks where Castro and 125 men attacked the dictator Batista's garrison on July 26, 1953. A guide explained the battle, Castro's strategy, and showed where the fighting occurred, some of it where we stood. Castro was captured as were many of his men, some of whom were tortured and summarily executed.

We also went to El Cemetario Santa Ifiginea where the tomb of Jose Marti, Cuba's national hero, is located. All was appropriately very solemn, until distorted martial music began blaring from loudspeakers and an honor guard of three Cuban soldiers marched from the main building to the tomb thrusting their legs with each step waist high and perpendicular to the ground.

One can't believe that the simple man who this monument rightly honors for his words and deeds would have been comfortable with this display of extreme distortion of the body in service to militarism. Close to the Marti tomb is one commemorating the martyrs of July 26 with the names of the fallen inscribed on it. Many of Castro's comrades were no more than 18 and one was 14.

From the cemetery, we traveled through the city to the Casa de Las Religeones Populares, a dwelling that houses practitioners of a type of Santeria or vudu. The people there performed music and ecstatic dance numbers for us. This is not usually done for visitors, who are rare. Next door, incongruently, was the headquarters of the District Committee of the PCC (Partido Communista Cubano). The remnants of the primitive adjacent to the representative of the modern, bureaucratic state.

In Baracoa the next morning, we toured Sendero Socio-cultural del Cacao, the Socio-Cultural Chocolate Trail, which is set up to receive tourists, but like so many other places in this region, we were the only ones there. On site is a 100-year-old working chocolate factory and the cacao is grown on the grounds, as well. Che, himself, is said to have sparked the resurrection of cacao production in 1963 according to a local billboard.

The cacao pods have a sweetish flesh which can be eaten fresh, but the seeds are what produces the chocolate and are extremely bitter to the point of being inedible until dried, ground, and sugar added. Our guide was Alejandro Hartmann, Baracoa's historian and preservationist, who explained the cacao production process. Then, chocolate bars! This facility is also managed by the Army.

Probably the most moving moment of the trip for all of us was when we were welcomed to the compound of the Grupo Nongon y Kiriba people, who identify themselves as the descendants of the few original Taino people not wiped out by Spanish genocide. We were greeted warmly by them and presented with an elaborate feast consisting of roast pig that was rotating on a spit when we arrived, roast fish, and 20 other dishes of corn, beans, coconut, and vegetables. After welcoming festivities and the meal consumed, dancing commenced with musical accompaniment. Soon, we were invited to dance with the participants, and many of us accepted.

As we prepared to leave, our tour leader gave a heartfelt speech of appreciation for their hospitality, which they returned in kind. All of us were fighting back tears at such a moving experience, perhaps made much more so because this remaining remnant of a people wiped out by our ancestors left us wondering how long they can survive in the modern world.

We left Baracoa for Guardalavaca along a badly rutted road, but each mile of scenery was described interestingly by our guide in both ecological and political terms. We stopped at Bahia de Taco for a rest and a group photo. The rest area features a statue of Alejandro de Humboldt, the cartographer for Castro's rebel band.

We later passed an ominous looking factory which is the first industrial site we had seen, so it is striking in its contrast to the lush eastern province vegetation in which it is located. It was a joint Canadian/Cuban nickel refinery (images of Sudbury, Ontario, eh?). Workers there are also a privileged strata. A billboard at the entrance exhorts those entering to "Imagine El Futuro," surrounded by an illustration of smoking, industrial facilities. Is this the future to be imagined? It raises the question of how does a country generate wealth, particularly when its population wants better conditions and more commodities? This signals complete immersion in the world market and all that it brings; heaven and hell, if commodities are heaven.

Seeing this plant brought to mind the condition of Cuba's workers, all represented by official unions, which, as in all socialist countries, function to assure state production norms are met and discipline the labor force rather than represent the interests of the workers. The Cuban government and its Western leftist apologists say class conflict has been suppressed, and it is the socialist government itself that represents the interests of labor. It's hard to believe many workers buy that.

Cuban anarcho-syndicalism was a major force on the island, including the IWW, militantly fighting for worker rights and revolution since the 1880s. The movement survived Spanish rule and that of a succession of Cuban dictators following the island's War of Independence, but has been suppressed by the Castro regime since it took over a half century ago. This is related powerfully by in his.

There's still a small, resilient, clandestine anarcho-syndicalist movement deep inside Cuba whose ideals have never been extinguished that can provide a mass movement away from both state and private capitalism. The desire for an authentic Revolution, distant from the world of iPods, still beats in many hearts on the island. May our Cuban comrades make it so.

Suggested reading:
Cuban Anarchism: The History of a Movement, Frank Fernandez, See Sharp Press, 2000

Cuba
From State to Private Capitalism
Adios Socialismo
Summer 2010

We entered the elevator on the ground floor of Havana's renowned FOCSA building in the city's Vedado district and were quickly whisked, non-stop, to the 33rd floor. When the doors opened, tuxedoed waiters welcomed us to La Torre, an elegant, candle-lit restaurant with floor to ceiling windows overlooking the city and its harbor twinkling in the night below us.

"Damn," I thought, "if the communists come back, we're screwed."

Of course, they never left, but the incongruity of eating an expensive meal (by Cuban standards) in opulent circumstances seemingly contradicts the island's slogan of "Socialism or Death," but it actually neatly sets the context for what may be the country's future.

Dinner at an improbably elegant restaurant occurred on the final night of my third trip to Cuba with a Toronto-based tour group. After having previously traveled with them to the eastern and western sectors of the 700-mile-long island, this trip featured a week in the nation's capital. I was the only American among 25 Canadians, mostly professionals in social services who were anxious to see how their Cuban counterparts work in related fields of medicine, social work, juvenile crime, women's issues, etc.

I am able to circumvent the U.S. blockade which prohibits Americans from going to the island by an exclusion from the law allowing journalists to travel there. [More on this at the end.] Through fortuitous occurrences, I wound up with accommodations at the Hotel Nacional de Cuba, an historic luxury hotel located on the Malecon, the broad esplanade, roadway, and seawall that runs along Havana harbor.

The building's lobby and rooms are so steeped in Cuba's pre-Revolutionary history that one can almost feel the presence of the multitude of American gangsters, movies stars, athletes, writers, and corporate managers who lodged there during their stay in the corrupt Latin playground for the wealthy. Some of the rooms are even named after the famous, such as the "Frank Sinatra and Ava Gardner Room," which a couple from our group was able to score.

Stories set in the Nacional fill books, but one hit me particularly as I was reading *The Mafia in Havana* by Enrique Cirules during my stay. The tripartite ruling powers of the island from the 1930s through to the 1959 revolution were the Mob, U.S. intelligence agencies, and American corporations, all abetted by the criminal state whose last president was Fulgencio Batista.

In 1946, the U.S. mafia called a summit meeting convened by Lucky Luciano in Havana to decide how to split up the American rackets and newly expanding ones in Cuba. They reserved all of the Nacional's 500 rooms for their meetings, and were met by chauffeured limousines at the airport to transport them to the hotel.

The gangsters' first big meal at the Nacional consisted of grilled manatee, roast flamingo, and turtle. From then until they were run off the island in 1959, the Mob increased its revenues as it expanded into casinos, hotels, and entertainment, much of it connected with Hollywood stars such as George Raft and Sinatra.

As on my other visits, we were bussed around by an able crew of guides and interpreters to local projects that showed the ingenuity and spirit of a people living under great economic and political stress. City residents reacted to us like the tourists we were and none offered political opinions. They were pleased, however, to show us their projects.

For instance, at the Organoponico Vivero Alamar on the outskirts of Havana, the director and several workers proudly explained how the vast urban gardens on Havana's outskirts, of which this was one component, provided the majority of the city's vegetables. Many of the workers were retirees from other sectors of the economy and used their labor at the farm to supplement their pensions and to continue as part of the social fabric of the area:

Workers are paid wages by the state and the farm has a small retail outlet for local consumption.

Back in the city, we took a walking tour of Old Havana, a UNESCO World Heritage Site, with its restored colonial buildings housing museums, shops, and restaurants which mostly cater to tourists. It is here that one encounters panhandlers and scam artists not usually seen elsewhere on the island.

In Cathedral Square, where mostly Canadian and European tourists congregate to drink mojitos, smoke Cohibas, and take in the sights, it occurred to me that if Americans were permitted to visit, which looks like it may happen soon, there would have been thousands of people in the square rather than hundreds. One thing glaringly missing are the normally ubiquitous signs with revolutionary implorations for socialism that are present everywhere else in the city, so as perhaps not to offend the capitalist sentiments of visitors.

In a corner of the square, four elderly Cuban men were playing and singing traditional island songs. Suddenly, a group of school children rushed up and stared at the music makers for a second, and then began enthusiastically singing along with them, obviously familiar with the song.

Wow, I thought, there's still a traditional folk culture here that hasn't been superseded by the global industrial music machine. However, later that night, still in the Old City, we witnessed the Canonazo, the Cannon Blast ceremony, a tradition dating from the Spanish colonial days, when shots were fired signaling the closing of the gates of the walled city and the raising of the chain across the entrance to the harbor. The tradition of firing a cannon every night at 9:00 pm has been maintained as a pageant even though the wall was torn down a hundred years ago. Re-enactment performers marched to the rampart and fired off the cannon to the delight of several thousand assembled Havaneros and a few dozen tourists.

As the dark encompassed the centuries old Morro Castle, we trekked back to our bus and came across about a hundred or more Cuban young people dancing wildly under a canopy. Upon listening, I realized it wasn't the Cuban rumba or cha-cha-cha animating them, but the music of the LA-based, hip-hop band, The Black Eyed Peas coming from a portable CD player. The young people knew all the words and loudly sang the choruses in unison.

It's not news that American popular culture has become globalized to the point of total domination at the expense of other countries' traditional forms, but in Cuba, even a seemingly innocuous song can be seen as one of the many signals of the re-penetration of U.S. capital. Washington and Wall Street have never given up their goals of moving the island back into its military and investment portfolios.

Such occurrences, even small ones, are usually hailed as signaling the end of a dour, authoritarian "failed state," one "stuck in the last century." Liberal critics, at least, are willing to allow that there are many admirable features on the island such as the always vaunted Cuban universal health care system and other state provided social services. The government's domination of most aspects of economic activity, to say nothing of its vice grip on the political apparatus, is something all critics agree is a vestige of another era, one long ready for "reforms" and "transition." Or, so goes the narrative by all but the most unreconstructed leftists who see little or nothing wrong with the current state of Cuban affairs, and are blind to the changes occurring.

Leaving aside the question of which nation, the U.S. or Cuba, suffers worse from a creaky bureaucracy, a repressive police apparatus, and more readily qualifies as a failed state, it's worth a look at what so-called reforms advocated for Cuba would look like. One only need to recall the collapse of the Stalinist dictatorships in Eastern and Central Europe to realize how quickly the transition from state to private ownership can occur.

Are the former Soviet bloc people better off today? Probably not in Mother Russia from whence the state socialist forms were imposed on its satellite nations, but in many of the latter, life has improved for most, but certainly not all.

Most countries under Soviet domination had already achieved a status of modern industrial capitalist economies, so their transition back to private entrepreneurial economies wasn't difficult, particularly when Party bosses quickly grabbed the reins of the previously socialized enterprises.

Castro and his band wrenched an island with little modern infrastructure other than in big cities, an impoverished peasantry, and an economy looted and corrupted by foreign imperialists, gangsters, and domestic elites, from the hands of U.S. corporate and military interests. Following the Revolution, attempts to build a modern industrial economy under the auspices of the state, and now, increasingly utilizing the market, all the while surrounded by a hostile major power, has proved and continues to be daunting for the little island.

The results were and are a fragile state capitalist economy, albeit with equitable forms of benefits for the population, and a rigid, authoritarian political command structure. There are more democratic modalities on a local level than is generally realized, but ultimately, policy is top down. Recent media accounts celebrate that "[Cuban president] Raul Castro is trying to modernize the system without jumping to full-scale capitalism." This in a BBC News web site report about how Cuba is turning over hundreds of state-run barber shops and beauty salons to employees "in what may be the start of a long-expected privatization drive."

The article notes that "other communist countries such as China and Vietnam have long since pushed through market reforms while maintaining political control." If those countries are a model, it's not much to look forward to for the Cuban people.

Cuba recently turned over a quarter million plots of unproductive state-owned land, laying fallow since mass sugar production ceased, to private farmers. Some taxi drivers are allowed to work for themselves.

Some, anticipating the re-introduction of private capitalist forms, are almost delirious with anticipation. Timothy Ashby, an official in the Reagan and Bush, Sr. administrations, and a specialist in privatization issues, writing in *Travel Wire Industry,* says, "Cuba is positioning itself for a China-style economic leap forward." The island, he writes, "remains a hugely untapped market of 11 million consumers."

So, it's, adios, socialismo, or, what passed for it. Ashby sees the lifting of the 50-year American trade and travel embargo as benefiting the economies of both countries, creating a modern, efficient economic infrastructure for the island and a shot in the arm for the U.S.' beleaguered employment situation. He estimates "that lifting travel restrictions alone would increase [U.S.] domestic output by between $1.2 billion and $1.6 billion annually, and create between 17,000 and 23,000 new jobs–yes, in tourism, but also in real estate, retail, food processing, transportation and associated sectors." He further reports that the Cuban government, with foreign partners, is planning 14 new condominium and golf resorts, part of a new, massive tourist infrastructure.

He writes further: "The same projections see U.S. airlines, cruise ships and tour operators generating more than $522 million from Cuban trade add-ons in the first year alone, increasing to $1.6 billion by the fifth year, and creating more than 10,000 jobs. An estimated 60 cents out of every dollar spent by Americans in Cuba reliably would end up back in the United States."

This all has a familiar ring, doesn't it? It sounds just like the equation which immiserated the Cuban people during the period up until 1959. Cuba as the recreation zone for Americans and others with the cash to vacation there while the people of the island will mix mojitos and make beds in resorts for them. Definitely, the Mob won't be allowed back in, but the other control sectors formerly excluded certainly will. But, what about the almost 6,000 American corporations and businesses the Cuban revolution nationalized for which the U.S. still demands compensation? Lawyer Ashby has a plan for that as well.

He writes, "American law requires that claims against Havana for 1960's-era U.S.-owned property that was seized, must be resolved before full relations can be re-established."

So, the new Cuba will enter the modern capitalist world in debt to the corporate gangsters who looted the island unrestricted for years. Maybe Cuba could get an IMF loan to pay off its debt and impose a little austerity along the way as the bankers almost always demand.

Ashby is quite enthusiastic about the future "once American visitors descend on the island." And, descend they will just like before and just like they do on other Caribbean island resorts, Jamaica, perhaps being the best comparison.

As I noted in the Summer 2008 Fifth Estate article about another Cuba trip, "Socialism or Cell Phones," there is a growing class of Cubans with disposable incomes thirsting for all of the technological gadgets and fashion available to modern citizens. The process Ashby advocates and the direction in which it looks like the Cuban government is headed will lead to the Jamaicaization of the island–another swell tourist destination.

But, there's no reason to think that the rising class stratification won't also produce the worst elements of Kingston which in late May necessitated a state of emergency declared by the Jamaican government following clashes between police and heavily armed *narcotraficantes* which left 30 people dead. A lot like that other bastion of tourism and democracy, Mexico. Right now, Cuba has none of that.

In a new, reformed Cuba, IMF-imposed austerity would undoubtedly mean that the extensive social services extended to all citizens will disappear, as would state subsidies. Currently, prices for most basics, such as food and housing, are now subsidized or very cheap.

For instance, at Havana's famed Heladeria Coppelia, a solid block of ice cream shops, a 4-scoop sundae costs about 20 cents in the local currency, but often entails a 45-minute wait. Fast service is available using CUCs, the tourist money, but the cost soars to $3 to $4. The same is true for venues such as the Morro Castle where canonoza takes place which also has two-tier pricing. No one goes without on the $20 guaranteed monthly income the U.S. media never fails to mention as proof of how poor the country is.

Much of the social services operate at a local and neighborhood level. We visited a Casa de Orientation a la Mujer y la Familia, a center for the guidance of women and the family, where support and information are supplied. The all-women staff explained the programs that deal with women's issues including health, and violence in the family. Cuban television airs ads against spousal and child abuse which they define, besides the obvious, as the withholding of affection.

In a Mother's Day Index, the international charity, Save the Children, rated Cuba, among less-developed nations, as the best place to be a mother based on access to education, jobs, and health care for women and children. By contrast, the U.S. came in 28th on the index of developed nations.

The week visiting Havana was exhausting with days filled with stops such as at the Antonio Nunez Jimenez Foundation for Nature and Humanity, founded by the cartographer for Castro's rebel band. It is in the forefront of creating sustainable development and ecological consciousness which probably puts it at odds with the planned centralized official vision.

A trip to development centers for children, the "House of Grandmothers," and neighborhood community centers, demonstrated a highly organized society. How much of it serves the political apparatus is a separate but important question.

We also were guests at a moving ceremony recognizing the 20th anniversary of Cuba's treatment of victims of the Chernobyl nuclear accident. Up to 800 children at a time from Ukraine, many with crippling conditions still being caused by radiation poisoning, were present in their wheelchairs. The Ukrainian ambassador to Cuba spoke and entertainment was provided by La Colmenita, a Cuban children's ensemble who played and sang as well as any adult group. The songs were all traditional.

A trip to one of the poorer barrios brought us to the Muraleando Cultural Project where local artists have festooned the neighborhood with wall murals and sculptures created from cast off junk. Some of it was reminiscent of Detroit's Heidelberg Project which also makes art from society's detritus. One mural featured quotes from American socialist and labor leader, Eugene V. Debs.

After three visits to the island, one of my friends remarked that I'm "getting soft on Cuba." I definitely am, but towards its people, certainly not its government.

Even as the rulers act like bosses and cops, there are many Cubans who take the island's official ideology of socialism and creating a new world seriously. Their results are in the many scattered exciting projects in education, music, art, ecology, science, culture, agriculture, and other endeavors that in many ways we mirror in our small efforts in this country.

However, the small projects we found admirable are a weak bulwark against the massive economic forces howling at Cuba's door. It is much more likely, sad to say, that the island's future is already determined by its re-integration into global capital. Perhaps it is a mistake to suggest that the island's economy has previously been independent of global economic forces. From the misery engendered by Columbus' visit which presaged the arrival of the Spaniards and slavery, through the island's colonial period, its domination by the U.S., and then its dependence on the Soviet Union, Cuba has had little capacity for self-reliance.

Since the early 1990s, following the Soviet Union's collapse, increasingly the island's economy has been based around tourism and foreign investment. Even with the U.S. trade embargo in place, Cuba still imports hundreds of millions of dollars' worth of American goods yearly. The dinner I ate at La Torre had as its main course fish imported from Canada.

Octavio Alberola, active with GALSIC (Support Group for Libertarians and Independent Trade Unionists in Cuba), a support and information network, and the Cuban Libertarian Movement in Exile (MLCE), remains a steadfast opponent of the Castro government. In an interview with the Kate Sharpley Library available online, he recognizes there is little or nothing left in Cuba today of the organized anarchist workers movement that Castro ruthlessly suppressed.

This publication desires, as I assume most readers do: a Cuba which experiences a real revolution that abolishes all forms of capitalism, private and state, and the government apparatus along with it which is what anarchists have always fought for. We should support our Cuban comrades when possible, but I doubt if their day is near.

I checked out of the Nacional at 6am, boarded a Chinese-made Yutong bus and roared across the Cuban countryside to Varadero 90 miles away to catch a plane for Toronto. Sixteen hours later, I was crossing the border from Windsor, Ontario to Detroit, arriving at a snow-covered customs booth staffed by grim faced, heavily armed border guards at the ready.

Been to Cuba? Out of the car. You've violated the terms of the Cuban Assets Control Regulations.

I'm a journalist qualified to travel there. I write about the island as well as do radio broadcasts about my visits.

You don't qualify. Empty your pockets. Get up against the wall. Spread your legs.

I bet you don't do this to reporters from NBC.

You'll hear from the Treasury Department.

Welcome home.

Author Note: I was never sanctioned for any of my four visits to the island, nor contacted by the State Department.

Venezuela
An Anarchist at the World Social Forum
Spring, 2006

Barrel-assing around hair-pin turns at 6:00am in a crowded bus on a road with no barriers between us and a two-thousand-foot drop was not the manner in which I anticipated arriving in Venezuela for the Sixth World Social Forum (WSF).

This anus-clenching adventure was made necessary by the fact that a key viaduct on the highway from the airport into Caracas was recently determined to be on the verge of collapse. All traffic was forced to take an old mountain road, so what was normally a 40-minute ride had turned into a gridlocked six-hour nightmare journey.

In order to alleviate the traffic jams, the government decreed specific hours for different types of vehicles, and bus time began at 5:00am. When we arrived, after a sleepless night on a flight from Newark, rather than being met by steely-eyed, suspicious immigration officials, the most obvious indication that we weren't in Kansas was a huge banner reading, *"Bienvenidos a Venezuela y el Foro Mundial Social: Otro Mundial es Posible"* (Welcome to Venezuela and the World Social Forum: Another World is Possible).

This was an official government sign welcoming us and similar ones were displayed all over the city for the January 24-29 events.

These now yearly forums came in response to the World Economic Forum held in Davos, Switzerland, where the international imperial chieftains gather annually to discuss how to keep the world exactly as it is, or, if it is to change at all, how they can still squeeze the most swag out of the world's poor. The first WSF anti-forum forums were held in Porto Allegre, Brazil, but this year, interest had grown to such an extent it necessitated a "polycentric" event with co-forums held in Mali and Pakistan as well as Venezuela. As it was, almost 100,000 activists showed up in Caracas to discuss and compare strategies for social justice and how to pull the fangs of the U.S. empire.

Representatives of social movements and non-governmental organizations are invited, whereas, those from political parties, governments, and armed groups are supposedly asked to not attend. The latter meant that the Zapatistas and Colombian guerrillas did not come, but the Chavez government had a major presence and weighed in with a $500,000 contribution to cover event expenses including airfare for 100 welfare rights organizers from the U.S. Also, representatives of the Cuban government took part in forums and had an official exhibit tent, and at least one political party, the Partido Communista do Brasil, was there in full force complete with musical groups and its members bedecked in t-shirts sporting hammers and sickles.

Caracas is interesting and exciting, but also dirty, crowded (5 to 7 million people we were told, which is quite a spread for an estimate), polluted (gas is 14 cents a gallon, so anyone who can drive, does), noisy, and somewhat dangerous. Other than that, it was fine, with all of the rhythms of life and culture one expects from a bustling Latin city. The modern, efficient subway system is always crowded, but costs only 17 cents and was free to WSF delegates as well as retired citizens.

The city is crisscrossed with pedestrian malls which are swamped with endless kiosks selling every sundry item imaginable. Crowds are often so thick one can hardly walk and music blares from stalls at concert level decibels. It seems unimaginable that people could consume the vast number of items for sale.

A friend, who attended the 2004 Forum in Mumbai, India, described her experience as "life transforming," so I arrived with great expectations. Unfortunately, much of my enthusiasm was dashed, in part because of the immense scope of the Forum itself. There were two 128-page tabloids published listing 2,000 workshops that were located in venues spread across the sprawling city. Events were often canceled, frequently with no advance notice, and although most probably took place, it seemed that the ones we most wanted to attend didn't happen. I spoke to the head of a WSF organizing group who said this was the worst planned of all five forums.

Most sessions were conducted in Spanish although the major talks featured simultaneous translation. The majority were on expected subjects such as human rights, youth, women, workers, and the environment, ones that would concern those opposed to globalization and neo-liberalism. However, there weren't many sessions that sounded engaging or innovative enough for me to warrant struggling through them with my rudimentary Spanish or spending an hour wearing headphones for their translation. A number of the formal sessions took place in the Caracas Hilton which is as elegant as in any U.S. city. However, this facility, besides the ubiquitous WSF signs, sported posters of Bush taped on almost every meeting room wall declaring, *"Bush: Asesino"* (Bush: Assassin). No one took them down.

Along with seemingly thousands of others, I spent most days in the outside plazas adjacent to the hotel taking part in informal discussions and watching an unscheduled variety of music and theatrical performances. The Hilton plaza area continually swarmed with ostensible opponents of capitalism, and the usual venue of the rich was transformed into a merchandise bazaar for South America's traditional left. Want a Che scarf or a Trotsky t-shirt or a Chavez poster? It was all there.

On January 24, there was a mass march of about 100,000 participants and Caracaquenos to the opening WSF ceremonies. All along our route we were flanked by ominous looking, battle-ready, Venezuelan army troops wearing Kevlar body armor and carrying automatic weapons. They were dispatched there to guard us against any provocation from the city's still formidable anti-Chavez right wing, unlike American cities where troops are mobilized *against* demonstrators.

After a seemingly endless march through the city, the opening ceremony, projected to the throng on a giant video screen, featured music and speakers, including American anti-war activist Cindy

Sheehan. When we passed a McDonald's during the march, thousands of people chanted, *"Arepas, Arepas; No Hamburguesas!"* referring to a preference for the local sandwich over the American shitburger.

All across Caracas, much like U.S. cities do for art fairs and the like, banners were hung welcoming people to the WSF, although most billboards urge buying commodities or watching *King Kong* or *Desperate Housewives*. As in all other Latin American countries, except Cuba, abortion is illegal in Venezuela, and Chavez is unlikely to stir up a hornets nest by doing anything about it. There were, however, many posters and banners demanding, *"Para Legalicacion el Aborto"*—For the Legalization of Abortion.

Perhaps my greatest disappointment of the trip was not being able to locate the anarchist-organized Foro Mundial Alternativo— the Alternative Social Forum (ASF). It was the announcement of that event as a counterweight to the essentially leftist and reformist orientation of the main gathering that made the whole idea of traveling there appealing. I've read reports of it since returning, so some people found it, but our constant inquiries about its whereabouts were unsuccessful.

On their extensive web site (nodo50.org/ellibertario; English version at bottom), the anarchist El Libertario group states that it wanted "to open and maintain spaces for debate and the construction of the dynamics of transformation," but doubted that the WSF is a "pluralistic, open, self-managed" event.

The ASF described itself as independent for its refusal to accept funding from the Venezuelan government, banks, tourist ministries, and even the Rockefeller Brothers Foundation and Christian aid organizations that contribute to the WSF. But it's more than just funding and WSF's uncritical stance toward Chavismo. *El Liberatario's* Rafael Uzcatequi, in several withering attacks on the Bolivarian Revolution of Hugo Chavez, available on the above web site, calls the WSF a "shroud for Venezuela's social movement."

He writes that rather than encouraging autonomy and anti-capitalist policies, the government's "imposition of organizational models directed by a single hand," the much-vaunted Bolivarian Circles and other organizations within the poor barrios, become "immobilized to raise their own demands."

Uzcatequi says what are billed as revolutionary social movements have experienced a "progressive incorporation in the cumulative politico-electoral logic" of the Chavez government and are "mortgaging their own autonomy." He ticks off the many facts that have led to the "paralysis of the Venezuelan social movements," such as a lack of mobilizations against energy concessions to multilateral companies, whereas, thousands turn out at rallies to hear Chavez give 4-hour speeches filled with anti-capitalist and anti-globalization rhetoric. The ASF gave voice to criticism of Chavez and advocated for social movements independent of the government.

The material available from El Libertario is extensive and argues powerfully that Chavismo is only capitalism with a human face. This means expanding the economy to allow previously excluded sectors of the population to reap some of its benefits by redistributing Venezuela's record high oil wealth more fairly. But this process also allows the co-optation of the independent movements which become the government's electoral machine and social base for its battle against the old ruling classes to whom Chavez is Castro and Hitler combined.

Uzcatequi views this process, thusly, "There are those in the Circulos Bolivarianos with the best of intentions, with priceless grassroots activity, and others, to my knowledge in a greater number than the previous, to whom the word 'revolution' is synonymous of a 'sure wage.'" This is much like Cuba, which I visited last year, where the strongest supporters of the Castro government are those who get paid by it. And, one can understand this.

While those of us, including the comrades of El Libertario, want an authentic revolution that eliminates capitalism and the state, most of Venezuela's poor are extraordinarily grateful for what the ersatz one has brought them. Venezuela, like the other countries of Latin America, have experienced intense looting, first by the Spanish colonialists and then by Western, primarily U.S., imperialist interests.

It doesn't bear repeating to this readership the bloody and exploitative history of the Western destruction and domination of the people, land, and animals of this hemisphere. On the sorry day Columbus was discovered by Arawak Indians, he wrote in his diary, "They would make fine servants." And, so it has been for over 500 years–servitude for the people of Latin America, first to bail out the collapsing economies of Europe, and later to enrich the corporations of North America and the local governing elites.

The colonialists and imperialists established a domestic class of rulers of European origin who were cut in on the racket of wealth extraction and have governed the native people of the region while swiftly and murderously extinguishing any resistance. When the local rulers couldn't do the job, the imperial power would intervene directly to insure the maintenance of the racket. The U.S. Marines invaded and occupied Latin countries over 100 times since 1900 to protect American interests including overthrowing elected governments.

Recently, however, the old fashioned invade, kill the rebels, and install a local fascist, such as occurred in Chile on September 11, 1973, has become unworkable. Indigenous social movements have grown to such a degree that they have been able to install leftist presidents in Brazil, Venezuela, and most recently, Bolivia. These leaders speak the language of socialism and anti-globalization, refusing the economic models of exploitation pressed upon them in the past by the World Bank and International Monetary Fund.

When Chavez took office, the official poverty rate was 54 percent. Now, if one takes into account the massive government spending in the poor districts, it's less than 30 percent. Millions receive previously unavailable health care; education spending has increased greatly, and food subsidies through Mercal, a chain of state-subsidized supermarkets, have combined to alleviate the most grinding poverty. Still, on a bus ride through suburban barrios, a Westerner is shocked at housing conditions. Chavez says that problem will soon be addressed.

But is this socialism as Chavez and his international supporters trumpet? Maybe in the Scandinavian sense of social democracy, but not within any precise definition of the word as it's been historically defined. Economist Mark Weisbrot, an American adviser to Chavez, told me as we spoke in his room at the Hilton overlooking the hotel swimming pool, that the government's policies are "gradualist reform." Still, the reforms are such a departure from the nation's past that no one looks askance when they are referred to as "21st century socialism."

Chavez is so popular that his poll numbers come in at a dizzying 77 percent, and like Che in Cuba, the Venezuelan's likeness is plastered everywhere. His popularity ends at the doors of Caracas' daily papers and commercial television stations that are so virulently over-the-top anti-Chavez that they make Fox News actually look Fair and Balanced. There is no censorship inhibiting these mainstream, corporate media which let loose a daily barrage of invective, mostly lies, against the government—a situation unlike anywhere else in the world. The papers and the TV stations were the spark plug for the 2002 coup against Chavez that overthrew the country's constitutional institutions and declared it a democracy. When Chavez was quickly re-installed, not one person was arrested nor any paper or station closed.

One day, when we traveled up to the Altamira district for a demonstration against Canadian and Brazilian occupation of Haiti, we stopped to eat some arepas and cachapas at a middle-class restaurant. After our meal, we were approached by a professor who claimed he was like a Jew under Hitler and had been blacklisted for signing an anti-Chavez recall petition. We had no way to verify his story, but then he went into a predictable rant: Venezuela used to be a wonderful place where everyone was happy until Chavez came along. Now, children were starving in hospitals. In reality, it seems little has been done to the traditional ruling class other than to diminish their absolute privilege. For instance, the one thousand freshman spots in medical schools, which were previously reserved solely for the children of the rich, are now open to students from the barrios as well. Hence, the wealthy feel like the Jews of Germany? They need to read a little history.

Socialism or not, there definitely is a new day in Venezuela and the other poor countries of Latin America. Some of the change is material such as improved living conditions, but it's also in the stirring of the poor populations to make their demands heard. Much of the transformation is in the way people conceive of themselves and the governments they are depending upon to change their lives. They exhibit a self-confidence that the poor have entered the stage of history en masse and things will never be the same.

At one WSF session, coca-leaf chewing Bolivians told the audience that if newly-elected Evo Morales doesn't do the bidding of the people, he will be removed just as were the two previous presidents. Venezuelans carry copies of their country's Bolivarian Constitution in their pockets almost like a Bible or talisman.

What are we to make of all of this? In terms of reform, it would be hard for anyone to oppose what the Chavez Bolivarian Revolution has brought to millions of Venezuelans. Also, it's heartening to hear Chavez denounce Bush as Mr. Danger (a Venezuelan literary illusion) and make utterances like, "The imperialist, mass-murdering, fascist attitude of the president of the United States doesn't have limits. I think Hitler could be a nursery-baby next to George W. Bush."

When Chavez isn't trash talking El Asesino, he speaks in terms that the Western capitalist rulers hoped had disappeared with the collapse of the Soviet Union. He has resurrected a dialogue in which capitalism is an issue, not a given. In a speech Chavez gave during the WSF at a Caracas arena, he denounced the U.S. as "the most perverse empire in history...This century we will bury the U.S. empire." We watched it on the government TV channel at our hotel which repeated the 2.5 hour harangue several times. I suspect most Caracaquenos were either viewing the U.S. sit-coms playing on the other channels, or, most likely, the Venezuelan baseball championships.

Before Chavez spoke, the 50,000 in attendance sang the "Internationale," (the international workers' anthem). Everyone seemed to know the words of the radical working-class anthem except for Cindy Sheehan, who sat on the dais, and, surprisingly, Chavez.

He told the crowd, "Time is short. If we do not change the world now, there may be no 22nd century for humanity. Capitalism has destroyed the ecological equilibrium of the earth." He quoted Marx, Jesus, and Noam Chomsky and called for "creating a worldwide anti-imperialist movement...We must urgently build a new socialist movement."

But what exactly is a "new socialist movement" these days and what does a "world-wide anti-imperialist movement" have as goals? If it is simply to improve the lot of the world's poorest and to stop allowing the Western economies to penetrate local ones for the purposes of imperial looting, this can only be seen as a positive reform.

However, Venezuela remains solidly enmeshed in the world market system and industrial capitalism. In fact, under Chavez, that process is accelerating, and not just with oil sales. Pablo Hernandez Parra, an oil expert quoted by Rafael Uzcatequi, says, "[N]ational and international capital headed by oil companies, have donned the red beret and sash [of Chavez] and advancing with triumphant strides impose their privatization program under the guise of socialism for the 21st century."

While including the poor in wealth distribution, Chavez, as Venezuelan presidents before him have, makes deals with the worst of the oil giants, but negotiates much better terms for his country from them. Also, plans for massive mineral and coal extraction are in the works that will displace some of Venezuela's indigenous people from their ancestral lands, and, along with the construction of two coastal superports and planned continent-wide oil and gas pipelines, do intense damage to the environment, contradicting Chavez' concern for ecology quoted above.

Probably the most dramatic display of autonomous opposition in Caracas during the WSF came when two thousand representatives of Bari, Yuka, Anuu, and Wayuu people and their supporters demonstrated in the Capitolio district demanding an end to mineral and coal extraction in the Zulia state by a host of multinationals. When I mentioned this to Mark Weisbrot, the Chavez adviser, he blithely said there was always some sacrifice associated with industrial development. Yeah, like whole continents and entire peoples.

There's no reason to think that Chavez has anything other than the best of intentions. He appears to genuinely despise what is done to the world's poor, and wants reform. But, what is being created is not "Another" world, but rather the same one made fairer. Again, it's hard to oppose this given the levels of poverty, but the question becomes, can capitalist development of the industrial infrastructure and wealth producing enterprises be accomplished utilizing existing resources without sinking the planet ecologically? Is a fairer deal a sustainable model for the billions of poor?

There's enough wealth in Venezuela currently to accomplish everything Chavez wants, but much of it is parked disproportionately in the hands of the traditional ruling class. So, he could take the route of 20th century socialists and expropriate the wealth of the rulers and distribute that. However, authentic class war would create a perhaps untenable political crisis. Instead, he turns to generating new wealth through standard capitalist means.

What emerges is a model that ends intensive imperialist looting and uses new wealth creation to alleviate the worst suffering of the poor through food coops, medical clinics, small business cooperatives, etc. Still, it's industrial capitalism which Marxist modernizers such as Chavez view as the road to be taken to lift the region out of poverty.

Chavismo essentially raises the question: is this the only type of revolution possible in the modern era? We advocate a world based on decentralization, yet every region of the planet is now intricately interconnected and the planet has a massive population of over six billion. Perhaps within "21st Century Socialism," the state would cease playing its historic role as a racket protecting the wealth and privilege of society's rulers, and instead become the arbiter of social justice. The spheres of wage work, private property, and profit, which revolutionaries have struggled to abolish for almost 200 years, would remain, but be used to promote the common good.

Under this concept, human community would be reassembled outside of the economic arena. As a species, we've gotten pretty domesticated over the eons to the culture of work and consumption. We would become fully human following our exit from the daily activity of wage work and commodity exchange through our connection to others. Maybe that's the best we can hope for. The major problem with this is that it still leaves humanity at the mercy of the state, hoping that it will function in the manner of Sweden and not as it usually has throughout the thousands of years of its brutal history.

On the surface, the vertical integration of classes under the aegis of a fair and just state sounds appealing given what we are currently confronted with, but it is also the philosophy of classic fascism.

It seems too much of a gamble to not continue struggling to bring about the world we want rather than accepting what we are told is "possible." As well, this dream of 21st Century Socialism is predicated on an expansion of the chemical/industrial/nuclear work economy.

The planet cannot sustain even current levels of extraction, production, consumption, and waste—even when they are cloaked in the intoxicating rhetoric of anti-imperialism and socialism. Only a radical retreat from authoritarian and technological solutions can restore balance and stave off catastrophe.

Final Words

Is There Hope?
Interview with Peter Werbe
from *Passionate and Dangerous*
St. Louis, 1999

Mark: From a theoretical perspective, what are some ideas that you've been considering lately?
Peter: The last few years have been sobering. A certain humility has crept into our thinking and way of life. It doesn't look like much of what we advocate is on the agenda. The machine rules everywhere. We are in a period of the total domination of capital where even the pseudo-opposition of capital's major 20th century rival, socialism, has left the scene. There is no longer any significant area, geography or thought that technology and capital hasn't extended itself into.

I'm not saying we should step away from radical critiques of capital and technology, but increasingly we're being forced into rearguard actions whose demands step away from the confronting the totality and sound more like, "Please, sir, don't kill everything so fast."

The idea that because we at the Fifth Estate make critiques of technologized capital doesn't mean that we escape the consequences of what we describe. We are at a critical point now trying to preserve those ideas which are at risk of being pushed from human consciousness. The Appendix to Orwell's wonderful dystopian novel, *1984*, is instructive. The idea of Newspeak, the language ordained by Big Brother, was to remove words from language and finally the ideas they represent. I see our projects and journals as repositories of anti-authoritarian ideas which include an understanding that technology as manifested under industrial capitalism is a major factor in the domination of the human spirit. We want to fight to keep that language and those ideas of revolt alive.

Mark: When you say humility do you mean that you have opened up or softened your views?
Peter: It doesn't mean I'm going to buy an electric steak knife. At one level, the modern world is as depressing as it always has been, but that's not to say we can't find elements of joy in our resistance and within an alternative culture we build around it.

At the same time, we have to recognize we are in a precarious position. We are in a biological, social, and spiritual (and I don't mean religious which I don't care about) decline. There's nothing left to hang our hats on that has substance. But people retain something in spite of this, even those immersed in the spectacle and commodity society.

An inherent sociobiology rooted in our basic humanity manifests itself in our wanting to be communal beings like we were for 95 percent of human existence on the planet, even in things that may appear as ordinary as a bowling league or a Star Trek convention. People want to do things together that are affirming and convivial no matter how much the culture of capital tries to domesticate us.

We've been domesticated by the state; we've been domesticated by capital; we've been domesticated by technology, but there's a million instances where people act contrary to that. But people could forget how to do it. As it is, the Star Trek convention holds no capacity to effectively confront our domestication. Worse examples, such as rooting for sports teams or worse than that, wars, take the impulses of communality and manipulates them for commodity consumption or the needs of the imperial state.

That's why it's critically important for us to continue our projects on the margins of this society, even if it looks absolutely hopeless. For one thing, if we want to live out our lives as distant as possible from the dominant society, we better work hard to create an alternative culture and communities, hopefully ones that have the potential to eventually confront the dominant paradigms that currently rule us.

Mark: So, there is some ray of hope?

Peter: I don't think we can live without it. We continue to fight against the worst excesses of technology and the empire and hope that something will occur—some incident or some sense of the harm this world does to everything and everybody that will impel people to move in a direction that reasserts human community and our own humanity. Maybe it will happen; maybe it won't.

Mark: Does distant human history offer any guidance?

Peter: The cooperative forms that nurtured every form of pre-historical, pre-state, pre-technological society gave them the capacity to exist. Anarchism is a clumsy way of enunciating the Old Ways, as poet Gary Snyder calls them; ancient wisdom and sensibilities about how to live on the planet and with each other. This doesn't mean that I or the *Fifth Estate* are advocating going back to the caves.

It means looking at the ideas that were operative in societies that did much better than us in living their lives. The Ottawa people in our bioregion, for instance, had a society where the major aspects of social and personal relationships were worthy of emulation. The culture brought here by the European invaders was a disaster for both the carriers of it as well as their victims. Unfortunately, we are the inheritors of that culture which is a planet-eater and not the one that knows how to live in harmony with the earth.

The task of resurrecting the Old Ways as a basis for a new world is challenging, but also rewarding. Actually, we have no other choice if we have any hopes for our children and the future of the planet.

Eat the Rich
Wealth and Poverty: In the
Shadow of an Exclusive Club
Summer 1991

Expensive new cars–Lincolns, Cadillacs, Mercedes, Jaguars–arrive at the entrance to the Detroit Athletic Club (DAC). Rich, white men dressed in $750 suits, $200 wing-tip shoes, custom tailored shirts, sporting $2,000 Rolex watches are greeted brightly but obsequiously by uniformed black attendants.

Members of Detroit's exclusive men's club stride up the walk bordered by an immaculate lawn and intricate floral patterns leading to the building's entrance. Each of them displays the arrogance and bursting self-confidence wealth and privilege bestow upon the rich and powerful.

Inside, ostensibly the purpose is sports and health, but on the squash and handball courts, in the steam baths, on the massage tables, deals are cut, partnerships are made and broken, politicians bought and sold, economic decisions affecting an entire city or even a distant nation are decided upon. The old, elegant, cut-stone building, with its crystal chandeliers, leather furniture and deep pile rugs, is the venue for the men who constitute the city's ruling class to gather.

A scant three blocks away is a building which once exhibited a similar elegance in the era when the DAC was constructed.

It is now one of only three remaining structures on the block, the others having long ago met their demise beneath the wrecking ball. Inside the Barclay Apartments, the first floor windows are boarded, the plumbing is broken, and the gas was turned off two years ago.

In a third-story room, where Detroit's bourgeoisie once supped, three young African Americans are arguing over possession of a rock of crack cocaine. As the dispute gets more heated, one of the men reaches behind his back for the .25 caliber automatic stuck in his belt which presses cold against his skin. The cops will be here soon. All three will test positive for the HIV virus, but none knows it at the moment. The one woman present is pregnant and her baby will be part of a statistic of infant mortality identical to those of who live in the slums of Mexico City's hillside squatter villages. The men have less of a chance of reaching 40 years of age than do their counterparts in Bangladesh.

Rarely do those at the Barclay Apartments or the DAC think about the connection between each other's social class, but each, in their poverty and in their wealth, create the other.

The rich and the poor, workers and owners, represent a profile of the American empire: a pyramid-shaped maldistribution of wealth based on the industrial plunder of the planet. The richest 10 percent of Americans own 83 percent of all personal wealth, while the rest of us share the remaining 17 percent.

The richest one-half percent of the population, the sector which personifies the ruling class, owns close to 50 percent of all privately held wealth, and it is this concentration which translates into political and social power. The life of opulence and leisure the rich lead, combined with their command position in the economy and politics, comes as a direct result of a system of looting. All they possess and control is at the expense of billions of workers and poor, both here and in the Third World.

The rich maintain a state of permanent class war against the poor. They are willing to kill to protect their wealth and privilege as they've done in Vietnam, Central America and most recently in the Middle East. Our vision of a free, ecologically sound world will never come to pass if we allow these planet-wreckers to continue in power. To them, we are nothing but dog meat for their industry and businesses, and cannon fodder for their wars.

We want to wipe the smug smiles off the faces of this selfish, swinish elite by challenging and destroying the rule of money and power. Our efforts for now may be small and isolated, but we intend to have them grow until the earth is free of this class of parasites.

One day, we will surely EAT THE RICH!

Chapter Image Credits

Page 5: Fifteenth century map of what the early explorers from Europe designated as the New World. It was only new to the travelers in desperate for riches, but not to the Indigenous people who had no need to go beyond their geography.

Page 29: Photo(detail): Millard Berry. Demonstrator holding a *Fifth Estate* Convention Extra at the 1980 Republican National Convention held in Detroit's Cobo Arena.

Page 63: Photo: Peter Werbe. The bathroom at Honest John's Bar and Restaurant in Detroit's Cass Corridor.

Page 106: Easter 1976 *Fifth Estate* parody issue of the local daily, *The Sunday News*.

Page 117: Image – Kathy Rashid. In 1983, *Time* magazine granted its annual "Man-of-the-Year" award to a "Machine-of-the-Year," the computer. This drawing was the cover image for the article, "*Fifth Estate* Tool of the Year: The Sledge-Hammer," in the Spring 1983 edition.

Page 135: Photo (detail): Adbusters. Occupy Wall Street poster, 2011.

Page 175: Photo (detail): Rebecca Cook. Bassist, Ralph Franklin, and drummer, Mel Rosas, of the Detroit band, The Layabouts. Live performance at Alvin's Twilight Bar in Detroit's Cass Corridor.

Page 189: Image: Dreamstime.

Page 217: Wilhelm Reich, 1950.

Page 231: Photo: Garten-gg. Traffic jam of capitalism. Consumers alone in their private cars, surrounded by truckloads of commodities. All going nowhere.

Page 265: Detail of the bronze statue of John Lennon in the park bearing his name – Havana, Cuba.

Acknowledgements

Thank your for reading this selection of my writing. The essays in this book are taken from the online archives of the *Fifth Estate* at FifthEstate.org/archive. They contain the original headline and the publication date.

The archives are the work of Robby Barnes and Sylvie Kashdan who have so far scanned into an easily accessible format over 5,000 articles that have appeared in the *Fifth Estate* over the last almost 60 years. I owe them great thanks. Without their extraordinary effort, it is doubtful that this book would have appeared. The archive is a valuable resource for research and for those wanting to read the recorded history of resistance and the desire for renewal.

As with the formation of my ideas, the essays are not a solitary undertaking. Those friends and comrades, too numerous to list, who originally edited my writing, deserve my great appreciation for making the essays readable, as good editors do.

Lorraine Perlman, co-founder with her late husband, Fredy, of Black and Red Books, deserves special thanks for publishing my texts that appear among so many impressive titles and authors the imprint has published since its founding in 1968.

And, to Ralph Franklin who designed the attractive cover and interiors of this book, and my novel. Great appreciation always to my wife, Marilyn, who has the unenviable job of being the first reader of what I write.

I welcome your comments at pwerbe@gmail.com. More information is available at my website www.PeterWerbe.com

www.PeterWerbe.com

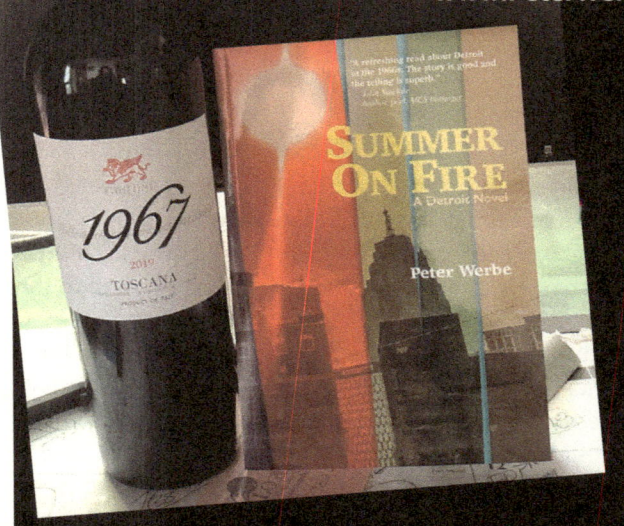

Summer on Fire: A Detroit Novel
by Peter Werbe

The temperature is scorching in Detroit during the summer of 1967 and so is everything else in this fictionalized memoir of the Fifth Estate. The staff members are thrust into rock and roll at the Grande Ballroom, drugs, anarchism, the White Panther Party, the Detroit Rebellion, anti-war demonstrations, fighting fascists, Wihelm Reich, and a bomb plot.

FIFTH ESTATE
Radical Publishing Since 1965

"The Fifth Estate supports the cause of revolution everywhere."
—1970 FBI Report

STILL TRUE TODAY!

Subscribe
to the longest running English language anarchist publication in U.S. history. Featuring articles of ideas and action.

4 Issues: $15 U.S.
Order and see content of current issue & archives at
www.FifthEstate.org
Sample copy: $4

Fifth Estate
P.O. Box 201016
Ferndale MI 48220

Black & Red Books
Publishing books and pamphlets with an anti-authoritarian perspective since 1968

Black & Red books record contemporary and historical attempts to lead principled lives. They examine social relations within our community and in the wider world, hoping to preserve the planet and the living beings who reside on it.

From theory to poetry, Black & Red publications focus on the coercive restraints of Capital, its authoritarian social relations and the deceptive abilities of political leaders who desire its power.

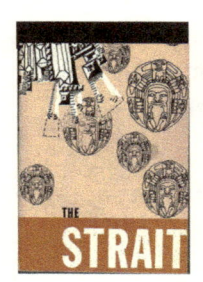

The Strait
Fredy Perlman

Against His-story; Against Leviathan
Fredy Perlman

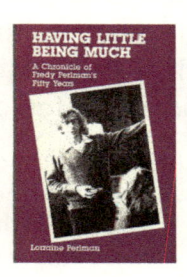

Having Little; Being Much
Lorraine Perlman

Lives of the Saints
Alan Franklin

For a catalog & ordering information: **Black & Red**
P.O. Box 02374
Detroit, Michigan 48202
www.PMpress.org www.BlackandRed.org

PM Press is an independent, radical publisher of books and media to educate, entertain, and inspire. Founded in 2007 by a small group of people with decades of publishing, media, and organizing experience, PM Press amplifies the voices of radical authors, artists, and activists. Our aim is to deliver bold political ideas and vital stories to all walks of life and arm the dreamers to demand the impossible. We have sold millions of copies of our books, most often one at a time, face to face. We're old enough to know what we're doing and young enough to know what's at stake. Join us to create a better world.

PM Press
PO Box 23912
Oakland, CA 94623
www.pmpress.org

PM Press in Europe
europe@pmpress.org
www.pmpress.org.uk

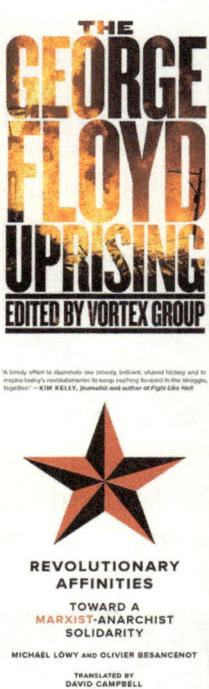

Find more revolutionary reads at:

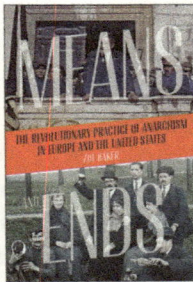

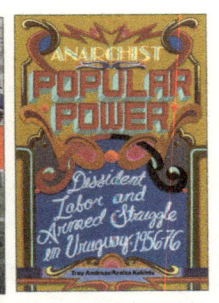

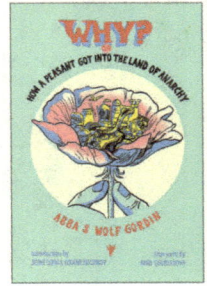

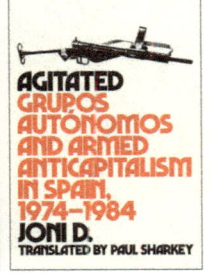

AK PRESS

Sign up as a Friend of AK Press
and get every book we publish!

AKPRESS.ORG